A CITY IN TERROR

ALSO BY FRANCIS RUSSELL
THREE STUDIES IN TWENTIETH CENTURY OBSCURITY
THE AMERICAN HERITAGE BOOK OF THE PIONEER SPIRIT
THE FRENCH AND INDIAN WARS
TRAGEDY IN DEDHAM
LEXINGTON, CONCORD, AND BUNKER HILL
THE GREAT INTERLUDE
THE WORLD OF DÜRER
THE SHADOW OF BLOOMING GROVE
THE MAKING OF THE NATION
THE CONFIDENT YEARS
FORTY YEARS ON
THE CONCISE HISTORY OF GERMANY
SACCO AND VANZETTI: THE CASE RESOLVED
ADAMS: AN AMERICAN DYNASTY
THE SHADOW OF BLOOMING GROVE
THE KNAVE OF BOSTON AND OTHER AMBIGUOUS
MASSACHUSETTS CHARACTERS

A CITY IN TERROR

Calvin Coolidge
and the 1919 Boston Police Strike

---

by
Francis Russell

BEACON PRESS, BOSTON

Beacon Press
25 Beacon Street
Boston, Massachusetts 02108-2892
www.beacon.org

Beacon Press books
are published under the auspices of
the Unitarian Universalist Association of Congregatons.

First published in 1975 by The Viking Press, Inc.
First Beacon Press edition published in 2005.

09 08 07 06 05 7 6 5 4 3 2 1

This book is printed on acid-free paper that meets
the uncoated paper ANSI/NISO specifications
for permanence as revised in 1992.

*Map of Boston orignally by Graphic 70
Redrawn in 2005 by Bruce Jones Design*

LIBRARY OF CONGRESS CATALOGING IN PUBLICATION DATA
Russell, Francis, 1910–1989
A city in terror: Calvin Coolidge and the 1919 Boston police strike.
Bibliography: p.
Includes index.
1. Boston—Police Strike, 1919. I. Title.
HV8148.B72R56   331.89′281′36320974461   74-31306
ISBN 0-8070-5033-4

CONTENTS

A Personal Recollection   1

The Year of Disillusion   7

The Boston Police Department   26

Overture to a Strike   47

Summer's End in Boston   73

On a Tuesday in September   97

The Riots   131

Law and Order   171

After the Strike   205

The Ghost of Scollay Square   236

Postscript in Baltimore   242

Acknowledgments   245

Selected Bibliography   246

Index   249

BOSTON
1919

1. BOSTON COMMON
2. BURIAL GROUND
3. STATE HOUSE
4. COURT HOUSE
5. CITY HALL
6. CITY HALL ANNEX
7. FANEUIL HALL
8. POST OFFICE
9. NEPTUNE FOUNTAIN

10. BRIMSTONE CORNER
11. ADAMS HOUSE
12. UNION CLUB
13. POLICE HEADQUARTERS
14. PUBLIC LIBRARY
15. TRINITY CHURCH
16. PARK SQUARE THEATRE
17. SOMERSET CLUB
18. CHAMBER OF COMMERCE

19. OLD SOUTH MEETING HOUSE

CAMBRIDGE STREET

CHARLES RIVER

MOUNT VERNON STREET

⑰

BEACON STREET

LONG WALK

ARLINGTON STREET

PUBLIC
GARDEN

CHARLES STREET

BOSTON
COMMON

BOYLSTON ST.

⑯

BOYLSTON STREET

COLUMBUS AVENUE

TREMONT STREET

⑭

HUNTINGTON AVENUE

⑮

COPLEY SQUARE

STUART STREET

A
PERSONAL
RECOLLECTION

The Boston Police Strike of 1919 was an event that reached far beyond itself, even into our own day. Its set of curious chances took an inconspicuous governor of Massachusetts, Calvin Coolidge, and placed him in the White House. It also made any future strike by the police force of a large American city all but impossible. Most police in that immediate postwar period were being carried along on the rising tide of unionization. The failure of the Boston strike saw the tide ebb for the police, leaving the strikers high and dry. Since then America's various police forces have formed their own associations, but after the Boston debacle few have chosen to affiliate with any national labor group. Boston's strike was unique in that when the police quit their posts there was no counterforce to replace them. To the public in that Red-haunted year the unchecked rising of the Boston mob came as an ominous shock. For many middle Americans—and for a few spellbound radicals—it seemed the germinal event, the harbinger of an American October Revolution. Respectable Bostonians, viewing the rogues' carnival in their staid streets, thought back to *A Tale of Two Cities* read long

1

ago in school. For a few hours the lid had been off their stratified social structure, and the glimpse of what lay underneath was cruel, bestial, something they did not like to think about.

That strike is one of my more coherent childhood memories. We lived then on Wellington Hill in the Mattapan section of Dorchester, four and a half miles distant from Beacon Hill, though considerably farther socially. Our Hill was a small lower-middle- to middle-class community where life during the hectic days of the strike ran on with a placid neighborliness that neither war nor civic commotion could disturb. Proletarian Blue Hill Avenue and the Dorchester streets below us remained equally calm. The second day of the strike my father came home from the office in a singularly buoyant mood. From the baize bag he had acquired in the Harvard Law School, he took out a service revolver and a shield-shaped nickel badge stamped BOSTON POLICE. He was now, he told my mother, a special policeman for the duration of the emergency. That evening he spent several hours going through trunks and boxes hunting for a pair of white kid gloves that he had worn at a Masonic installation eight years before.

"Nobody can ever find anything in this house," he muttered, a perennial complaint of his.

"Don't be an Uncle Podger,"* my mother told him, her time-worn retort. She finally found the gloves in the old steamer trunk under his tennis-racket press.

One of my father's fixed beliefs was that he had a natural talent for things military, a talent under which he now subsumed police work. The police strike became a kind of compensation to him for not having served in two wars. Twenty-one years before, as a seventeen-year-old Dorchester High School senior, he had stood in line with my Uncle Charlie to join the Roxbury Horse Guards for service in Cuba. However, somebody tipped off my grandfather at his South Boston paper factory, and he whipped down in his buggy to intercept his two boys before they reached the recruiting officer's desk.

In August 1914 my father had taken the German side, either out

---

* See Jerome K. Jerome's *Three Men in a Boat*. My father did indeed have much in common with Uncle Podger.

of contrariness to the general feeling on the Hill, or from recollections of an elementary psychology course under that staunch Harvard Teuton, Professor Hugo Muensterberg, or because he had had a German grandfather in the Franco-Prussian War, or perhaps to bait my English mother. I expect all four motives were inextricably combined in him. But the sinking of the *Lusitania*, in which my mother had returned to this country in 1913, muted his pro-German opinions, and with the United States War Declaration of April 1917, he did a complete about-face. From then on no one on the Hill was more uncritically and ardently patriotic. As head of the local Red Cross drive he saw to it that his Mattapan section had the highest percentage of contributions in the city. He served on the Mattapan Legal Advisory Board, which entitled him to wear a bronze pin in his buttonhole showing a hand holding a pair of scales over which was inscribed LEGAL ADVISOR and underneath, U S SELECTIVE SERVICE SYSTEM. The long field behind our house was ploughed and divided up into war gardens, and along with most of our neighbors my father took an allotment. His agricultural zeal was brief, however. Our garden was by autumn easily the weediest, the least hoed, the most neglected on the Hill. Beetles devoured our potato plants, rabbits from the Hollow chewed off our emergent peas and beans, cutworms leveled our tomatoes. Only the summer squash, planted at random in the rubbish pile, grew lushly. I do not think our family efforts helped the starving Belgians much. Still, my father was very proud whenever he came up the back stairs with those elongated and overripe yellow squashes.

At that time he was serving the first of several terms in the legislature. As a state representative, as a married man with two children, he was not subject to the draft. I am still rather puzzled that he did not volunteer. Instead he became a home-front zealot, in the legislature, in the Red Cross and Liberty Bond drives, at the Legal Advisory Board (whose functions I have never been able to determine). His wartime views, once adopted, remained fixed. During the pacifist drift of the twenties he would continue to argue that America's entry into the war had been necessary to keep the victorious Germans "from coming over here." He once told me that if he had joined in 1917 he could have been a major. Over half a century later I still find it a shuddering thought, unless he had been kept penned up in the judge advocate's office. His martial spirit later found a part outlet in the legislature when he sponsored a bill to create a Massachusetts State Police. After the bill was passed Governor Coolidge presented him with the pen he had used in signing it. It was a white goose quill, the nib stained with ink. Though the pen has long since been lost, I still have the governor's letter following my father's election to the legislature, with the somewhat questionable observation that "our House of Representatives is an ancient and honorable body and worthy of the highest type of service that our Massachusetts citizenship can bestow upon it."

The calm of our district was probably quite a disappointment to my father. His single adventure was in commandeering a private automobile to chase a suspicious character who had been noticed boarding a streetcar at Mattapan Square. The character was suspicious because he was foreign-looking and had tried to change a ten-dollar bill at McHugh's drugstore. However, he turned out to be merely an Italian laborer, and the bill was what was left of his week's pay.

For several days my father in his white kid gloves directed traffic at the corner of Morton Street and Blue Hill Avenue, the busiest intersection between Franklin Park and Mattapan Square. In those days there were only about a twentieth as many cars on the road as today, but somehow each morning he managed to create a traffic jam of dimensions previously unknown in Dorchester and not to be seen again until the introduction of traffic lights. He maintained that the tie-up was caused by all the drivers coming in town after the strike, and that no regular policeman could have managed better. Whatever the jam, he enjoyed himself thoroughly. Badge, revolver, whistle, and white gloves were authoritative symbols that made his law office seem tame when he went back to it a week later.

Before the strike, the police of Boston still wore dome-shaped helmets like those of the English police. They also wore high-necked frock coats above which protruded the ends of a wing collar. With their leather outer belts they resembled the old Keystone Kops. The only policeman I knew by sight was Mr. Fitzgibbons. "Iron Mike" they called him at Mattapan's Station 19. His daughter Susy was in our fourth-grade room. Susy was a bright, aggressive little girl who wore paper hair-ribbons, could write in Palmer Method without making blots, and got double promotions. As I look back now at our old fourth-grade picture, I can see that she was the most attractive one of our group, but I did not think so then. She was the oldest of seven children.

The Fitzgibbonses lived in a square little two-and-a-half-story house down the street from the Martha Baker School. They were neat, well-behaved children, all seven of them, and they went to St. Angela's, not like those tough shanty Irish who lived on Mulvey Street. Mrs. Fitzgibbons belonged to the Mothers' Club. There were such a lot of Fitzgibbonses that they used to have benches along the dining-room table instead of chairs. People like my mother were dubious about so many children, but they thought Mrs. Fitzgibbons was a wonderful manager.

I can remember Mr. Fitzgibbons coming up over the Hill on the way home from Station 19, a tall, striding figure in his grey helmet and blue coat with the shining badge and buttons. Even the Mulvey Streeters who used to yell "Cheese it, the cop!" when they saw other policemen were quiet when he went by. No one would have dared to challenge his presence. Mr. Fitzgibbons, that proud and handsome man, walking up the street with the sun shining on his helmet, saluting Miss Sykes, the head teacher, as he passed with courtly reserve, was the Law. But on that Tuesday afternoon he went on strike with the others. "If I hadn't been in my last month, I'd have seen that Mike never walked out," Mrs. Fitzgibbons told my mother afterward.

For several months after the strike the policemen of Station 19, almost all of whom had struck, were replaced by the state guard. The aspect of these overage and underage guardsmen was ludicrously unmilitary. They scarcely knew the manual of arms, and they still wore the laced gaiters and felt campaign hats of the Mexican Border Campaign of 1916, which had been replaced in the American Expeditionary Force by spiral puttees and overseas caps.

To us in the fourth grade, though, they were impressive indeed, soldiers in the flesh, objects of military might. It was like having Memorial Day every day in the week to see so many uniforms. The guardsmen carried rifles with fixed bayonets rather than revolvers, just like the pictures of soldiers in the war. That Halloween I was chased by a guardsman who caught me shinnying up a lamppost to put out the gas light in front of the Sandses. As soon as I saw him I jumped and tried to get away by ducking through the backyards, but he ran after me and the fear went down into my legs. I still recall my side glimpse of that looming khaki figure in his wide-brimmed felt hat, his rifle at port, and the light sparkling on the bayonet as he chased me across lots and under clotheslines. At each step he took I could hear the slap of the leather sling against his rifle stock. I was so frightened I wet myself.

By the end of the year a new police force had been recruited and the drab uniforms of the state guard disappeared. The new policemen had different uniforms. The long coats and wing collars had been discarded. Caps replaced the helmets. It was the close of an era: the end of the patrolman in his high helmet walking his beat under the gas lamps past the corner saloon, the beginning of prowl cars and bootleggers.

Even in the fourth grade I could sense the change. I remember one sunny October afternoon passing the Fitzgibbons house on the way home from school. The Fitzgibbonses had a tree in their yard that Susy called an umbrella tree. It had wide leaves almost two feet long and a pink fruit that ripened in the autumn and looked like a magnolia bud. Most of the leaves had fallen, and the yard behind the clipped privet hedge was buried under them. One of the Fitzgibbons children who was too young to go to school yet was gathering the leaves in his express wagon. Another, still younger, sat on the edge of the curb in front of the house playing with an old spoon and a grey policeman's helmet.

THE
YEAR OF
DISILLUSION

November 11, 1918. By the time the first cloth-capped workers with their tin lunch boxes stood waiting for the Boston streetcars in the long-shadowed morning, the newspapers were already shouting in jubilant headlines that the armistice had been signed. Church bells and fire bells rang out in the suburbs, small boys built fires in the streets, and the downtown air quivered from the shrillness of tugboat whistles and foghorns in the harbor. For Boston, as for all the other thronged and delirious cities, that morning was the beginning of the new, the bright promise of a future that combined the ineradicable American belief in progress with the memory of a prewar golden past that never existed but was now to be recaptured.

In that first World War the patriotic slogans had rung as true as newly minted silver coins. Keep the World Safe for Democracy! The war had been the struggle of light against darkness, against the sinister forces led by the Kaiser, the very essence of militarism with his spiked helmet and insolently upturned moustache. Beat the Hun! Those barbarians had started it all by attacking brave little Belgium and marching through that green and peaceable land, butchering women and children and even worse, as one could read in the nightmare pages of the Bryce Report. Only barbarians would have bombarded an open city, as the Boches did when from seventy-five miles away they shelled the French capital with their Paris Guns. Only Boches would have sunk the unarmed *Lusitania* carrying innocent American women and children.

Through the little streets of the Boston suburbs, of Roxbury, Dorchester, Everett, Somerville, South Boston, Liberty Loan posters, flaunting a high-breasted Columbia draped in the Stars and Stripes, filled the front window. Often there was a serviceman's flag beside the posters—the blue star on the red-bordered white background—and a Red Cross transparency behind which it was suggested one light a candle on Christmas Eve—until the fire commissioner objected.

Our boys would not come back until it was over Over There, the Old World redeemed by the New. For this Americans cheerfully had accepted meatless days and lightless nights, substituted rice and cornmeal for wheat flour, used Karo corn syrup instead of sugar, huddled without grumbling before a portable Simplex oil heater when coal grew scarce. In the public parks through the summer evenings, men who had never touched hand to hoe before trenched and weeded in war gardens among rows of potatoes and corn and beans and tomatoes. Can Vegetables and Fruit and the Kaiser Too! Families ate more peaches for the sake of the stones that in some mysterious way had become vital to the manufacture of gas masks. Peach-stone collection barrels dotted Boston Common. All the large cities held Wake Up America parades. Such celebrities as Douglas Fairbanks, Charlie Chaplin, and the opera singer Geraldine Farrar gave four-minute pep talks to persuade even the most hesitant to buy Liberty Bonds. Arthur Guy Empey, the heroic American author of *Over the Top*, who had rushed to join the British Army after the sinking of the *Lusitania* and who had fought and been wounded in the trenches, announced that he was now giving away an autographed copy of his book to everyone who purchased a $100 bond. Buy a Bond! Feed a Fighter! Those who could not afford a Liberty Bond could at least buy War Savings Certificates, and even schoolchildren could save their nickels and dimes for the green twenty-five-cent Thrift Stamps sold by the postman, sixteen of which could be exchanged for a War Savings Certificate. Lick the Stamps and Lick the Kaiser!

America in those nineteen war months had been overwhelmed by a euphoria such as the nations and cities of Europe had experienced in the summer of 1914. War, unknown for fifty years in the United States except for the three-month Spanish-American incident, became a heart-moving experience that cut through class and ethnic barriers to knit Americans together in a mindless unity. As one contemporary versifier, caught up in the patriotic fervor, explained:

> There's a certain sort of glory
>   That is throbbing in the street;
> You can read the battle story
>   In the faces that you meet.

Wilson, delivering his war message in the chamber of the House of Representatives, had called the German submarine warfare a warfare against mankind. "There is one choice we cannot make, we are incapable of making," he told the assembled senators and congressmen, almost all of whom were wearing or carrying small American flags, "we will not choose the path of submission." At those electric words Chief Justice Edward Douglass White, old Confederate soldier and Ku Klux Klan night-rider of Reconstruction, rose from his front-row seat in exultation, the tears streaming down his cheeks. Following his spontaneous gesture, all the others in the chamber stood up. Almost everyone in the country felt the same patriotic surge. In the weeks that followed, Harvard's Professor Francis Peabody returned his Order of the Prussian Crown to the Kaiser via Switzerland. Not to be outdone, the trustees of Brown University revoked the honorary degree they had earlier conferred on the German ambassador, Count von Bernstorff. Let's Keep the Glow in Old Glory! Several state legislatures passed laws forbidding the teaching of German. Others banned the use of any language but English in telephone conversations. Sauerkraut was reborn as liberty cabbage, and even German measles was transmogrified to liberty measles. Small boys took to stoning dachshunds. Wagner's music gave way to the strenuosities of John Philip Sousa, and the German-born conductor of the Boston Symphony Orchestra, Karl Muck, was driven from the podium.

There was of course a dissenting if diminished minority that declined to wave flags. Six senators and thirty-one congressmen had voted against Wilson's war resolution, and Wisconsin's Senator Robert La Follette spoke for three hours against it. Nevertheless, a few days later, House and Senate backed the war unanimously by passing the loan bill—the largest financial measure in the history of the country. Dissent, peripheral though it might be, found itself confronted with vigilante patriotism. In September 1917 government agents raided the headquarters of the Wobblies, the anarchist-oriented Industrial Workers of the World (IWW), in twenty-four cities, confiscating their records and making ten arrests. Two months later seventeen Wobblies were tarred and feathered and then whipped near Tulsa, Oklahoma, by the "Knights of Liberty." Wisconsin patriots hanged Senator La Follette in effigy, and the American Defense Society urged his expulsion from the Senate.

Socialists and their sympathizers had remained the chief opponents of the war, but after America's entry many—perhaps most of them—caught the patriotic fervor as long-time party members resigned to support the war effort. Those who refused, who remained intransigently unpersuaded, were led by the dynamic and voluble Eugene V. Debs, as ingrained a Hoosier as his friend James Whitcomb Riley. Most of these stubborn holdouts, however, were the foreign-born socialists of New York and other big industrial cities, brought up in the European tradition of the class struggle, for whom the war was merely the ultimate capitalist deception that Debs denounced so boldly in a speech at Canton, Ohio, in June of 1918.

In response to this challenge from the left, Congress passed laws against espionage and sedition, prescribing stringent penalties for speaking, printing, or otherwise expressing contempt for the government or the Constitution or the flag or the uniform of the army or navy, using language calculated to aid the enemy's cause, using words favoring any country with which the United States was at war, or saying or doing anything likely to restrict the sale of United States bonds. Under this draconian legislation—unparalleled since the Alien and Sedition Acts of 1798—Debs was sentenced to ten years in prison for his Ohio speech. The IWW leader Big Bill Haywood and ninety-eight other Wobblies were also tried and found guilty under the same statute, receiving sentences ranging from ten days to twenty years, with fines amounting to $2,300,000. To most Americans such men were slackers if not downright German agents and spies, deserving of far worse. The genteel Princeton essayist and versifier Henry van Dyke spoke for the flag-waving majority when he announced that he was ready to "hang everyone who lifts his voice against America's entering the war."

Professor van Dyke would have found few to disagree with him in Boston. For the Massachusetts capital was one of the most perfervidly patriotic of American cities, the headquarters of the Twenty-sixth Yankee Division, the pride of New England, in whose ranks the Irish and the Old Yankees had managed to suspend if not bury their animosities. Formed from units all over New England but with its nucleus in Boston, officered by Back Bay Brahmins and South Boston politicians, the Yankee Division had been the first of the American Expeditionary Force to be organized, the first to cross the Atlantic, the first to be committed to battle. Professional military men considered the Twenty-sixth mediocre, handicapped by its Saturday-night soldiers and its amateur officers, whom for political reasons it was impossible to remove. Not so the citizens of Boston, who had absorbed the belief that their own Yankee Division was vital in winning the war. This the local papers proclaimed day after day. The Boston *Globe* even sent its star reporter, Frank Sibley, overseas as a special divisional correspondent.

Boston dissent huddled obscurely in the Roxbury side streets among the members of the Lettish Workmen's Association, Russian-born revolutionaries, many of whom had served with bands of Lettish terrorists in the 1905 Russian insurrection. The Boston Letts, belonging to the pro-Bolshevik Russian Federation of the Socialist party, were a tough-minded group who provided Soviet Russia with secret couriers, propagandists, and at least two leaders who at various times were in charge of illegal Communist operations in the United States. They owned a hall and a printing plant in Roxbury and had brought Louis Fraina from New York to edit the underground weekly *Revolutionary Age*. Fraina, an Italian-born left-wing intellectual, was one of the more extreme Socialist leaders, fanatically devoted to the Bolshevik revolution and looking to a similar revolution in the United States with himself playing the role of the American Lenin.

There was no consciousness of dissent in the city on that first armistice morning. The first rush of cloth caps was followed an hour later by felt-hatted clerks and tellers and salesmen funneling in from the inlying suburbs of Dorchester and Roxbury to the elevated stations at Forest Hills and Egleston Square and Dudley Street, or moving by ferry and streetcar from East Boston, Winthrop, and beyond. Still later the more solid middle-class commuters began arriving by train at the North and South Stations from outlying Winchester and Medford and Melrose, Dedham and Needham and Wellesley and the Newtons. They were succeeded within the hour by staid brokers and bankers and lawyers of the Back Bay and Beacon Street, walking with prissy briskness through the Public Gardens and across the Common under the shadow of Bulfinch's gilt-domed State House, where the 160-year-old bell that had rung out during the Revolution had been pealing since daybreak. A day unlike any other, for no one was intent on job or office; yet in contrast to the usual holiday exodus, more people thronged the narrow Boston streets than ever before, packing into Newspaper Row on lower Washington Street, milling in front of City Hall and the State House, jamming together to the despair of traffic in an atmosphere of furious festivity, relief, joy, triumph, and hope. The War to End Wars was over.

It was an incandescent moment that could not last much beyond the impromptu parades that marked the war's end. Americans had sustained their patriotic ardor by imagining a postwar country of

> Peace, prosperity and health
> Private bliss and public wealth.

Soldiers, shortly to be demobilized with a bonus in their pockets—$50 for a private, $200 for an officer—looked forward to home as they had pictured it in the tedium of barrack and trench. Industrial workers, who had never been so well off in spite of the sharp price rises, expected that their wages would stay at the peak. The many whose income had remained stationary in the face of the High Cost of Living—as inflation was then more naïvely called—expected that prices would recede to their prewar level. Middle-class suburbanites expected industrial peace. Those who had made fortunes out of the war expected to be let alone.

"*WHOLE WORLD IN DELIRIUM OF JOY*" the *Globe* headlines of November 11 proclaimed, and "Uncle Dudley" in that same paper editorialized that "it is victory, victory at last. The old day is over; its long, dreadful night of war is past. A new day dawns." The day was climaxed by an impromptu victory parade featuring an effigy of the Kaiser carried on a stretcher by white-aproned market men and led by Mayor Andrew J. Peters and his small son, each holding a flag. The parade as it passed the State House was reviewed by flint-faced Governor-elect Calvin Coolidge. Yet even by the week's end, even as the city celebrated the return to a familiar routine beyond the shadow of war, there were other shadows darkening the landscape. War industries, employing nine million workers, were now preparing to shut down abruptly. Four million soldiers and sailors would soon enter a labor market already swollen by the unemployed of closed or reconverting factories. Four days after the armistice President Samuel Gompers of the American Federation of Labor, uneasy at the industrial prospect, warned that any reduction in wages or increase in hours would mean a bitter fight from organized labor. Two weeks later the Boston Elevated Street Railway Company announced a raise in fares from seven to eight cents. Two years earlier it had been five cents. El ticket collectors won a fourteen-cent increase to forty cents an hour. The price of coal jumped overnight from nine dollars to ten dollars a ton. Though the war was over, the High Cost of Living was obviously not.

On November 27 the Boston horizon lightened briefly when the Yankee Division's former commander, Major General Clarence Edwards, arrived from overseas. The plodding, too-talkative General Edwards had fallen foul of his superiors in the late months of the war and had been relieved of his command. His removal had caused much indignation in the city and the state. Governor Samuel McCall, as one of his last gestures in office, designated November 27 as General Edwards Day. At a public reception at the State House the general reassured a large group of mothers, troubled by rumors of their sons' conduct overseas. "Your boys," he told them, "were so good and pure I was afraid they wouldn't fight, but they proved the greatest of soldiers."

On December 4 President Wilson sailed for France and the peace conference. Even before he landed, the police and firemen of Montreal had gone on strike for higher wages and union recognition. For several days the Canadian city was in the hands of rioters, who wrecked fire stations, looted the stores along St. Catherine Street, and beat up and robbed those who stood in their way. By New Year's of 1919 the bright promise of Armistice Day had noticeably dulled. That surly and troubled year—as it would seem in retrospect—ushered in a wave of strikes. There was the great steel strike, there were railroad and transit strikes, strikes of factory workers, carpenters, pressmen, butchers, cigar-workers, actors, bank clerks, even rent and buyer strikes, and strikes against the High Cost of Living. Wherever one turned, in industry or transportation or public service, there seemed to be a strike or threatened strike. To add to the malaise, prices, instead of falling, continued to rise. The value of the 1914 dollar had dropped to only forty-five cents. Food costs had gone up 84 per cent, clothes, 114 per cent. For the average American family the cost of living was double what it had been five years earlier, and income had lagged behind. Professional classes from clergymen and professors to clerks, state and city employees, firemen and police, found themselves worse off than at any time since the Civil War.

Veterans of the AEF marched off the troop ships amidst the blare of brass bands to a homeland riven with strikes and protests. What ex-soldiers and civilians alike expected—with some improvements—was to resume the pattern of life that the war had interrupted. The bumbling Harding would soon sum up the mood in his neologism "normalcy." Normalcy meant 1914 with a halo. But by 1919 it was disillusioningly apparent that normalcy was not just round the corner. During the first postwar year there would be thirty-six hundred strikes involving some four million workers.

Nineteen hundred and nineteen, that year of strikes and lockouts, was led off the second week in January by a walkout of New York harbor workers. On January 25, thirty-five thousand dress and waist makers—most of them young women—struck in New York for a forty-four-hour week and a 15 per cent pay increase. Such strikes, whatever bitterness they may have aroused, were in the familiar pattern. The Seattle general strike of February 6 was something else again. When news of it splashed across the headlines of the country's press, many uneasy Americans saw the shutdown of an American city as a prelude to revolution. Such was certainly not the intention of the strikers, whatever the inclinations of some of their leaders. The strike developed from a walkout of thirty-five thousand ship workers who, in spite of the fact that their contract with the Emergency Fleet Corporation still had two months to run, struck for higher wages and shorter hours. Then the radically minded Seattle Central Labor Council, whose secretary was close to the Wobblies, decided on a sympathy strike to aid the ship workers and to challenge the growing militancy of the generally antiunion Northwestern employers. On February 3 the Central Labor Council issued a proclamation for a general strike to begin on February 6. The Seattle *Union Record*, spokesman for the council, tried to reassure the public, promising that everyone would be fed, that babies and the sick would be cared for, that all industries necessary for the public health and welfare would continue to run, and that law and order would be preserved. But a *Record* editorial concluded ominously: "We are undertaking the most tremendous move ever made by LABOR in this country.... We are starting on a road that leads—NO ONE KNOWS WHERE!"

On February 6, sixty thousand workmen struck, and the seaport city was at a standstill. Streetcars lay idle in the car barns, schools closed, business shut down. Vital services did continue to function and the city was never without food, coal, water, heat, or light. The strikers remained orderly. There was no violence. Not a single arrest occurred while it lasted. Nevertheless Seattle's businessmen and middle-class inhabitants were badly frightened. The Wobbly-hating Mayor Ole Hanson, a former Progressive who had supported Wilson in 1916, declared that it was not a strike at all but a plan to establish a Soviet and kindle a flame of revolution in America. That same day, at the mayor's request, soldiers from Camp Lewis moved into the city. The next day Hanson notified the strike committee that unless the strike was called off by eight o'clock on the following morning, he would use federal troops to crush it and to operate all essential enterprises. However some of their leaders may have felt, the rank-and-file strikers had no larger interest than to aid the ship workers and to assert labor's strength in the Seattle area. Seattle's American Federation of Labor locals, who had hesitantly backed the strike at the beginning, now feared that any prolongation would destroy unionism in the city, and they brought pressure on the strike committee to end it. On February 11 the strikers capitulated. Though the hostility of the public and lack of support from the AFL really brought the strike to an end, Mayor Hanson absorbed most of the credit. Across the nation he was hailed in the press as "the man of the hour," becoming overnight a national hero.

The Seattle general strike focused public attention sharply on domestic radicals. They in turn had been revitalized by the success of the Russian Revolution, which they saw as a preliminary to world revolution. "Follow Russia's lead!" the anarchist leader Emma Goldman had urged anticonscription audiences in New York in 1918. If the "people's government" had already come to Russia, could it be far behind in America? That was the question Socialists, anarchists, and IWWs asked themselves belligerently as they met in grubby back halls. John Reed had returned from Russia to thrill Socialist activists, most of whom nursed bitter memories of czar and kaiser, with his incandescent account of the ten October days that shook the world.

Not all Socialists were prepared to follow the red star in the East. The Bolshevist seizure of power had, in fact, split the Socialist party into the "Slowcialists," who believed in reaching their Socialist goal legally through the ballot, and the Left Wing, direct-action revolutionaries, who scorned such bourgeois democratic notions. Led by determined radicals like Reed, Jim Larkin, the pugnacious hawk-nosed Irish organizer, and the persuasively earnest Ben Gitlow, the Left Wingers—who before the end of the year would break away to form the Communist and Communist Labor parties—were resolved to re-enact the October Revolution across the Atlantic as soon as a suitable revolutionary situation could be created. In February 1919 the Left-Wing faction of the Socialists' Greater New York local issued a manifesto calling for the overthrow of capitalism and the establishment of socialism through proletarian dictatorship. A month later, after the founding of the Third International, Carl Sandburg, returning from a surreptitious trip to the new Russia, smuggled in a copy of Lenin's letter, "To the American Workers." It was printed in Fraina's *Revolutionary Age,* and some five million copies were then distributed in the United States, urging the American workers to follow their Russian brethren and shake off the shackles of capitalism.

To this challenge of a militant minority, the American majority reacted with fear and hatred. As Ben Gitlow noted, "The anti-Red hysteria was fanned into a high pitch of frenzy by reactionary politicians who hoped thereby to gain political advancement, by all the open shop and anti-labor interests of the country, by a large section of the press and by labor spy agencies, who now saw a splendid chance to sell their stock-in-trade to the industrial interests." The affinity of domestic radicals for Bolshevism gave the National Security League, the American Defense Society, and the National Civic Federation a new target in their drive for patriotic conformity. Supporters of Soviet Russia were labeled variously "criminals," "anarchists," "Wobblies," "beasts," and "economic imbeciles." Almost overnight the bristling term "Bolshevik" became synonymous with "treason." Shortly after the Third International came into being in Moscow, the American Legion was founded in St. Louis "to foster and perpetuate a one hundred per cent Americanism" and by the year's end had enrolled a million ex-soldier members.

Following the Seattle strike, Mayor Hanson toured the country crying up the Red menace. But Seattle was a continent away, and Bostonians and the Boston press were more concerned with the strike in the mills of Lawrence, the drab and polyglot company town thirty-seven miles to the north. That strike of foreign-born workers was seen by both sides as a sequel to the great Lawrence strike of 1912, when the founder of the IWW, the one-eyed giant Big Bill Haywood, had come to the city in person to rally the workers. With him in that turbulent struggle, in which one girl worker was shot dead, were the anarchist leader Carlo Tresca, the anarchist poet Arturo Giovannitti, and Tresca's mistress, the (then) slim young firebrand Elizabeth Gurley Flynn.

The second Lawrence strike began three days before the one in Seattle, following a demand by the textile workers for a reduction of their six-day nine-hour week to one of eight hours at the same rate of pay. The companies were willing to compromise by granting a forty-eight-hour week at the same rate plus time-and-a-half for overtime. Although United Textile Workers of America officials were ready to accept the offer, the more radical local leaders were not. The strike took on political overtones when a general strike committee repudiated the Central Labor Union and the AFL, and called on the IWW for help. Ime Kaplan, a Russian alien, took over the leadership of the strike. To Kaplan the six hours in dispute were irrelevant. He saw the strike as part of a larger pattern of capitalist disintegration preliminary to the seizure of power by the proletariat. Tresca and Giovannitti again traveled to Lawrence to spur the workers on, and Larkin put in a firebrand appearance. The strike committee sent out an appeal in twenty languages calling for a general strike of all textile workers. Factory owners refused to negotiate further. Lawrence police forbade all meetings on city land. A house was bombed, a striker killed by a shot in the dark. Some of the mills defiantly reopened. But the strike dragged on for months.

The narrow streets of Boston had a grim aspect when President Wilson landed there on February 23 on his return from the Paris Peace Conference. Secret Service men armed with rifles lined the roofs, and all windows were ordered closed as he drove past. The day before, two Spanish anarchists of the Groupa Pro Prensa had been arrested for plotting Wilson's assassination. Nothing untoward occurred during the President's Boston visit, but the fear remained, a fear that Secretary of Labor William B. Wilson gave voice to when he warned an apprehensive middle-class audience that "recent strikes at Lawrence, Seattle ... and other places were not industrial, economic disputes in their origin but were results of a deliberate, organized attempt at a social and political movement to establish Soviet Governments in the United States." News from overseas reinforced such fear: the earlier Spartacist revolt in Berlin, a Soviet Bavaria under the Left Socialist Kurt Eisner, in March Béla Kun's Communist dictatorship in Hungary, the wounding of Premier Clemenceau in France by a "Bolshevik agent." Could it happen in America? men increasingly asked themselves.

Telephone service in New England went dead on April 15 as twenty thousand telephone operators, headed by the Boston local of the telephone workers' union, pulled the switches and walked off their jobs. The girls, earning sixteen dollars a week, demanded twenty-two dollars, finally settled for nineteen dollars. That strike lasted only a week, but it disrupted and alarmed the business community. It seemed one more ominous sign.

Something of the mood of Armistice Day in the grey seaport city was recaptured when on April 25 the returned Yankee Division held its final parade in Boston. The Commonwealth of Massachusetts appropriated thirty thousand dollars for the victory reception. Stands had been run up in front of the State House and on both sides of the Commonwealth Avenue mall. For hours on that cold spring day, the men of the Yankee Division marched by the gilt-domed State House to the applause of the assembled politicians, down Beacon Street and up and down Commonwealth Avenue, company after company in their high-collared tunics, spiral puttees, and steel helmets, led by their new commander Major General Harry Hale. But all eyes were on the former commander, General Edwards, mounted on a skittish bay and conspicuously wearing an overseas cap instead of a steel helmet.

Three days later the country received its first bomb scare. Already in February, when there was talk of deporting every radical, anarchist posters had appeared in New England defiantly proclaiming:

GO AHEAD

The senile fossils ruling the United States see red!
. . . .
The storm is within and very soon will leap and
Crash and annihilate you in blood and fire. You
have shown no pity to us! We will do likewise.
. . . .
We will dynamite you!

Then on April a package containing a home-made bomb was sent to Mayor Hanson in Seattle. Acid from the detonator leaking through the package revealed the bomb before it could explode. Another bomb, sent to Georgia's ex-Senator Thomas Hardwick, was more disastrous, exploding as a maid opened the package and blowing off both her hands. On April 30 thirty-four "May Day" bomb packages were discovered in the mail before delivery, addressed to such people as Ellis Island's Commissioner of Immigration Frederick C. Howe, the commissioner general of immigration, the chairman of the Senate Bolshevik Investigating Committee, Postmaster General Albert S. Burleson, who had earlier barred radical literature from the mails, Judge Kenesaw Mountain Landis, who had sentenced Big Bill Haywood and the other Wobbly leaders, Supreme Court Justice Oliver Wendell Holmes, Attorney General A. Mitchell Palmer, Secretary of Labor William Wilson, John D. Rockefeller, and J. P. Morgan. Headlines announced to an alarmed public that *"REDS PLAN MAY DAY MURDERS."* Until 1919, except among the foreign-born of the large cities, May Day had never taken on the political significance that it had developed in Europe. But radicals were determined to dedicate this May Day to their cause, to make the day a real Red Letter one. In cities across the country they held mass assemblies and staged Red Flag parades. Riots followed as indignant opponents, often ex-soldiers and sailors still in uniform, attacked the Red militants. Major disturbances took place in New York, Cleveland, and Boston.

In New York ex-servicemen invaded a Tom Mooney protest meeting that overflowed Carnegie Hall while other men in uniform stormed the Russian People's House on East Fifteenth Street and forced a Socialist gathering to sing "The Star-Spangled Banner." Seventeen Socialists were injured. Some four hundred soldiers and sailors then broke up a reception at the new offices of the Socialist *Call*, smashed furniture, and forced the guests into the street.

In Cleveland, Victory Loan workers led by an army lieutenant stopped a mammoth Red Flag parade, and the lieutenant tore a red banner from the hands of a soldier leading the column. Paraders and their opponents at once flung themselves on each other with fists and clubs. In Public Square another uniformed lieutenant confronted several soldiers wearing red flags pinned to their uniforms. As he snatched at the flags the soldiers struck back, and the parade turned into a riot so violent that it required army trucks and a Victory Loan tank to break up the fighting. One man was killed and over forty were injured. Police arrested 106 Socialists, most of them aliens.

In Boston the Roxbury Letts were denied a permit to parade by the City Board of Street Commissioners. Nevertheless, on May Day morning they formed up in front of the Dudley Street Opera House and unfurled their red flags and revolutionary banners to shouts of "To hell with the permit!" Led by Fraina, marching arm-in-arm with a huge gorilla-like Lett by the name of Jurgis and the frail Willy Sidis, the mathematics prodigy who had graduated from Harvard five years earlier at the age of fifteen, the Letts trudged off toward Boston. Near the Dudley Street el terminal they came up against a squad of police, who ordered them to halt. Instead they rushed the police, who gave way, vainly swinging their billies. Some bystanders dashed in to aid the police and to snatch at the red flags. When police reinforcements arrived, the Letts went at them with fists, knuckle-dusters, short lengths of pipe, blackjacks, and even revolvers. One policeman, Arthur Shea, was shot in the hand; another policeman in the foot. Several men were stabbed, while still others were clubbed, stoned, and attacked with ice picks. In the swirling brawl a police captain died of a heart attack. Not until mounted police appeared did the Letts finally disperse. Confronted by such a Red menace, Boston reacted savagely. Patriotic vigilantes spread through Roxbury beating up anyone looking too suspiciously foreign or wearing a scrap of red. District Attorney Joseph Pelletier (shortly to be disbarred) called on every citizen to "be on guard and active against the malignant enemy of democracy." Before the melee ended, 116 paraders had been arrested. Taken before Judge A. F. Hayden at the Roxbury Municipal Court, fourteen of them were found guilty of disturbing the peace and sentenced to several months in prison.

Two weeks after the May Day outbreaks, the Winnipeg Trades and Labour Council in Manitoba, Canada, called a general strike. With its onset the Winnipeg city government, the police and fire departments, the post office, and other municipal offices fell completely into the hands of a strike committee. Although the strike collapsed after two weeks, many Canadians and Americans believed it another Bolshevik forerunner. Samuel Gompers of the AFL, fearing the spreading reaction against all organized labor, labeled it an "evil." Secretary of War Newton Baker told the Ohio Federation of Women's Clubs that "in our country, since the armistice, there has been a growing agitation and unrest manifesting itself sometimes in race riots and mob disorder, but for the most part evidenced by widespread industrial controversies. Our

21

newspapers are daily filled with accounts of violent agitation by so-called Bolshevists and radicals courting violence and urging action in behalf of what they call revolution."

As if to bear out his warning, on June 2 bombs exploded in eight American cities. The chief target was the Red-hunting attorney general, A. Mitchell Palmer. Just as he was going to bed in his Washington town house on R Street, a tremendous explosion blew off the front of the building and shattered the windows of neighboring houses, including that of Assistant Secretary of the Navy Franklin Roosevelt across the way. Copies of a pamphlet entitled *Plain Words* were found near the site of each explosion. It read, in part:

> There will have to be bloodshed ... we will destroy and rid
> the world of your tyrannical institutions....
> Long live social revolution! Down with tyranny!
>   The Anarchist Fighters

The bomb destined for Palmer went off prematurely, blowing its carrier to bits. Only his head was found, on a rooftop several blocks away. Not until some time afterward did the police finally identify him as Carlo Valdinoce, a New Jersey anarchist.* Judge Hayden's house on Wayne Street, Roxbury, was almost demolished by a bomb made of an iron pipe stuffed with shrapnel and dynamite, although the judge himself was unhurt. Copies of *Plain Words* were found in the debris. In suburban Newtonville a similar bomb blew off the side of a house belonging to State Representative Leland Powers, who had sponsored an anti-anarchy bill in the Massachusetts legislature. Attorney General Palmer declared that the latest bombings were another attempt on the part of radical elements to rule the country.

Spring gave way to the Red Summer, so named by James Weldon Johnson, the black poet, who was thinking more of the color of blood than of politics. It ushered in the most savage racial strife in a generation as four hundred thousand Negro soldiers returned to civilian life. Race riots broke out in twenty-five Ameri-

---

* Valdinoce's sister Susie went to live with the Sacco family in Boston after the arrest of Nicola Sacco and Bartolomeo Vanzetti.

can cities. With the wartime shortage of labor, rural Negroes from the South had migrated to the Northern industrial centers. After the war such migration continued, even though falling employment brought blacks and whites into increasing confrontation both in jobs and housing. One sign of conflict was the spectacular growth of the revived Ku Klux Klan. In Chicago the conflict erupted into a race war after the death of a young Negro at a Lake Michigan beach. He had swum into water customarily reserved for whites, who threw stones at him. Although they failed to hit him, they so terrified him that he drowned from exhaustion. Negroes felt he had been murdered and began to attack whites on the streets. The whites turned on the Negroes, and rioting raged for thirteen days. Even when after four days the militia was called out, the guardsmen were unable to contain the riot that soon expanded into a miniature civil war. Before it was over fifteen whites and thirty-eight blacks were dead, with over five hundred injured on both sides. More than a thousand houses were burnt down, mostly in the Negro district. Other race riots followed in the District of Columbia, Tennessee, Nebraska, Omaha, Arkansas, and Texas. During the year some seventy Negroes were lynched, a figure that included ten returned soldiers.

As the 1919 Fourth of July neared, it seemed in prospect as ominous a day as the first of May. Radicals took the lead in demanding a general strike in protest against the conviction of Thomas Mooney, who with Warren Billings had been arrested in July 1916 and sentenced to death for his supposed part in setting off a bomb during a San Francisco Preparedness Parade in which nine people were killed and forty injured. Doubts as to their guilt, carefully fanned by propaganda, made them into a symbol of the working class's fight for justice. Liberals and radicals of all the shades from pink to red embraced their cause. Again apprehension spread among the more naïve patriotic Americans. *"REIGN OF TERROR PLANNED,"* newspaper headlines announced as the Fourth neared; *"PLANS FOR WIDESPREAD VIOLENCE AND MURDER."* Mayors and governors grew increasingly nervous. In New York City, eleven thousand police and detectives were placed on a twenty-four-hour alert guarding all public buildings. Two companies of infantry were rushed to Chicago. In Boston several platoons of soldiers with rifles stood guard at the Federal Building.

July Fourth itself turned out to be an anticlimax. The much-vaunted strike never took place, and there were no signs of other radical activity. Nevertheless, the very anticipation of more labor violence heightened antiradical emotions and increased public suspicion of unions in general.

The annual convention of the American Federation of Labor, meeting at Atlantic City in June, had gone out of its way to demonstrate its hostility to radicalism. Delegates voted against recognizing the Soviet Union, declined to take any part in a proposed general strike for Mooney and Billings, opposed "one big union," and demanded more stringent immigration laws. The AFL did, however, reverse an old policy by announcing that it was now prepared to grant charters to police unions. Over the large protests of Gompers the convention rank and file endorsed the Plumb Plan providing for the federal government's permanent ownership of all the United States railroads, already taken over as a wartime measure by Wilson in December 1917. The four Railroad Brotherhoods supported the plan, which called for the purchase of the railroads and a division of the profits between the government, the managers, and the other employees. Many Americans, including many members of Congress, saw the Plumb Plan as "a bold, bald, naked attempt to sovietize the railroads."

The summer grew increasingly turbulent. President Wilson, already repudiated in the 1918 midterm elections, was fighting a desperate rear-guard action for his League of Nations. Attorney General Palmer, still unnerved by the bombing of his house, made preparations to purge the country of Reds once and for all. Strikes, riots, and terror spurred on the fanatic conviction of men like Fraina, Reed, and Gitlow that this turbulence would usher in a revolutionary wave to sweep away the old. Middle Americans yearned for the assurance of stability. Patriotic zealots saw their fears embodied in the unruly radicals. Strikes rose from 248 in April and 303 in June to 360 in July. On July 4, five thousand New England fishermen began a thirty-eight-day walkout, to be followed by the maritime workers. On July 13 Boston streetcars and elevated trains stopped for four days after the elevated railway workers left their jobs, refusing to return until their demands were met. The Boston *Herald* observed angrily that "every self-respecting person must have a feeling of disgust over the thought that an army of public service employees can get their wages raised by so despicable a performance as quitting their jobs while an adjustment is pending, to which they had agreed to adhere, the terms of which would have been retroactive."

Some of the crustier Republican elders blamed Governor Coolidge for being too conciliatory to the Boston elevated strikers. Undoubtedly the el strike made a preceptive impression on the Boston policemen, whose static pay scale had long been a growing source of discontent to them. At a December meeting of the representative police organization, the Boston Social Club, a member suggested calling in an American Federation of Labor agent. The matter was dropped without a vote. But by February 19, 1919, more than a thousand Boston policemen attending a meeting of the Social Club in Intercolonial Hall, Roxbury, "to discuss the advisability of affiliating with some other organization" declared themselves in favor of joining the American Federation of Labor. A large majority of those present voted to grant their executive board full power to act in the matter.

An announcement, following the American Federation of Labor June convention, that the federation was now prepared to grant charters to police unions resulted in a surge of union activity among police all over the country. By August the police forces of thirty-seven large cities had already been accepted into the AFL. On July 23 the *Herald* noted that "Boston Police wish to join the A. F. of L." According to the *Herald*, petitions were already circulating in each of the nineteen police districts requesting the formation of a union with an AFL charter.

THE
BOSTON POLICE
DEPARTMENT

Like the city itself, the Boston Police Department traced its roots to the earliest Colonial period. In 1631, a year after the settlers arrived on the Trimontaine peninsula and renamed it Boston, the "Court"—that is Governor John Winthrop, Deputy Governor Thomas Dudley, and their assistants—ordered "that *Watches* be set at sunset, and if any person fire off a piece after the watch is set, he shall be fined forty shillings, or be whipped." Two days later, as set down in the spidery handwriting of the record, "we began a Court of Guard upon the *Neck*, between Roxburie and Boston, whereupon shall always be resident an officer and six men." Those seven, on night watch against knaves, thieves, straggling Indians, wolves and bears, runaway servants and slaves, were Boston's first police force. Five years later at Town Meeting the watch's position was made more regular when "upon private warning, it was agreed y^t there shalbe a watch taken up and gone around with from the first of the second month next for ye summertime from sunne sett an houre after ye beating of ye drumbe, upon penaltie for every one wanting therin twelve pence every night."

All able-bodied males from the age of sixteen, subject to certain property qualifications, were made liable to keep "watch and ward," watching at night to prevent any danger of fire and to see that good order was maintained, and warding on the Lord's Day. As the village grew to a town, the burden of staying up all night proved too onerous for the more well-to-do citizens, and a paid watch was substituted under the charge and command of a "sober, discreet, able-bodied householder," whose badge of office was a "quarter pike with spire on the top therof." Ordinary watchmen carried a "staff with a bill fastened theron." By the end of the seventeenth century watchmen were being paid forty shillings a month and watching became a kind of public welfare. In 1733 Mathew Young was appointed watchman "that he and his children do not become a town charge."

In the winter the watchmen with their billhooks went on duty at nine in the evening, in summer at ten. They were instructed to walk their rounds "slowly and silently, and now and then stand and listen." After midnight, however, they were "to cry the time of night and state of the weather, in a moderate tone—One o'clock, clear, and all's well."

In 1703 a John Barnard built two watchhouses with sentry boxes for the town, one next to the Town House, the other near the powderhouse on the Common. A decade later the first watchhouse was moved to Queen Street by the school house with "a cage and whipping post to be added." The watch was then increased by two men, and the number continued to grow with the town. By 1723 there were five divisions of the watch; Old North, New North, Dock Watch, Townhouse Watch, and South Watch, with four watchmen and a captain at each house. By 1748, able-bodied watchmen were being paid in inflated paper currency at the rate of seven pounds ten shillings a month, but fined a pound whenever caught "getting asleep" on duty, a perennial weakness. As a countermeasure to dormancy, watchmen were ordered to patrol by twos. Among their duties was that of arresting "all negroes found out after dark without a lantern."

In the turbid years before the Revolution, when the mob ruled the Boston streets, the watch kept itself discreetly apart. There is no record of any watchmen caught up in the annual Pope's Day brawls, the sack of the house of the stamp distributor-designate Andrew Oliver, the gutting of Lieutenant Governor Thomas Hutchinson's mansion, the Boston Tea Party, or the Boston Massacre. In 1765 Captain Seemes of the South Watch reported that "Negro Dick came to the watchhouse and reported rowdies under his window. Watchmen were sent, and met a gang of rowdies, one of which drew a sword. The watch cried murder and fled to the watchhouse, and the rowdies escaped."

Then and after the Revolution watchmen were not held in very high esteem. In August 1789 a group of citizens, angered by a succession of burglaries, complained that the watchmen "have been asleep since New Year's. The Captains are generally men in their prime, aged from ninety to one hundred years, and the crew only average about fourscore, and so we have the advantage of their age and experience, *at least the robbers do.*" Whether the watch had anything to do with it or not, two men and a woman were hanged that October on Boston Common for highway robbery.

The first mention of police as such occurred in 1785 when John Ballard, William Billings, Christopher Clarke, and a Mr. Webb were appointed inspectors of police. In 1796 the legislature passed a law recognizing the Boston Watch. To the city's twenty-four constables fell the duty of supervising the "jaded stevedore, journeyman and mechanic" who made up the watch and whose own orders were "to walk their round once an hour, to prevent damage by fire and to preserve order ... taking particular observation and inspection of all houses and families of evil fame." The constables—coeval with local government—were the embodiment of authority, acting for the courts and sheriffs as arresting officers. By the early nineteenth century Boston had twenty-four of them. Besides their various legal and court fees they received an additional sixty cents for night watch duty. The watchmen received fifty cents. The five watchhouses were each manned by one constable and six watchmen. Watchmen, in addition to their billhooks, now wore badges of office and carried slatted wooden rattles that could be heard for a quarter of a mile. They continued on their rounds every other night at the same hours as in the previous century; nine o'clock in winter, ten o'clock in summer. Most of the watchmen had daylight jobs as well.

By 1810 the town of Boston, with 33,234 inhabitants, was consolidated into three watch divisions staffed by a police inspector,
two assistant police officers, seventeen constables, and thirty
watchmen. Two years later a captain of the watch was appointed,
and the pay of constables raised to seventy-five cents. Watchmen on
duty were instructed "not to talk loud, or make any noise, nor suf-
fer any one to enter a watchhouse without a certificate from a
Selectman." Besides the regular watch, a hundred special watchmen were now employed to patrol the town. Yet, in spite of badges
and billhooks and rattles, all was not well with the watch, as many
citizens were prone to observe. A committee of selectmen making
a surprise night visit to the various watchhouses found too many
watchmen doing duty inside, and at the South Watch "two constables asleep." An inspector of police on his rounds found a constable asleep at the South Watch at one in the morning and at "one
and one-half o'clock at Centre Watch found constable and door-
man asleep, and a drunken man kicking at the door to get in." A
group of indignant citizens complained that the watchmen "care
for nothing but their pay, and are sure to get that; give us a private
watch."

In 1822, by an act of the legislature, the expanding town became
the City of Boston, governed by a mayor, an executive board of
seven aldermen, and a common council of forty-eight councilors,
four from each of the twelve wards. Under the new government the
watch still remained the old watch, and it was found necessary to
post an order that all watchmen found asleep on duty would be discharged. As the self-contained town expanded into an amorphous
city "dangerous riots, routs and tumultuous assemblies" made the
lack of adequate protection all too apparent. The burning of the
Ursuline convent in Charlestown in 1834 by a mob was followed a
year later by the assault on the abolitionist William Lloyd Garrison.
Constables stood by helplessly as an inflamed crowd roped and
dragged the editor of the *Liberator* through the streets. Even the
mayor himself was roughly handled. In 1837 it took a cavalry regiment of militia—called out for the first time in its history—to
restore order after volunteer firemen returning from an alarm had
clashed with an Irish funeral procession on Broad Street. Finally in
1838 the exasperated legislature passed a law allowing the mayor

and board of aldermen to appoint daytime police officers with all the powers of constables except that of executing a civil process. The Boston Police Department as such came into being on the twenty-first of May when the board organized a police force under the direction of the city marshal. Six officers were appointed. The new department had no connection with the watch.

In 1846, under Mayor Josiah Quincy, Jr., the police department was reorganized under the flamboyant, tough-minded city marshal, Francis Tukey, a police official of the French school with "a thorough knowledge of the weaknesses of human nature." There were now twenty-two day and eight night police officers. The day officers remained on duty from eight in the morning till nine in the evening, reporting to the marshal at eight and at two. They were paid $2.00 a day, whereas the night force, whose function was chiefly to keep an eye out for burglars, received only $1.25. Watchmen's pay had risen by degrees from $.60 to $1.00. They continued on their independent and somnolent way, for it was noticed that after a round or two at the beginning of their watch they had a habit of wrapping themselves in their long coats and sleeping in the watch boxes until relieved. In 1848 Marshal Tukey issued a general order to cite all persons smoking in the street. As a demonstration that no one, not even the marshal, was above the law, Tukey himself was fined for fast driving.

The watch and the police continued side by side. Gradually the balance swung in favor of the police. By midcentury, with Boston's population at one hundred forty thousand, Mayor John Prescott Bigelow could announce that "there are 50 Police Officers, 225 Watchmen, the beat of each man averaging over a mile. The expenses of Police and Watch, $113,000 per year." Police officers had their appointment renewed each year.

Eighteen fifty-one was the year of the Great Descent, when police and watch combined to raid the disorderly houses of Ann Street. Some 165 persons "of all ages, sexes, nations and colors" were taken into custody for "piping, fiddling, dancing, drinking and all their attendant vices," receiving three to six months in various reformatories. The aftermath of the Great Descent proved unfortunate, for with the breaking up of Ann Street its inhabitants scattered all over the city to form new and expanding centers of criminal activity. Marshal Tukey's reformist zeal had more success in forcing theaters to abolish their "third row," a section traditionally set apart for the special accommodation of prostitutes. In 1852 the marshal found his office abolished and himself appointed chief of police, a position he held only briefly, for the newly elected mayor, Benjamin Seaver, discharged Tukey and all the night force as well as most of the day force and replaced them with those politically more amenable. At about the time of Mayor Seaver's purge, a harbor police detachment of a captain and ten men was formed. For some years police officers had been identified by leather hat bands bearing a number and the lettering POLICE in silver. Now a six-pointed oblong brass star, worn on the left lapel, was substituted for the leather band. About as large as one's hand, the badge was much ridiculed as looking more like a sculpin's head.

In 1853 the legislature authorized the city council to combine the watch and the police, and on May 26, 1854, the 229-year-old Boston Watch and Police ceased to exist and the Boston Police Department came into being. The new department, with headquarters at City Hall, had a chief, two deputies, a superintendent of hacks, a superintendent of teams, and five detectives. Eight police stations divided up the whole territory of the city, each with a captain, two lieutenants, and anywhere from nineteen to forty-four patrolmen. A station had three divisions or shifts, one for day and two for night duty. Day patrolmen went on their beats at 8:00 a.m. and remained out until 6:00 p.m., when, after being relieved by the night division, they reported back to the station house. Often they found themselves detailed for special duty at places of amusement, for which they received extra pay. The first night division was on duty from 6:00 p.m. to 1:00 a.m., the second until relieved by the day patrolmen. Every other night the divisions alternated. Each night man had to do day house duty once every six days. Captains now received three dollars a day, patrolmen two dollars. But although the pay was the same, the night division remained essentially the old watch, and day duty was much more sought after. Police officers, night or day, were now required to devote their full time to their work and to have no other employment.

The basic structure of the Boston Police Department was now fixed. As the city grew, the police force expanded. Each year brought innovations to the department: a sailboat for the harbor police, telegraph lines linking the stations, a photographer for the rogues' gallery. New duties fell to the police as well. Each station provided nightly "lodgings" to homeless strangers. In 1854 the city was stricken with cholera so severely that one person in twenty died. When the epidemic was at its height, it fell to the Boston police to do what all others refused: to remove bodies from tenements and "smoke" the rooms, to bring those who were stricken in the street to the station houses, and to care for the sick and the dying.

In 1858, under Mayor Frederick W. Lincoln, the police were at last given uniforms—a blue frock coat with brass police buttons, blue trousers, and black vests; a dress coat for the chief and his captains. The ridiculed sculpin badge was at last replaced by a smaller silver one, and the old billhook after 154 years gave way to a fourteen-inch club, carried in a leather waist-belt. The night men still retained their wooden rattles. Some ardent democrats and libertarians objected to a uniformed police force and accused the mayor of copying the "liveried servants" of the Old World. The new uniforms coincided with the first open scandal in Boston police history when in 1860 six night patrolmen were found guilty of stealing cigars and similar items from shops along their beats.

During the first year of the Civil War, 136 police details were required for the various military processions, parades, receptions, and reviews. Police were kept equally busy keeping an eye out for deserters. A military man, Colonel John Kurtz, having been appointed chief of police, ordered his men to assemble at Faneuil Hall for drill under his command. Such drill was afterward continued at each station house. The annual renewal of appointments to the force was now abolished, police being kept on during good behavior and usefulness, subject to removal only by the mayor.

When in June 1863 President Lincoln issued his draft call for three hundred thousand men, Boston's quota was set at thirty-three hundred. But in July, as the provost marshals began distributing their call-up notices, a riot broke out near the gas works close to Prince Street after a woman screamed that the soldiers were coming to take away her husband. At once the streets and alleys filled with infuriated men and women. When a detachment of police arrived, the officers were overpowered and two almost lynched. Others were knocked to the ground, beaten and trampled. A threatening crowd of some two thousand then gathered in front of the Hanover Street station as alarm bells sounded throughout the city—eleven strokes, three times repeated—calling out the whole police force. The riot proved too much for the police, and not until troops arrived from Fort Warren in the harbor was it finally put down. Pillaging was general. No policemen were killed, but seven were badly injured. Boston would not see such turbulence and disorder again for fifty-six years, not until the Boston Police Strike of 1919. One effect of the riot was to arm the police for the first time. From then on patrolmen took to carrying revolvers.

By 1869 traffic had so increased in the central city that police had to be stationed on the chief street crossings. Three hundred police were called out on special duty that year for the National Peace Jubilee, a stupendous occasion climaxed by a rendering of the "Anvil Chorus" from *Il Trovatore* by 10,000 choral singers, an orchestra of 84 trombones, 83 tubas, 83 cornets, 75 drums, 330 strings, and 119 woodwinds, while members of the Boston Fire Department in red shirts, blue trousers, and white hats pounded a hundred anvils. The next year the police department's first grand ball was held at Faneuil Hall, with police and public dancing together under a great banner reading: CHARITY—BOSTON POLICE—FRATERNITY. By this time the force numbered five hundred, and with a new sense of cohesiveness the men formed a Police Relief Association.

In the years following the Civil War, Boston's Fourth of July celebrations had grown into a carnival of misrule that took fifty-five separate police details and 275 special police appointed for the day to control. By 1873 the Fourth had become so riotous that Mayor Henry L. Pierce abolished the usual fireworks, the annual balloon ascension, and other festivities on the Common. In the more "quite and rational" Fourth that followed, he was able to dispense with the special policemen. On November 9 and 10 of that same year, Boston was devastated by the Great Fire that in two windy days destroyed most of the commercial and mercantile sections of the city. All 524 police remained on constant duty. As the fire swept toward the stores near and on Sumner Street, merchants, seeing that their stocks were doomed, invited all present to help themselves to anything they could carry away. Many of the poor used the occasion to obtain a free pair of boots, a shawl, a hat, garments, and bolts of cloth. A number of thrifty-minded citizens of the better class also accepted the invitation, retreating from the oncoming blaze with their arms full of merchandise. The police, however, insisted on regarding them as thieves, and the lockups and jails were soon full not only of city rabble but of solid citizens, including several aldermen, councilors, and at least one clergyman. Finally the police gave up arresting anyone, merely confiscating the goods while letting the takers go. In the end the police department collected four hundred thousand dollars' worth of assorted merchandise, though no one could determine afterward to whom it belonged.

After the independent towns of Roxbury and Dorchester voted to annex themselves to Boston, new police stations were set up in these semi-suburbs. The growth of the police department continued to parallel that of the city. Departmental changes were minor, confined to periodic reorganizations and amendments to the rules and regulations, and occasional alterations in buttons and badges. Since the powers of the mayor, the aldermen, and the chief of police over the department were not clearly defined, the result, Mayor Pierce complained, was lax discipline. In 1878 he was authorized by the legislature to appoint three commissioners to supervise and direct the police department. Each was to serve for three years.

Meanwhile in 1885, with the cooperation of dissident Yankee Democrats, Boston elected its first non-Yankee mayor, Alderman Hugh O'Brien, a man of great dignity and integrity but nevertheless foreign-born. A generation after the beaten survivors of the famine years had overrun the brick complacency of Boston, the Irish were emerging to political power. To the more astute Republicans who controlled the State House on Beacon Hill, it was clear that the days of the Boston Yankee mayors with their English-derived, New England-acclimated names were numbered. Phillips, Quincy, Otis, Eliot, Chapman, Brimmer, Bigelow, Seaver, Lincoln, Wightman, and Pierce would in a decade or so give way to Fitzgerald and Curley. The newcomers were already waiting in the wings. To put at least the strategic police department beyond the reach of the Celtic intruders, the Massachusetts legislature in 1885 passed an act creating a State Board of Police. This board consisted of three citizens of Boston appointed by the governor and the governor's council to administer the Boston Police Department. Boston was required to supply the funds to run the department, but the only powers retained by the city were the right of the mayor to increase the size and the pay of the force and to assume control in case of emergency. The reason given for the Commonwealth's takeover was that the police department had been too lax in enforcing regulations governing liquor licenses. But the real reason, as every politician knew, was the election of Hugh O'Brien.

For all that Massachusetts controlled the Boston police, the racial center of gravity in the department had been shifting. In 1851 the appointment of the Irish Barney McGinniskin to the force stirred up such violent opposition against "untrustworthy foreigners" that when he appeared at police headquarters, announcing himself as "Barney McGinniskin, fresh from the bogs of Ireland!" Marshal Tukey refused to assign him to duty. Mayor Seaver in his shake-up of the department kept McGinniskin on, but in 1854 he was discharged by the newly elected "Know Nothing" mayor, Jerome Van Crowninshield Smith. In 1861 there were no Irishmen on the force. But eight years later there were forty. Not for a number of years had a policeman's lot seemed a happy one to the old-line Yankees. But to the emergent Irish a police career was the third and the most practically attainable of the three P's—priest, politician, policeman. Any Boston Irish mother's highest ambition was to see her son a priest. A more deviously gifted boy might rise as a politician. Though the policeman might rank third, his was a rank more readily attainable. In his neighborhood he was highly respected. Not only did he embody authority, but his pay was at least double that of the average laborer and somewhat more than that of a teller or bookkeeper. With the new century the Boston police adopted a domed helmet—grey in summer, blue in winter— similar to that of the English police. Splendid in helmet, wing collar, long coat with a row of glittering buttons, polished leather belt fastened by a buckle bearing the city seal, and with a night stick tucked in his belt, the Boston patrolman walking his beat was a figure imposing enough to fill any mother's or wife's heart with pride.

Running the police department with three commissioners, often of different views, proved both unwieldy and inefficient. Graft and corruption, while not as blatant as in most American cities, were still evident. Finally in 1906 the legislature abolished the State Board of Police, and the three commissioners were replaced by a single commissioner with virtually complete authority over the department, as defined by the Act of 1906:

> The Police Commissioner shall have authority to appoint, establish, and organize the police of said city, and make all needful rules and regulations for its efficiency. He shall from time to time appoint a trial board to be composed of three captains of police to hear evidence in such complaints against members of the force as the commissioner may deem advisable to refer to said board. Said trial board shall report its findings to said Commissioner, who may review the same and take such action thereon as he may deem advisable. Except as otherwise provided herein, all the powers and duties now imposed or conferred by law upon the board of police of the city of Boston are hereby conferred and imposed upon said police commissioner.
>
> Present rules and regulations ... for said city shall continue in force until otherwise ordered by said police commissioner.

To fill this post for a five-year term, Governor Curtis Guild named Stephen O'Meara. The new commissioner was that anomaly, a Republican Irishman. Pockets of Yankee Democrats existed, survivors of the pre-Civil War scene, but an Irish Republican seemed an oxymoron. Some thought O'Meara's political aberration could be accounted for by his childhood in Charlottetown, Prince Edward Island. But whatever his politics, he was much respected by his fellow Celts and even by the native Yankees.

Tall, of soldierly bearing, he carried himself with an innate air of authority that scarcely any subordinate would feel inclined to challenge. As a man of integrity he ranked with such early Boston Irish leaders as Hugh O'Brien, the poet John Boyle O'Reilly, and Mayor Patrick Collins, who had died in office the year before O'Meara's appointment. It was of Collins that ex-President Grover Cleveland wrote, "In public life he was strictly honest and sincerely devoted to the responsibilities involved." The same could be said for O'Meara. It could scarcely have been said of Collins's successor, John F. Fitzgerald, better known as "Honey Fitz" for his tenor rendering of "Sweet Adeline." John Cutler, Honey Fitz's sympathetic biographer, would entitle his chapter on Mayor Fitzgerald's first term, "Thieves in the House." Entering office in the same year, the two Irishmen formed a curious contrast: the austere commanding police commissioner and the dapper, venal little mayor.

Stephen O'Meara's parents brought him from Canada to Charlestown, Massachusetts, when he was ten. He grew up in that rugged Celtic enclave where babies were said to be born with their fists clenched. A bright, eager pupil at Charlestown High School but too poor to go on to college, he found his first job as a cub reporter for the newly founded *Globe*, then two years later moved to a better job on the Boston *Journal*, the morning mouthpiece of Republican New England. A few years later he went back to the *Globe* as a police reporter, then shifted to political and legislative affairs, becoming one of the most skilled and knowledgeable reporters in the city. Returning once more to the *Journal*, he advanced successively over the next twenty years from city editor, to news and managing editor, to editor and general manager, and finally in 1895 to editor, publisher, and part owner. By 1899 he had secured majority interest in the *Journal*, holding this until 1902 when he sold his paper to Frank A. Munsey.

O'Meara received a measure of acceptance in frosty Yankee Boston rare for an Irish-American of his era. He was a member of the Exchange, Algonquin, St. Botolph's, and Union clubs, the latter being only a cut below that Boston club of clubs, the Somerset. He was a speaker much in demand by numerous social, political, and religious organizations. He served as treasurer of the New England Associated Press and as director and vice-president of the National Associated Press. Dartmouth awarded him an honorary degree. Harvard appointed him a lecturer on municipal government. When President McKinley attended the 1898 Atlantic Peace Celebration, he chose O'Meara as the New England speaker. O'Meara numbered among his correspondents Joseph Pulitzer, Henry Cabot Lodge, and Theodore Roosevelt. Roosevelt was so taken with him that in 1912 he begged him to run for governor on the Bull Moose ticket.

After selling the *Journal*, O'Meara took his family on an extended trip abroad. He was in Europe when he learned that Governor Guild had appointed him police commissioner. Guild explained that O'Meara was a man above politics. The governor was not, however, unmindful of Boston Irish sensibilities when he appointed him. O'Meara returned to Boston at once and was sworn into office on June 5, 1906.

The new commissioner made his presence felt in the department at once. In his first weeks he tightened up discipline and issued new regulations on appearance. He let his men know that at all times they must be clean-shaven, with boots and belts gleaming, trousers pressed to a razor-edge, white collars spotless. Rough conduct and unjustified assaults on citizens—there had been assorted complaints—were to cease.

While mayors Honey Fitz and James Michael Curley alternated at the municipal trough, the Boston Police Department under its austerely upright commissioner remained a towering exception to the corruption of City Hall. O'Meara in his years as a police reporter had come to know all the ins and outs of the department, the sources of graft and handouts, the links between police and politicians and the underworld. No subordinate could pull the wool over his eyes. He brooked no favoritism or favors, insisting that his policemen were there to maintain order and to keep the law, not to break it. The men found him strict but just, sympathetic to their needs, a man to be trusted. In spite of his Republican aberration, he was still one of their own, a Charlestown boy, an Irishman, a Catholic. Any policeman with a personal problem was free to talk it over in the privacy of the commissioner's office. He saw to it that all officers were selected and promoted on a merit basis. Discipline was enforced without regard for political connections. "The fairest man anyone could ever hope to deal with," one of his patrolmen called him years after his death. In his early months in office he encouraged his men to form the Boston Social Club, accurately described by its name, for although he was willing to listen to the suggestions of its various committees, he gave the new organization little or no say in the running of his department.

At the end of his first year in office the *Globe* in an editorial, "One Year of O'Meara," praised his reforms and declared that "members of the whole department are frank in their expression of their unqualified confidence in their ruler.... The Commissioner's leniency in dealing with offenders in the department has brought the men closer to him.... Today the commissioner is more popular with the men than any commissioner in recent memory."

In his first annual report, the commissioner himself wrote: "The first efforts of the police commissioner were directed to the task of convincing the men of the admirable police force over which he took control, that they were absolutely free from outside interference; that the commissioner himself in coming to the department had no entanglement and no obligation and that his duty was to the law alone; and that they, in turn were to look only to their department superiors for rewards and punishments."

When Honey Fitz tried to have four special policemen appointed who did not meet the commissioner's requirement, O'Meara wrote him that if he as mayor wished to increase the size of the police department, he had the legal right to do so, but the commissioner would still make the appointments. When his friend Senator Henry Cabot Lodge interceded for a Francis McDonald who had failed to meet the physical standards, although his own doctor had pronounced him fit, the answer was still No. Lodge wrote, "I take real interest in this case and should be much indebted for anything you can do." O'Meara replied, "The trouble with Mr. Francis McDonald ... is that he walks very badly and for a policeman that is a fatal defect.... We are obliged to be more particular than doctors."

Boston under Commissioner O'Meara remained and would continue to remain singularly free of the scandals so recurrent in the police departments of most major American cities. Even petty graft all but disappeared. As Raymond B. Fosdick wrote in his study of American police systems, "Particularly after the creation of a single-headed management in 1906, the administration of the Boston police force was conducted with a disregard for political consideration rarely encountered in American cities."

At the end of his five years O'Meara was reappointed by Gov-

ernor Eugene Foss, an elderly corporation lawyer who resembled
Humpty Dumpty with a moustache, and who was known generally
as "the Old Boy." Long a Republican, Foss had turned to the
Democrats in pique after failing to be elected to Congress as a
Republican in his own district. The Republican old guard–progressive conflict in 1910 enabled him as newly minted Democrat to get
elected governor. Democratic politicians now urged him to replace
the commissioner with a loyal Democrat, pointing out that
O'Meara had criticized him repeatedly in the *Journal* and opposed
him for Congress. Foss asked them rhetorically to "show me a
Democrat as honest, as intellectual as Stephen O'Meara and I'll
appoint him."

As he began his second term, O'Meara could boast that "in all
the criticism to which the police department and its commissioners are sure to be subjected, not one person and not one newspaper has ever alleged in five and a half years that the department as
a whole, or any members of it, were concerned in any way with politics, except as voting citizens." In that time only one police officer
had been convicted of taking a bribe.

O'Meara appointed his new men from the certified lists of the
Massachusetts civil service. These "reserve men" then served a one-
and-a-half- to two-year period of probation. But high rank alone in
the competitive examination did not assure a place in the department.
The commissioner also considered age, weight, height, health, and
above all character. "No written examination," he wrote, "can possibly disclose the qualities and habits which are of vital importance to
a police officer of rank and can be known only to superiors. Among
them are judgment, coolness, moral as well as physical courage, executive ability, capacity for the command of men, sobriety and other
moral qualities, standing among his associates and in the community,
powers of initiative, temper, integrity, energy, courtesy."

Promotion remained in O'Meara's hands, based on his personal
observations and the reports of ranking officers. While these sub-
jective reports were open to bias and at times caused resentment
among the rank and file, the Boston police cadre grew to be among
the best in the land. The public-minded Richard Henry Dana, son
of the author of *Two Years Before the Mast*, thought that the Boston
police were "physically finer than West Point cadets."

Every year the annual report of the police commissioner carried lists of punishments and dismissals for violations of discipline and behavior unbecoming an officer. In 1908 the report disclosed that twenty-seven policemen were convicted of wrongdoing and fourteen dismissed. O'Meara recorded with stern pride that "the number is the largest number of dismissals for various reasons of rigid discipline with two exceptions in 55 years and probably since the department was established." The commissioner was equally alert to root out the violence so taken for granted by most police. He informed his men that the "third degree" had no place in the Boston police force, and in 1916 he even outlawed the use of night sticks. Ernest Hopkins, writing long afterward in *Our Lawless Police*, noted that "O'Meara trained his men to take verbal abuse or a punch in the jaw without replying in kind. That unrestraint is the spirit of crime, restraint is the spirit of law, is the hardest lesson for Americans or their police to learn." Under O'Meara the Boston police force became one of the most law-abiding and law-conscious in the country.

O'Meara showed himself a stern moralist, much concerned with enforcing liquor laws, Sunday closing laws, and the "blue laws" still on the statute books. In interviews with newsmen he declined to discuss police matters except such as appeared in his official reports. He did, however, tell a reporter from his own *Journal* that he was completely opposed to the teaching of "sex hygiene" in the schools, since "a foreknowledge of that subject would serve as a stimulus to curiosity."

Neither Republican nor Democratic politicians were overly fond of O'Meara with his self-righteous denial of patronage, nor was he of them, for in 1907 he denounced both major parties openly and called for a formation of a third, a citizens' party. Overwhelmed by the Honey Fitzes and the Jim Curleys, the reform elements in Boston, the Good Government Association in particular, several times appealed to him to run for mayor. Each time he refused, telling them that his only ambition was to improve the performance, discipline, and efficiency of the police department. One of his first acts as commissioner was to forbid police officers to accept rewards for the performance of routine business, until then a commonplace practice and, for strategically located officers, a tidy source of additional income. He also discontinued the presentation of medals to officers who performed heroic acts, maintaining that to give a few individuals excessive recognition detracted from the honorable, if routine, performance of duty by the majority.

In 1916 Republican Governor Samuel McCall reappointed the commissioner almost as a matter of course. After ten years O'Meara could truthfully claim that he had kept his department "free from party politics and graft." An article in *Human Life* singled him out as "Stephen O'Meara: Police Chief Extraordinary." During his tenure the department personnel grew from 1358 to 1877. O'Meara ran his department from his headquarters at 29 Pemberton Square as if he were commanding a ship, subject only to the nominal authority of the governor. Demanding much of himself, he demanded much of his men, with little regard for human frailty. There were those who saw him as essentially a negative reformer. Leonard Harrison, in *Police Administration in Boston*, wrote:

> Warding off political favor seekers, counteracting unfair criticism, preventing injustice to members of the department—these were the defensive activities of the commissioner's. At this time the police force developed a certain pride in its position in the community. It maintained a high standard of integrity and self-respect, accompanied by a sense of satisfaction that everything was all right as it stood. Tradition for the most part determined the course to be followed. Imagination and experimentation were apparently not encouraged and a deep rut of conservatism was worn in this period.

There were problems O'Meara would have had to deal with, chiefly matters of pay, hours, and quarters, that had remained more or less in abeyance during the war. But on December 14, 1918, he died suddenly of a cerebral hemorrhage. The *Globe* wrote in tribute to its old reporter:

> Before his first term had expired it began to be noised about the land that Boston had a police department of peculiar excellence. Mr. O'Meara had impressed it on his men that their's were not "jobs" but "positions," and that they had been chosen for their work because of special fitness of which they had a right to be proud and to which they must live up.... Visitors from other cities have commonly remarked a difference in the Boston policemen—their

pride of profession, their courtesy, patience, and good temper, and the singular tact with which men were chosen for just the districts where they would best fit in with the temper of the population.

Whatever their latent discontent at the war's end, the Boston policemen had not wavered in their confidence in and affection for their leader. Most of the members of the force visited his body as it lay in state, and afterward marched in the funeral procession. Every station and every branch of the department sent its separate wreath.

If O'Meara had lived out his third term, the Boston Police Strike of 1919 would probably never have taken place. Under his successor, Edwin Upton Curtis, it became almost inevitable. For if O'Meara had been an autocrat tempered by understanding, the fifty-seven-year-old Curtis was an uncompromising martinet with no previous experience in police administration and no great affection for the Boston Irish. William Allen White characterized him with malicious accuracy in *A Puritan in Babylon* as

> a large, serious man, addicted to long double breasted coats, with a reserve which passed easily for dignity in the pre-Civil War era; a reserve which men in his own day were moved to call pomp; one of these solemn self-sufficient Bostonian heroes who apparently are waiting in the flesh to walk up the steps to a pedestal and be cast into monumental bronze. Boston parks are peopled with them.
>
> He ... embodied the spirit of traditional inherited wealth, traditional inherited Republicanism, traditional inherited skepticism about the capacity of democracy for self-government and a profound faith in the propertied classes' ultimate right to rule.

A quarter of a century earlier at the age of thirty-three, Curtis had taken office as Boston's youngest mayor. On that chill January day in 1895, his career seemed full of promise, with City Hall merely a way station on the glittering political road upward. The bright prospect never materialized. The road led nowhere. A year after his election he was defeated for a second term. His further career, until he became police commissioner, was a series of negligible interludes. In 1896 Governor Frederick Greenhalge appointed him a member of the Metropolitan Park Commission. A year later he married Margaret Waterman of the well-known family of undertakers. In 1906, as a further reward for Republican virtue, he was made assistant United States treasurer in Boston. In 1908 he became chairman of the Republican State Convention. A year later President Taft appointed him collector of customs for the Port of Boston, and there he remained until the advent of Wilson in 1913.

The Curtis genealogy was as old and established a one as could be found in New England. In 1632 John Curtis, born in England, had settled in Roxbury across the neck from Boston. Seven generations of Curtises had grown up there, none of them living more than a mile from the family homestead, which was torn down shortly before Edwin Curtis's birth in 1861. His father, Major George Curtis, had built a new home on Highland Avenue less than a mile from the old, a spacious square house with oval windows and a cupola. The major had been a Roxbury alderman and became a Boston one after annexation. But the Boston of Back Bay and Beacon Hill, the opulent mercantile Boston, passed the Curtises with a cursory nod. Unfashionable Roxbury remained a world apart from the Boston of the so-called Brahmins—the term the kindly Oliver Wendell Holmes had originally coined to mean no more than a bread-and-water intellectual asceticism but that had come to mean a class-conscious membership in the Back Bay–State Street oligarchy.

If Edwin Curtis had been brought up on Beacon Hill, he would no doubt have gone to Milton Academy or St. Paul's School and then Harvard. Instead he attended the solidly respectable if unfashionable Roxbury Latin School that a remote ancestor, John Eliot, the translator of the Indian Bible, had founded. After four years of the school's six-year course, he transferred to the Little Blue School at Farmington, Maine. Then he entered Bowdoin, a sturdy, small college sixty miles south of Farmington. Graduating from Bowdoin in 1882, where he was more remembered as an athlete than a scholar, he returned to Roxbury. He decided to become a lawyer, following the old-fashioned pattern of reading law in a private office—that of former mayor and governor William Gaston—rather than going to law school. After two years he passed his bar examination and in 1885 started a law firm on his own with his Bowdoin friend William G. Reed. But as an ardent Republican, his most engrossing interest was politics. An adequate private income, though modest by Beacon Hill standards, freed him from too much concern about building up a law practice. Within a year of opening his law firm he was made secretary of the Republican City Committee, and the following year, 1889, when Republican Mayor Thomas N. Hart replaced Democrat Hugh O'Brien, he was elected city clerk. Curtis's tenure was notable chiefly for the introduction of the Australian ballot system.

A Yankee Democrat, Nathan Matthews, Jr., succeeded Hart as mayor and was twice re-elected. Then, in 1894 the Republicans decided to turn from the party elders to the young city clerk. Henry Parkman, placing Curtis's name in nomination before the Republican City Convention, spoke of the "need of a young person of vigor and manhood." The Boston *Daily Advertiser* commented that it would give the young Republicans the chance they had been asking for to show what they could do. The Democrats put up Francis Peabody, Jr., a pleasant nonentity with a distinguished genealogy and a reputation as a Harvard oarsman, a figurehead candidate nominated by the Irish ward bosses who, in spite of Hugh O'Brien's earlier success, did not yet feel confident enough to name one of their own. Curtis's election seemed to Boston Republicans a redemption from Democratic error. So confident were they in the dawn of a new Republican day that they persuaded the firmly Republican legislature to extend the mayor's term from one to two years. In 1895 Martin Lomasney, the mahatma of Ward Eight, with the other Democratic ward bosses, upset Republican hopes and Republican tenure by importing a mayoralty candidate from neighboring Quincy: Josiah Quincy III of the eponymous family, the direct descendant of the pre-Revolutionary Josiah Quincy, "the Boston Cicero." Quincy easily defeated Curtis and was the third of his name to become mayor of Boston.

Curtis's political career was cut short by his defeat. Never again would he be nominated for public office. His bitterness against the ward bosses remained. His people had governed Boston since the Revolution. Now they were being steamrollered by the second-generation Irish. He despised and feared this emergent group with its alien religion and its eye for political plunder. In his heart he was convinced that Boston would never again be a decent city until the ephemeral Honey Fitzes and Jim Curleys and Dan Coakleys had been replaced by Curtises. That was why at the 1917 Massachusetts Constitutional Convention he sponsored an amendment denying public funds to any private religious institution, school, or hospital, a measure aimed primarily at parochial schools and one that Boston's Cardinal O'Connell called "an insult to Catholics." That was why, in the period of Boston's decline, he accepted the office of police commissioner from Governor McCall.

When Curtis took over the Boston Police Department in 1918, he was an ailing man, suffering from a malignant heart condition which he attempted to conceal but which gave his face with its pendulous protruding ears a somewhat bloated appearance. It was a face that had grown increasingly set in middle age, with an uncompromising quality intensified by narrow, disillusioned eyes and a pugnacious chin clamped above a wing collar. At fifty-seven, in spite of his precarious health, he welcomed the new police post as a belated opportunity to demonstrate his abilities.

OVERTURE
TO A STRIKE

In February 1913, the *National Police Magazine* listed the recently increased salaries of the Boston Police Department as:

Commissioner $6000
Superintendent $4525
Chief of Detectives $2800
Inspectors $2600
Captains $2500
Lieutenants $1600
Sergeants $1400
Patrolmen (1227) $1200

This, the magazine felt, was a very fair pay scale, as indeed it was in the day when a laborer or mill worker often earned less than five hundred dollars a year. The new graduated scale had been set in 1898, but because of a running dispute between the mayor and the city council had not been voted into effect until fifteen years later. Those years marked the end of the post-Civil War deflationary cycle that had at last reversed itself during the McKinley administration. Already in 1913 living costs had risen 37 per cent above what they had been in 1898. By 1918 they had shot up another 79 per cent. Yet a new policeman, who had to be twenty-five years old, received only two dollars a day, what he would have received in 1854 when the police department was established.

A recruit, after he had passed his police examination, joined the Boston force as a probationer or "reserve man" at $730 a year. The following year he received $0.25 a day more or $821.25 annually, but usually during that year he became a patrolman at $1000. His salary then increased each year until it reached a six-year maximum of $1400. Out of his pay he had to provide his own uniform and equipment at a cost, by 1919, of over two hundred dollars.

What had been acceptable before the war grew less so after 1917. Rising expectations induced by the steady expansion of a consumer economy were accelerated by the slogans of the war years. With the High Cost of Living, discontent and restiveness among Boston's police grew. They were resentfully aware that in the wartime boom they had come to earn less than an unskilled steelworker, half as much as a carpenter or mechanic, fifty cents a day "less than a motorman or conductor on the streetcars." Boston city laborers were earning a third more on an hourly basis. Even the admittedly small wages of the female spinners in the Lawrence mills had quadrupled since 1914. As William Allen White noted: "The high wages received by comparatively unskilled labor, in the factories and shipyards, was probably the most potent force in stirring up insurrection in the heretofore staid Boston police force. Many of these officers living on less than twenty-three dollars a week were arresting shipyard and factory workers on their Saturday nights in Boston. Their spending was profligate. Wages of seventy-five dollars to one hundred dollars a week were common through the pyramiding of high overtime rates."

In 1917 a committee of policemen met O'Meara to ask about a raise. He was sympathetic, but advised them to wait for a more auspicious time. They did not raise the issue until the summer of 1918, when spokesmen for the Boston Social Club again complained about the inadequacy of their pay. The commissioner told them that while he himself favored an immediate increase, his hands were tied. The best he could do was to arrange for them to meet with the mayor. Boston's "reform" mayor, Andrew J. Peters, in reply to their demand for an across the board $200-a-year increase, explained that the city at present lacked funds, but if they would wait until the new budget was completed he would see what he could do. Not until December 7 were the budget plans announced. To their dismay the police found that a quarter of them were to get no raise at all. Those who had been at a maximum for at least a year would receive a $100 raise. Reserve men would enter into the force at $900 a year and after three months of satisfactory service would be given a $200 increase. No one else would receive anything.

The disgruntled police felt their patience had done them little good and that Peters had let them down. On December 25 a committee of four patrolmen from the Social Club, headed by Michael Lynch, met again with the mayor and the new commissioner, Edwin Curtis, who in the few days since O'Meara's death had not yet been officially sworn into office. The committee renewed the police demand for a $200 general increase, and again Peters refused. Lynch enlarged on what had happened in the Montreal police strike and asked Peters how he would like such scenes in Boston. He also warned that many of his fellow patrolmen were threatening to leave for better-paying jobs and that their leaving would disorganize the department. But he denied that "radicalism had entered the department to such a degree as to make the duties of the new commissioner difficult." Peters, with as much affability as he could muster, told the committee that the city could not afford such a pay hike. Lynch replied that he was "clearly disappointed." The mayor told the press afterward that "while the word 'strike' was not mentioned, the whole situation is far more serious than I realized."

Lynch in turn assured reporters that "the matter of a strike has not been considered by any patrolmen I know." But he added that "for four years we have waited patiently for some action regarding more money." He complained of the High Cost of Living and pointed out that other cities paid their police better. "Boston should live up to its high ideals," he concluded. "The situation could be summed up by saying that the men in the department are unable to make both ends meet." Finally, on New Year's Eve, seven hundred of the twelve hundred Boston Social Club members met in Longfellow Hall, Roxbury, and voted unanimously to stick to their demand for a $200 increase. The word "strike" still was not mentioned.

Although pay stood out as the primary grievance of the Boston police, other grievances were there, exacerbated by what seemed the intransigence of the mayor and the commissioner. Beyond the pay scale there was the matter of hours, unaltered in half a century. Patrolmen worked a seven-day week, with one day off in fifteen. Day men put in seventy-three hours a week, night men eighty-three hours, and wagon men ninety-eight hours. Night Patrolman James Long of the LaGrange Street station recalled:

> After my day off, I used to report and had to do what they called a "house day," that is I was on call at the station from eight in the morning to six at night, sometimes on command for a wagon run— to hop the wagon when it went out—sometimes to sit at the signal desk and record the duty, things like that.
>
> We got out at six, but we had to report back at the station house at nine. After we checked in, we usually went upstairs to the dormitory where we slept until 12:45 when the bell rang for roll call. Then we went out on the street till eight in the morning. After that we could go home, but had to be back at six for what they called an evening on the floor, the same sort of duties as house-day duties, a trip on the wagon, taking care of prisoners, whatever turned up. At nine we went to bed for three hours. Sometimes during the week we'd get an afternoon detail at a theater like the Wilbur and get two dollars extra. But for parade duty on our days off we got nothing— and Boston always had a lot of parades.
>
> That was the way it was day after day, round and round. We had no freedom, no home life at all. We couldn't even go to Revere Beach without the captain's permission.

Day men, in addition to their ten-hour day, had to spend one night a week in the station house on reserve. Although the commissioner and the mayor had agreed to give the police a twenty-four-hour holiday for every eight days of work, this day could be taken away at will. Even in their free time the patrolmen could not leave the city limits without express permission.

Many of the extra duties assigned to the police came to seem arbitrary and even capricious. Men did not see why ten or fifteen patrolmen should be assigned to a Sunday band concert where two would have sufficed. Nor did they feel that they should be delivering unpaid tax bills, surveying rooming houses, taking the census, or watching the polls at elections. Particularly after O'Meara's death, they objected to having a man's promotion hang on the judgment of his captain, who if he disliked him could keep him a patrolman indefinitely in spite of his qualifications and assign him to some undesirable beat if he attempted to protest. Then there were the "petty tyrannies" of the captains and higher-ups, who in many cases made errand boys of their men, sending them out to bring in lunches and Sunday dinners or to pick up the daily newspapers ("peanut graft," never paid for). One superintendent even complained about his free papers arriving late!

Finally, the police had much to complain about in the sorry condition of most of the nineteen station houses. Only four had been built during O'Meara's term and these—in South Boston, East Boston, Charlestown, and Mattapan—were far beyond the city core. In spite of all the commissioner's efforts, the inner-city station houses remained overcrowded, decaying, rodent- and vermin-ridden. Much of this state of affairs was brought about by the hostility of Democratic mayors to Republican police commissioners. In all but two of O'Meara's years, the mayor's office was occupied either by Honey Fitz or James Michael "Gentleman Jim" Curley. Neither Fitzgerald nor Curley was interested in improving the conditions of a department over which they had no control and through which they could parcel out neither jobs nor favors. Curley in 1913 was so piqued at the frosty integrity of the Republican commissioner that he attempted to undermine him by disallowing the new wage scale. Until 1912 there had been no new police station in thirty years, and some stations stood relatively unaltered since before the Civil War. In 1912 the city council at last appropriated thirty-seven thousand dollars for plans for new buildings. Those plans were drawn up, scrapped, and drawn up again, but except for the four semisuburban structures, nothing further was done. In May 1917, O'Meara prepared a lengthy report for the city council about the need for new or reconstructed station houses. After two years the council had taken no action.

As the station houses continued to deteriorate, ordinary patrolmen came to feel that their officers were little concerned about how
the men had to live as long as their own private offices were in
order. Captains were supposed to inspect the attic dormitories in
the station houses once a day but often had never so much as set
foot there. Beds were used by two, three, or even four men in succession in a single twenty-four-hour period, the man coming off
duty merely pushing the duty man out of bed and taking his place.
Bedbugs and roaches swarmed in the sleeping quarters until it
became a sardonic joke among the men that they carried visitors
home in their clothes. In the Court Square station house, just
behind City Hall, the bugs were so voracious that they ate the
leather of the police helmets and belts. That same station had four
toilets and one bathtub for 135 men. All the stations were overcrowded, so much so that at times two patrolmen had to share not
only the same locker but the same bed. At Dudley Street the
matron had to occupy a room with the female prisoners. Patrolman
Long at LaGrange Street thought the cockroaches there were the
largest in Boston and wondered if they were some new breed. His
attic dormitory was almost never cleaned, the two city laborers
assigned to do it contenting themselves with mopping the floor and
perfunctorily making beds. Next to the dormitory was the toilet-
washroom, and often at night he would be wakened by the stench
of it.

O'Meara had indeed created an efficient and smooth-running
police department, but his tightly organized system inevitably kept
him remote in spite of all his efforts to make himself available.
Proud of the *esprit de corps* of his men, he felt like a military
commander faced with imposing tasks. Duty came first; no burden
was too difficult! In a dozen years his force grew from 1358 to
1877. Yet the weight of work increased proportionately far more.
In 1906 the police had made 49,906 arrests; in 1917 the number
was 108,556. By order of the legislature the Boston police were
assigned the task of checking the backgrounds and character of
some twenty thousand prospective jurors. As auto traffic increased,
they were called to regulate it. Other special functions required
special details. The war greatly expanded the demand for police
services. In 1917 O'Meara's men did twenty thousand tours of duty

exclusively related to the war effort. During the war years grumbling and discontent in the police department, though shunted aside and belittled by the captains and the superintendent, finally reached the ears of the commissioner. In O'Meara's last year there was enough talk of the police forming a union for him to notify Governor McCall and to issue General Order Number 129 on the subject. His order, dated June 28, 1918, met the current rumors head-on:

> It is probable that the printed rumors to the effect that members of the police department are discussing the advisability of organizing a union to be affiliated with the American Federation of Labor represent no substantial sentiment existing among them. Under ordinary conditions no attention would be paid to such rumors, but even though unfounded, they are so likely to injure the discipline, efficiency, and even the good name of the force, and the times are so favorable to the creation of discontent among men who are bearing their share of the war burdens, though still at home, that I feel it to be my duty to make the situation clear.
>
> There is no substantial disagreement as to the wisdom and even the necessity of maintaining unions among persons following the same industrial occupations.
>
> Though a union of public employees, as distinct from those composed of employees of private concerns, is in itself a matter of doubtful propriety, such union in any case and at the worst could affect the operations only of a particular branch of the city service. The police department, on the other hand, exists for the impartial enforcement of the laws, and protection of persons and property under all conditions. Should its members incur obligations to an outside organization, they would be justly suspected of abandoning the impartial attitude which heretofore has vindicated their good faith as against the complaints almost invariably made by both sides in many controversies.
>
> It is assumed erroneously that agents of an outside organization could obtain for the police advantages in pay and regulations. This is not a question of compelling a private employer to surrender a part of his profits; it has to do with police service which is wholly different from any other service, public or private—a service regulated by laws which hold to a strict responsibility certain officials, of whom the Police Commissioner is one. The policemen are their own best advocates, and to suppose that an official would

yield on points of pay or regulation to the arguments or threats of an outside organization if the policemen themselves had failed to establish their case would be to mark him as cowardly and unfit for his position.

I cannot believe that a proposition to turn the police force into a union, subject to the rules and direction of any organization outside the police department will ever be presented formally to its members, but if, unfortunately, such a question should ever arise, I trust that it will be answered with an emphatic refusal by the members of the force who have an intelligent regard for their own self-respect, the credit of the department and the obligations to the whole public which they undertook with their oath of office.

On December 30, 1918, the Boston Social Club members again met at Intercolonial Hall to take up the salary question. After an individual roll call to assure that no strangers were present, the seven hundred present voted unanimously to reject Mayor Peters' proposal of December 26 and declared that they would accept nothing less than their $200 demand. There was still no mention of a strike nor any hint of any approach to the American Federation of Labor, but it was clear that in their frustration the men were growing increasingly militant. At the close of the meeting President Lynch, to correct rumors circulating in the press, issued a statement pointing out that the present wage scale had been voted over twenty years before and had not gone into effect until 1913; that when the war broke out and prices rose, the men had bided their time because of Boston's financial difficulties; that when in 1917 they had gone to the commissioner, he had advised them to postpone their demands; that when they had taken his advice, they had found no special consideration a year later for their patience.

Earlier on that same day the outgoing Governor McCall had administered the oath of office to Commissioner Curtis. In his first public statement the new commissioner announced bluntly that any member of the police force so dissatisfied that he could not perform his duties properly and cheerfully was free to resign. His sole advice to his men was to be patient. "No increase in salaries can be given the police department," he told them, "except by concurrent action of the mayor and the police commissioner. Undoubtedly we shall consult on the subject. Meanwhile, everyone should talk and act with moderation with regard to the matter. Knowing the member-ship of the department by reputation we are confident that they will gratefully accept our final decision."

Even Curtis realized that something must be done about the policemen's pay. In February, after Peters' piecemeal wage offer had been rejected, the commissioner suggested a compromise plan of a flat 10 per cent increase, amounting to an average $140-a-year raise. The men rejected the compromise, holding to their original demand while at the same time pointing out that salaries were only one of a number of their grievances.

In March Clarence W. Rowley, the lawyer for the Boston Social Club, challenged Curtis to debate whether the salaries of the policemen should be increased to meet the cost of living. Curtis refused. "Being in touch with the committee of the men them-selves," he replied, "I know that my attitude on this question is sat-isfactory to the men and I see no useful purpose to be gained in debating the matter. I do not share your fear that there is danger that our Police Department will be demoralized."

Rowley answered him tartly:

> Boston police officers have worked faithfully more than 60 hours per week throughout the war; they have received no increase in pay for more than five years, while the pay of thousands of alien work-men has been advanced from 50 to 70 per cent or more, during the same period. The pay of carmen has advanced very materially and the cost of living has increased 72 per cent.
>
> I wish you would consider whether it would be fair, both to the city and the men, to increase salaries in the same proportion that the cost of living has increased since July 1, 1914, which date I take because it seems to be a normal time before the disruption of the great war....
>
> The effect of a demoralized Police Department will be immediate and will endanger life and property. The maintenance of law and order and the prevention of crime demands [sic] a properly governed and fairly paid Police Department.

To this Curtis did not reply. Finally in May Governor Coolidge signed a bill increasing Boston's tax limit from $6.52 to $9.52, a limit that, like the police department, was controlled by the legislature. With the prospect of additional revenue, Mayor Peters announced on May 10 that police and firemen would now receive their $200 increase. Senior officers would get $200 by the end of the month, while privates in the lower grades would get the regular $100 advance plus $100.

But what might have been a cause for rejoicing two years earlier, and quite acceptable even in the previous year, now seemed inadequate under the lengthening shadow of the High Cost of Living. Some of the policemen were as much as five hundred dollars in debt. Policemen could read in the papers that government economists had now set $1575 a year as the subsistence minimum for a family of five. Even that minimum was still beyond the reach of the majority of the police. Nevertheless they were not yet prepared to challenge the commissioner. At a meeting of the Social Club on May 9, resolutions were unanimously adopted thanking Curtis for providing "at [his] personal expense" refreshments for police assigned to the Yankee Division parade. "This kindness as well as many others for their welfare put into active operation by you since assuming your important office, is highly appreciated by the patrolmen of the Police Department, for which we sincerely thank you."

In spite of their formally polite resolutions, the police found their new commissioner cold and unapproachable. When shortly after he had taken office a committee from the Social Club came to him to suggest a review of working conditions, he refused to deal with it. Instead he set up his own grievance committee, made up of men elected by ballot, one from each of the station houses. Since the division captains counted the ballots in the privacy of their offices, there was much suspicion that many of the elections were rigged. The new committee met only once, and at the commissioner's order. After that he scheduled no further meetings, and when the committee's president, the same Michael Lynch who was president of the Social Club, asked him when they would meet again to discuss departmental problems, he replied, "Search me!" Those members who went directly to Curtis with their complaints received scant satisfaction. When one such delegation complained that certain men in Division Sixteen earned forty to sixty dollars a month for extra duty while others with larger families were bypassed, he not only did nothing about it but saw to it that the complaining grievance officer was transferred and given strike duty at a shoe factory. Nor was anything done about the condition of the station houses. Curtis merely selected a committee of officers to inspect them and submit a report on their condition, which he then forwarded to Peters. Nothing was heard of it further in the mayor's office.

While the police simmered in their grievances, Boston itself moved from spring to summer. As the elms on the Common budded and then leafed, the turbulence of the country and the world outside impinged on the city only in headlines. Bostonians, proper and improper, were engrossed in casual day-to-day events: the opening of the baseball season at Fenway Park, the flight of the great navy seaplane, the NC-4, with its crew of five across the Atlantic from Halifax to Horta in the Azores, the intrepid aviators of the Flying Circus who looped the loop over the State House at over seventy miles an hour as a spur to the lagging Victory Liberty Loan drive. The last of the American Expeditionary Force was leaving France. Sergeant Alvin York of Pall Mall, Tennessee, the most decorated American soldier of the World War, again made the headlines by marrying. Governor Coolidge vetoed the Massachusetts legislators' efforts to raise their pay from $1000 to $1500. In the United States Senate, the debate on President Wilson's peace treaty opened, with Massachusetts' Senator Henry Cabot Lodge and other Republican stalwarts vindictively eager to separate the treaty from the League of Nations. Of more emotional concern to Boston were the mass meetings held to demand Ireland's freedom, some of which Cardinal O'Connell graced with his presence.

For several June weeks the city sweltered under a heat wave that was finally broken by the east wind. The plate glass windows of the sedate houses on Commonwealth Avenue and Beacon Street were boarded up as usual for the summer while their owners left for the North Shore or Bar Harbor. Children again rode on the swan boats that glided decorously under the bridges in the Public Garden. Macullar, Parker's Tremont Street window had its annual display of Harvard club hat bands.

Few in the city gave much thought to the police. The patrolmen had changed their blue winter helmets for summer grey; there seemed to be no other change. They walked their beats, high-headed, staid, reliable, "Boston's finest." Those passing them so casually on the streets would have been surprised to learn that anything like a crisis was developing within the police department, a confrontation looming up between the stubborn Yankee commissioner and his resentful Celtic force. Whatever their grievances, the members of the Boston Social Club still hoped to avoid such a confrontation. On July 16 the grievance committee wrote to Curtis: "We want to thank you sincerely in behalf of all the patrolmen of the Boston Police Department for the many vital and important benefits obtained and which were championed by you, including the non-contributory pension, corrections in the rule relating to unnecessary reporting by night men on their off days and excuses from different roll calls. We desire to express our deep sense of gratitude for your efforts in our behalf in obtaining the increase in salary."

The June reversal by the American Federation of Labor of its policy of not granting charters to police unions was seen as a great opportunity by the Boston police to turn their innocuous Social Club into an aggressive union. Unionization was in the air. In the preceding four years, aided by wartime prosperity and a friendly national administration, union membership had increased by 60 per cent. In 1919 alone almost a million new members had joined the AFL. The Boston firemen now had their affiliated union as did the clerks and office workers of City Hall. Police in other cities were rushing to sign up. An undercurrent of persuasive discussion ran through the Boston Police Department even as petitions for an AFL charter gathered signatures at the various station houses. When Curtis in his Pemberton Square office learned of this, he issued a statement to the press expressing his disapproval of the movement. Then he walked the hundred intervening yards to the governor's office to consult with Coolidge's officiously efficient secretary, Henry Long, left in charge while the governor was away on vacation. Curtis told Long of the strong unionization movement within the police force. As commissioner he planned to oppose any union and wanted to know if Coolidge would stand behind him. He declared he was ready to take whatever action was necessary but would nevertheless like the assurance of the governor's support. The secretary offered the assurance on his own. Curtis said this was not enough. The governor himself must make the statement directly. Long then telephoned Coolidge and gave him Curtis's message. Coolidge told Long to "tell the Commissioner to go ahead in the performance of his duties."

The remark, terse as it was ambiguous, was typical of the austere Vermont Yankee who occupied the austere, elegant governor's office in the Federalist State House. For Calvin Coolidge was a cautious man who measured his words with a teaspoon, put on his long winter underwear in mid-October and took it off in mid-May, and summed up his philosophy by remarking that if you see ten troubles coming down the road, you can be sure that nine will run into the ditch before they reach you. Harvard's self-consciously aristocratic Barrett Wendell described him as "a small hatchet-faced, colorless man, with a tight-shut, thin-lipped mouth; very chary of words but with a gleam of understanding in his pretty keen eye."

He was born John Calvin Coolidge in the remote hill-bound hamlet of Plymouth Notch, Vermont, the one state in the Union that always voted Republican, and that had fewer people in it than at the time of the Revolution. His father, a farmer and storekeeper, was also the local justice of the peace. The flinty Coolidge features had been honed by a slight admixture of Indian blood. Even in the waxworks museum that was Vermont the family had seemed atavistic, their very speech deriving from a remote psalm-singing Calvinist past. Young John Calvin's nasal accent had a twang that had made his Plymouth schoolmates giggle. He was said to be the last New Englander who pronounced "cow" as a three-syllable word. When the boy was fifteen, his father enrolled him in Black River Academy, one of the small pathetically named academies scattered across the New England landscape in the wake of the Greek revival, this one in Ludlow, twelve miles to the south of Plymouth and equally overborn by the Vermont hills. A shy and lonely boy, thrown back on himself, he took no part in sports or recreation, made no mark even in that petty world. After graduating from Black River he went on to Amherst, seventy-three miles to the south but still within his hill range, for the Berkshires are only an extension of Vermont's Green Mountains. There in upland Massachusetts the taciturn, diffident freshman hoped for acceptance, without knowing how to go about it. No one sought him out. No fraternity bothered to rush him. "I don't seem to get acquainted very fast," he wrote wistfully to his father. Sometimes in writing to Plymouth Notch during those first months he found his hand trembling from homesickness.

By his senior year he had won at least a half measure of acceptance. In that year he was asked to join a newly formed fraternity. Enough of his classmates had become aware of a certain caustic wit that lurked beneath his Vermont-granite exterior to elect him Grove Orator, the senior chosen to give the classday humorous oration. He managed to graduate *cum laude*. No soaring ambition filled him as he faced the world, no restless urge to move beyond the familiar range of hills that had always hemmed him in. He considered store-keeping and law as careers, finally deciding on the latter. When a friend asked him where he planned to settle, he replied laconically, "Northampton's the nearest courthouse."

Northampton was seven miles away. He moved there in September 1895. In the more primitive tradition of the early Republic he read law on his own, serving as a clerk in the Northampton firm of Amherst graduates John C. Hammond and Judge Henry P. Field, sitting at a table in the outer office learning to prepare writs, deeds, and wills, while reading Kent's *Commentaries* and legal text-books in his spare time. Judge Field thought the pinch-faced, sandy-haired clerk, who was already showing signs of baldness, a queer stick. Sometimes Field on coming out of his office would catch him leaning back in his swivel chair staring out into space. The judge did not find his new clerk a very hard worker, but then he was not paying him anything. Coolidge spent some twenty months at Hammond & Field's, an unobtrusive, solitary, inscrutable figure. Then one morning his table was clear of his books, and he was gone.

In those twenty months he had learned enough law to pass his bar examination. Using a minute inheritance he then rented two small rooms in the Masonic Building, hung out his shingle, and waited for clients. Northampton was then a city of fifteen thousand, its industrialism tempered by its rural past and by Smith College for women, just then completing a second decade. Its established middle and upper classes were undeviatingly Republican, but the newcomers, the Irish and "Canuck" mill workers, were usually numerically sufficient to elect a Democratic mayor. Northampton would seem to have no political future for a young Republican like Coolidge, but he had two hidden qualities that would become apparent in time, and that were both essential to political success. First of all, he was lucky. Secondly, for all his introvert taciturnity, he had the knack of winning the goodwill and even the liking of those at or near the working-class level—the cobbler, the barber, the deliveryman, the plumber, the news vendor, even the tavern keeper. With such people he could pass the time of day, whereas the upper-crust Northampton of the Fields and the Hammonds reduced him to silence. In times to come, it would be seen that French-Canadians and Irish, who would never vote for a Field or a Hammond, would even abandon their traditional party to mark their ballots for a Coolidge.

"Calvin," Coolidge now called himself with unconscious appropriateness, discarding the adventitious and seldom-used "John." After an impecunious start he managed to earn a modest living as a lawyer, but found more interest in local politics than in the law. His luck began here, for he lived in a furnished room on Round Hill in the one solidly Republican ward of the city. His Republican allegiance to the party of respectability, sound money, and business was as much part of his nature as his Vermont inheritance, and in his semisilent way he made his politics known. During the McKinley-Bryan campaign of 1896 he wrote an article for the *Hampshire Gazette* attacking Bryan and the free coinage of silver.

Not long after being admitted to the bar he became one of five chosen from his ward to serve on Northampton's Republican City Committee. Two years later he was elected as one of the ward's three members to the city council, a post that paid nothing but might with luck be the first step up the Massachusetts Republican escalator. That smooth-running machine, if one waited one's turn and minded one's place and held tightly to the rails, could carry an astute and adaptable politician a long way, from the precinct and the ward, to councilor or mayor of a small city, to the gilt-domed State House and even—with a certain winnowing at the higher levels— to Congress or the ultimate destiny of the governor's chair. Beyond that lay the blessedness of a directorship in a life-insurance company or the perfect peace of the Boston Safe Deposit or the First National Bank.

From the council Coolidge was appointed to the unfilled term of city solicitor. The next year he was elected to that office, though the following year he was defeated by a brasher and more plausible Democrat. It would mark his sole defeat in a lifetime of holding office. Republicans looked after their own, and following the death of the clerk of court of Republican Hampshire County, Coolidge was named to replace him. Though there were no outward signs, political ambition quickened within. He soon quit the profitable but dead-end clerk's job to run for the legislature, making few speeches but carefully visiting every voter in his district and taking particular pains with the Irish Democrats. "I want your vote. I need it. I shall appreciate it," he told them. Nothing more. To the surprise of everyone but himself, he defeated the Democratic incumbent. "An enigmatic little devil," Judge Field observed as he noted his clerk's slow rise on the escalator.

Representative Coolidge became one of the four legislators from Hampshire County, for which he received $750 a year plus his travel expenses. The mousy, middle-aged young man with the freckled flinty face and the high grating voice made no great impression in the Massachusetts House of Representatives. His colleagues suspected he might be either a schoolteacher or an undertaker. He took a small back room in the Adams House on Washington Street at a dollar a day and returned by train each weekend to his family in Northampton. After ten years in Northampton he had married Grace Goodhue, a young woman of such animated charm that neighbors wondered and continued to wonder what she had ever seen in him. She, living on Round Hill, had caught a first ludicrous glimpse of him one morning as he stood near his bathroom window in long underwear, a felt hat on his head, while he shaved. Nevertheless, after a prolonged and rather silent courtship, she accepted him. It is said that in the course of a walk, during which he had proposed and she agreed, he had remained silent for the next fifteen minutes. When she asked him why he said nothing more, he replied that perhaps he had said too much already.

The Coolidges lived in a two-family house on maple-shaded Massasoit Street, a duplex with three bedrooms upstairs, downstairs a front hall that opened into a bay-windowed parlor that in turn opened into a dining room. Coolidge himself had taken care of the furnishings. In the parlor the chairs and table were of mission oak. On the wall hung a framed sepia reproduction of "Sir Galahad" and a photograph of Plymouth Notch. The mantel displayed the embroidered quotation:

> A wise old owl sat in an oak
> The more he saw, the less he spoke;
> The less he spoke, the more he heard.
> Why can't we be like that old bird?

No one would ever accuse Coolidge of speaking too much, but he gave more attention to the legislature and its operation than did most of his colleagues, seldom missing a session, and being always on hand to vote, study bills, and attend the dullest of drawn-out committee meetings and hearings. The social world of Back Bay and Beacon Hill, the world of Symphony Hall and the art museum and the opera house and the Athenaeum, remained as remote from him as the arctic. He had no hobbies, no need of recreation. Evenings under the flaring gas jet in his room he read the *Evening Transcript* and the *Manual for the General Court*. In his loneliness he honed his political sagacity. The Democrats came to recognize him as a man of his word, yet not averse to doing favors. Gradually he built up a political reputation for faithfulness and reliability. Even western Massachusetts was feeling the reform currents engendered by Progressivism, and Coolidge as a legislator voted for a six-day week, limitation of working hours for women and children, direct election of United States senators, women's suffrage, and limitations on injunctions in labor disputes. But as Progressivism faded and as Coolidge rose on the escalator, his conservatism asserted itself. He grew more and more suspicious of innovation and what he considered radicalism. By inheritance and by his very place of birth he remained a Puritan. William Allen White, who knew him well, wrote in *A Puritan in Babylon*:

> He brought the habits which were inevitable in a meager but happy civilization; thrift, energy, punctuality, self-reliance, honesty and caution. These marked the man to the end. His morals were Hebraic. Plymouth Town, with its villages nestling in the hills, was

governed something as the ancient Hebrews were: the town meeting was supreme, the voice of the people was the voice of God. There was no doubt about God. In the morals of this boy God was the force outside himself that governed that inexplicable chance in the game of life which makes in the end for righteousness. There was no doubt about righteousness. Righteousness was neighborly consideration, justice between man and man, kindness institutionalized in various social forms and political works and ways. The barn-raising was one of the social forms of righteousness. The common school which guaranteed educational equality was a political work of righteousness. And the public care of the poor to eliminate begging was an economic way of the righteous life. And these morals which were founded upon the hypothesis of an orderly cosmos were ingrained in Calvin Coolidge in those years of his childhood. He never forsook them. Always he had faith in the moral government of the universe. He felt that God keeps books and balances them with men and with nations. He believed obviously that it pays to be decent and kindly and just. He had the Bible for it—that righteousness exalteth a nation and sin is a reproach to any people. When he came out into the world to fight his dragons he was never unsure. He never faltered, nor halted in a complex world; a cynical world, a world full of a thousand doubts, an order rocking in a flood of disconcerting and terrible facts. His truth was unshaken.

Some of the party leaders began to take note of the unprepossessing newcomer, one of whom described him as "like a singed cat—better than he looks!" Not so his distant and high-toned Coolidge relatives in Boston and Cambridge. Even after he became governor, that branch of the family declined to assert the relationship. "Calvin Coolidge," Harvard's Professor Julian Coolidge—who was also a Lowell—remarked with sniffy genealogical exactitude "is an eighth cousin once removed."

It was customary on the lower reaches of the Republican escalator for a representative to the General Court to serve two annual terms. Coolidge was re-elected after his first year, though by a perilously slight margin. The following year, 1909, he was unanimously endorsed by Northampton's Republican City Committee to run for mayor, and even in that Democratic center managed to win by a small margin. The close-mouthed Coolidge with his stony features, his quacking voice, his obvious rectitude, and his sixth political sense was on the way to becoming a political character, the subject of anecdotes, an enigmatic vote-getter for whom people voted at least in part because he reminded them of the past. He was re-elected mayor. From then on he would never be out of office until he left the White House. His luck held. In 1911, that Democratic year, when the president of the Massachusetts Senate, Allen Treadway, left his safely Republican district to run for Congress, Coolidge declared himself a candidate for the vacant seat and easily won the nomination and election. He served two terms in the senate, making himself increasingly felt as a deft and knowledgeable politician. Then, in spite of the informal two-term tradition, he decided with the backing now of the wealthy paper-manufacturer Republican boss of western Massachusetts, United States Senator Murray Crane, to run for a third term, since the president of the senate, Levi H. Greenwood, was considering running for lieutenant governor. Greenwood later changed his mind and decided to go back to the senate, but in the election he was defeated by a general Democratic sweep plus the antagonism of the suffragists in his district. In the same election Coolidge, even as he defied the rotation system, was almost automatically elected to a third term. At the age of forty-two he replaced Greenwood as president of the senate. Since a Democrat, David Ignatius Walsh, had been elected governor, Senate President Coolidge became the highest-ranking Republican official in the state, able to reward his friends and conciliate his enemies. In spite of his glum silences and still-rustic manner, he was recognized as a skilled parliamentarian. The Boston *Globe* noted under "State House Gossip" that

> those who have been in the State House in recent years say that the President of the Senate, Mr. Coolidge, is one of the keenest men who have filled that chair in a long time. When he first came to the Legislature, his nasal twang and other peculiarities made some of his Eastern colleagues laugh, and they used to call him—behind his back—David Harum.
>
> David himself was a pretty shrewd Yankee, and so is Mr. Coolidge.... If it is not injudicious to apply the word "countryman" to a man who is a graduate of Amherst College and has been Mayor of Northampton, the word might be used to describe the President of the Senate at first impression.

> That resemblance to David Harum may bring Mr. Coolidge still
> higher honors if he cares for them and the times are ripe.... The
> ability to appeal to the people who work the plough is an asset not
> to be disregarded. Mr. Coolidge has that.

Coolidge was re-elected in 1914, in spite of the opposition of
the Democrats and the Progressives. In 1915, after Republicans
and Progressives had buried their differences, he announced: "I am
a candidate for lieutenant governor." He won the nomination readily over a rather bombastic opponent, then, in that year of a Republican return to power in Massachusetts, led his party as a
vote-getter. The well-oiled escalator moved ahead with relentless
quiet.

Traditionally a lieutenant governor served three annual terms
before moving up to the governor's level. No lieutenant governor
took office without the thought and prospect of that goal. Coolidge,
biding his time, was rotated into the governor's chair in 1918. It
was an uncomfortably narrow rotation, for his Democratic opponent had been Richard Henry Long, an adder-tongued shoe and
shoe-machinery manufacturer who had made a dubious fortune on
government contracts during the war and whose chief political
motivation was a grudge against the United Shoe Machinery
Company for what he considered an infringement of patents.
Opposed for the nomination by a staidly conservative Colonel Gaston, Long had turned rabble-rouser, posing as a friend of labor in
spite of an ambivalent record at his factory, and espousing such
incongruent causes as Czechoslovak independence, the abolition of
the fish trust, government control of refrigerator cars, and public
ownership of utilities. Coolidge defeated him by a mere 16,773
votes.

"What is your hobby?" a feature-writer asked the newly elected
governor. "Holding office," Coolidge quacked at him. Yet he was
said by those who found his David Harum aspect less than
picturesque to be the laziest governor the Commonwealth had ever
had. Despite appearances, he was not so much indolent as lethar-
gic. And his political instincts were always alert. Every day after an
uncommunicative lunch at the Union Club, where as governor he
was an *ex officio* member, he would mince to his office, lean back in

his chair with his feet on the vast glass-topped desk, and smoke a cigar while he read the early edition of the *Transcript*. Then he would doze off for several hours. He had felt from the beginning that the troubles of Boston's police department were not his. In any case the impending crisis was one of those troubles that would probably run into a ditch before reaching his particular spot on the road. Yet, little as he might consider the prospect, he and Commissioner Curtis and Mayor Peters were the three Yankees destined to be the leading characters in the police drama that was gradually developing in the last weeks of July.

Unlike the dour Coolidge, Andrew James Peters had a sprightly manner, an affable air of good fellowship, and an eagerness to please. But whereas the governor was a political expert, the mayor was an innocent. James Michael Curley, his predecessor as mayor and himself no slouch at diverting public funds, wrote witheringly that Mayor Peters

> was a pawn of his palace guard, who were selling jobs and promotions right under his aristocratic nose. Peters was a part-time mayor with a passionate addiction for golf, yachting, hammock duty and other leisurely pursuits, and although a person of mighty moral muscle and admitted courtliness, he deserved the censure even his friends heaped upon him when they called him "an innocent dupe for a conscienceless corps of bandits."
>
> The vulturous palace guard who surrounded him made a travesty of the highest political office in Boston.... The wholesale pilfering of the city treasury reached such scandalous proportions in his do-nothing regime that Boston was left in a sorry condition, with a depleted treasury and little of a tangible nature to show for the funds that had disappeared.

Of an old if undistinguished Colonial family, Peters was that Massachusetts anomaly, a Yankee Democrat. Here and there such Democrats were to be found, of Puritan descent, with inherited wealth, Harvard graduates, yet through some twist of family allegiance standing outside the old Bay State Federalist tradition. Harvard's president-emeritus, Charles W. Eliot, was such a Democrat as were the Russells of Cambridge, Cleveland's Secretary of War William Endicott, the Quincys, Colonel William Gaston, and Winslow Warren, president of the Cincinnati and descendant of the Bunker Hill general.

The Peters family came from Jamaica Plain, a higher social as well as geologic level than neighboring Roxbury but still not the haunt of the Cabots and the Lodges. Peters remained on the fringe of the Brahmin world rather than part of it. Not until after his marriage to Martha Phillips of the rich and established Boston Phillips family was his name included in the Boston *Social Register*. As a boy he attended St. Paul's School, then entered Harvard with the class of 1895, but left no scholastic or athletic record behind him. In his sophomore year he "ran for the Dickey," the club within a club comprising the first eighty of those taken into the Institute of 1770. Members of the Institute generally became members of the Hasty Pudding Club the following year. (Some years later the two clubs would combine.) Those belonging to these threshold clubs—about a quarter of each class—were winnowed into the eight final clubs. Peters, to his chagrin, failed to survive the winnowing.

From the college he moved on to the Harvard Law School, and after receiving his degree in 1898 joined the law firm of Colonel William Gaston—son of the former governor—as a novice lawyer. In 1902 he was elected to the Massachusetts House of Representatives and, after a term there, served a term in the state senate. His Republican district was of singular advantage to him. A Democratic nomination there could be had almost for the asking. The Democrats voted for him because he was a Democrat, the Yankee Republicans crossed party lines out of allegiance to a Mayflower descendant. Politics was nothing he took very seriously, certainly not as seriously as club life. He was a member of the Eastern Yacht Club, the Tennis and Racquet, the Somerset, the Exchange, the Tavern, and the New York Harvard Club. In 1906 he ran for Congress and was elected to the first of four terms from his safe but shabby Eleventh District. Fifteen years out of Harvard, he finally married. By 1919 he had had five sons, the first born in 1911, the last in April of his second year as mayor. Peters lived in the white Regency house in which he was born, at 310 South Street, Jamaica Plain, opposite the Arnold Arboretum's Bussey Institute on a butte overlooking Forest Hills. One of the few genuine Regency houses in Massachusetts, graceful in line and elegant in expanse of window, it looked slightly incongruous in that increasingly plebeian neighborhood. One could scarcely imagine a Boston Brahmin living there. Peters felt as bound to his district as to his paternal home. Yet he could not fail to note that over the years the district with its growing Irish working-class electorate could no longer be considered safe. He prudently did not run for a fifth term in 1914, accepting instead an appointment from President Wilson—always considerate of Yankee Democrats—as assistant secretary of the treasury in charge of customs. Resigning from this post in 1917, he was appointed a member of the United States section of the International High Commission, a position he held only briefly until Boston's mayoralty election of that same year.

In 1917 Mayor Curley was finishing out his first four-year term, determined to succeed himself. Equally determined to drive him from City Hall were the ward bosses he had alienated, headed by Lomasney and his old enemy Honey Fitz. Boston's Good Government Association—founded by the chamber of commerce and derisively labeled the Goo-Goos by Curley—persuaded Peters to come out as a reform candidate. Peters had the backing of the minority Republicans, the proper Bostonians, the Goo-Goos, and various real-estate and business interests alarmed over the increase in taxes resulting from the free-spending Curley. More vitally, Peters had the indirect support of the Ward Eight mahatma and Honey Fitz. In a straight contest the ebullient Curley would have overwhelmed the lackluster Peters. To make sure that this did not happen, Lomasney inserted two Irish-American congressmen in the contest to split the Democratic vote, James A. Gallivan of South Boston and Peter Tague of Charlestown. The division was too much of a handicap even for a dynamic freebooter like Curley. Peters won the election with 42 per cent of the vote. The final figures were: Peters 37,923; Curley 28,848; Gallivan 20,255; Tague 1700.

As a minority mayor, unfamiliar with City Hall, Peters soon found himself beyond his depth and turned to the ward bosses who had elected him for help, filling his staff with the men they suggested, allowing them to assume the bothersome details of administrative work while leaving him serenely carefree. Subtly, almost without his knowledge, the underlings took over. While he sat in the mayor's office, bagmen did business in the anterooms, and greenbacks were passed routinely in the corridors. Under the rule of Honey Fitz contractors had had a habit of charging the city for each side of a granite paving block. Under Peters they sold the foundations of City Hall. His administration became the most graft-ridden in Boston's graft-ridden history.

By his late forties Peters had grown almost bald, resembling more an aberrant Scot than a Yankee. He had a domed forehead fringed with rufous hair that gave him the spurious look of a thinker, petulant too-full lips, and curiously tufted, almost Mephistophelian eyebrows. His tenor voice had a precise Harvard-Boston accent, the exaggerated broad "a" that is not quite English and not quite anything else. Preferring long summers at his Maine estate on the island of North Haven and other-season interludes at his clubs to hours at his City Hall desk, he was somehow able to shut both his mind and his eyes to the corruption of his administration. He gave the impression of an easygoing, superficial man, inclined to bore. Yet beneath his brownstone exterior lurked a perverse personality, recognized by a select few at the time and only to come to larger light long afterward. For, in spite of his affection for his wife and small sons, Peters had an uncontrolled and apparently uncontrollable passion for pubescent girls, those whom the lepidopterous Nabokov would come to classify as nymphets. Whenever he could create an excuse he would entice the local nymphets into his sedate Jamaica Plain house. In 1917, just before he declared his candidacy for mayor and when he was forty-five years old, he became involved with the eleven-year-old Starr Wyman, a distant relative living nearby whom he encouraged to visit as a playmate for his boys. After much maneuvering he finally managed to seduce her when they were alone by giving her ether. From then on she accepted and he continued his anesthetic advances, until in time she became something of an ether addict. As she grew older she would sometimes slip away for rendezvous with him in out-of-town hotels. She remained attached to him with a mixture of both affection and fear, if one can judge by her diaries that came to light after her death.

Neither the mayor nor the governor nor the police commissioner in that postwar August sensed the weight of the trouble that was advancing directly down the road toward them. But Curtis, increasingly disturbed by the buzzing talk of a police union, shook up the department, discharging eleven men he considered trouble-makers and dispersing a number of others within the department, an effort that was only to result in spreading the discontent. On July 29 he issued an order that he hoped and believed would meet the issue head-on. Once he had made himself uncompromis-ingly clear, he was convinced that the men, his men, would fall into line.

I note [the order read] that a movement among the members of the Boston Police force to affiliate with the American Federation of Labor is actively on foot. I had hoped that the older men in the service who have served under my predecessor, Stephen O'Meara, who understood his attitude on such matters would have speedily and effectually terminated such a movement. Mr. O'Meara issued a General Order to the police force on June 18, 1918. I repeat to the members of the force what he said in that General Order, and trust that every member of the force will weigh every word care-fully....

I desire to say to the members of the force that I am firmly of the opinion that a police officer cannot consistently belong to a union and perform his sworn duty. I am not an opponent of labor unions, and neither was Mr. O'Meara. He pointed out in well-chosen lan-guage that there is no question in the police department as to how much of an employer's profits should be shared with the workers. Policemen are public officers. They have taken an oath of office. That oath requires them to carry out the law with strict impartiality, no matter what their personal feeling may be. The laws they carry out are laws made by the representatives of the people assembled in the Legislature. Therefore it should be apparent that the men to whom the carrying out of these laws is entrusted should not be subject to the orders or the dictation of part of the general public. A man who enters the police force, as I have stated, takes an oath of office, and he should realize that his work is sharply differentiated from that of the worker in private employ. It is difficult to see, under these cir-cumstances, what a policeman can hope to gain by proposed affilia-tion, although it is easy to see how the other affiliated bodies may gain a great deal.

As Police Commissioner for the City of Boston, I feel it is my duty to say to the police force that I disapprove of the movement on foot; that in my opinion it is not for the best interests of the men themselves; and that beyond question it is not for the best interests of the general public, which this department is required to serve.

On August 1 the Boston Social Club scheduled an emergency meeting at Intercolonial Hall to consider Commissioner Curtis's adamant stand.

SUMMER'S END
IN BOSTON

Intercolonial Hall, rancid from decades of floor oil, sweat, and cigar smoke, was full to overflowing as more than fifteen hundred members of the Social Club met to deal with the commissioner's new general order. In spite of the recent salary raise the hall churned with discontent. Again the familiar complaints were aired, though in more strident tones: the old talk of hours and wages and conditions, of peanut graft and petty tyrannies. Even before the balloting it was clear that the policemen had committed themselves emotionally to the union. Of those present 940 voted to join the AFL. The rest abstained. Not one man voted No. Yet it was also clear that, though a minority group was ready to challenge the commissioner head-on, the majority were still anxious to avoid any such confrontation. They chose rather to ignore the last general order, as if it might somehow evaporate. President Lynch was so intent on smoothing matters over that he had even invited Curtis to address the meeting. The commissioner declined, ostensibly because of his health, but each speaker that evening went out of his way to compliment him for his efforts in winning the police a salary increase and in trying to improve their working conditions. If, however, they thought such soft words might make the commissioner more conciliatory, they obviously knew him as little as he knew them.

After that meeting the police were expected to announce the formation of a union in the next few days. A police sergeant told a *Globe* reporter that 891 patrolmen had already signed up. Yet the days slipped by and nothing happened. If quiescent Boston grew more conscious of the imminence of a police crisis, it was due more to police disturbances elsewhere in the nation and the world. Dwarfing all other such news that August were the reports of the strike of English police in Liverpool and London over the same matter of union recognition. The London strike resulted in few disturbances, but the one in Liverpool developed into one of the bloodiest in British labor history. For two nights the dockside city was given over to riot and pillage. Troops were called out, and pitched battles developed between the soldiers and the mob. The Admiralty finally sent three warships to guard the port and prevent destruction of the docks and shipping facilities.

In this country Jersey City police, attempting to form a union, were threatened with suspension by Mayor Frank Hague. Police in Washington, D.C., were negotiating with the AFL. The Massachusetts Police Association (consisting of the Metropolitan Park Police and those of other Massachusetts cities and towns except Boston) was asking in peremptory tones for a wage increase. In Brockton, a small shoe city forty-one miles from Boston, the police were organizing, while in Springfield, New Bedford, and Lawrence they were demanding substantial pay raises. The Lawrence City Council met hurriedly to consider police claims there, while in suburban Wellesley the selectmen hastened to forestall trouble by granting their minuscule force a raise. Worcester police halted their plans for a union to await the Boston outcome. The only news from Boston was that a new order now allowed the police to leave the city on their day off without permission. On August 9 this static calm was broken by a rumor that the AFL's New England organizer, Frank McCarthy, already had a charter in hand for a Boston police union. Unlike most rumors, this happened to be true, for the officers of the Social Club had sent a telegram to AFL headquarters requesting such a charter. Within twenty-four hours the document was on its way, making Boston the thirteenth city to be enrolled. Not for two days was the news made public. On learning of the charter Curtis at once issued an official addition to the rules and regulations of his department. Rule 35, Section 19, said:

> No member of the force shall belong to any organization, club or body composed of present and past members of the force which is affiliated with or part of any organization, club or body outside of the department, except that a post of the Grand Army of the Republic, the United Spanish War Veterans, and the American Legion of World War Veterans may be formed within the department.

Curtis defined a policeman as not "an employee but a state officer" bound to the impartial enforcement of the law. Police affiliation with any outside organization representing the interests of a segment of the population, rather than the population as a whole, would compromise his duty to carry out impartial law enforcement. But, he concluded, this new rule in no way interfered with a policeman's interests as a man and a citizen.

The police felt otherwise. Their commissioner's tight-lipped intransigence stirred them to stubborn opposition. Each move of Curtis's brought a hardening of spirit to both sides that lessened the chance of conciliation and compromise. As the strike-ridden months of August moved along in a succession of cool and rainy days, Bostonians began to realize that a crisis in their city was imminent. News of conflict between the police and the commissioner advanced from the back of the Boston papers to emerge at last in splashing headlines on the front page. The AFL's McCarthy called Curtis's order "amazing, unfair, coercive, unsound in law as it is un-American in principle." He denied that joining the AFL would create any conflict between the men and their duties, and went on to accuse Curtis of attacking their rights to obtain a standard of living more in keeping "with American ideals, and their honorable positions." James Vahey, the silver-haired grandiloquent labor lawyer and general counsel for the Street and Electric Railway Employees of America, protested that Curtis had "no right to take away from the men the liberty which entitled them to organize." Vahey, twice

Democratic candidate for governor, had recently guided the Bay State Carmen's Union through its successful strike, and he was now prepared to guide the police. He threatened the commissioner with an injunction that would restrain him from coercing his men. Rule 35, he insisted, was unconstitutional under Massachusetts law. City Councilor James Moriarty, an officer of the sheet metal workers' union, asked Acting Mayor Francis Ford—Mayor Peters being on his yacht somewhere off the coast of Maine—to call a special meeting of the city council in order to select a committee of councilors to meet with the governor and the commissioner. Labor leaders planted reports in the press that if Curtis continued to remain adamant, organized labor would force him from office.

Curtis's supporters were quick to come to his defense. The Boston *Herald*, which had long since replaced the *Journal* at New England's Republican breakfast tables, cautioned the policemen "to regard themselves as officers of the law, representing all the people," and to trust the public for a "satisfactory share of the product of the community." The tea-table institution, the Boston *Evening Transcript*, was pleased to note—what Curtis himself had not yet noted—that the governor fully supported the commissioner. In the *Transcript*'s editorial opinion the police were not employees but officers of the state who exercised a sacred trust of enormous responsibility, a responsibility that ought not to be abused "but must be protected."

After two years of debates the Massachusetts Constitutional Convention was still in the process of concluding its deliberations. But echoes of the police crisis penetrated even that languid atmosphere. On August 13 one of the delegates, former state Attorney General Albert Pillsbury, proposed legislation making it illegal for public-service employees to affiliate with labor unions. Carried away by the thought, he then moved to a general attack on all labor unions:

> The American people [he informed his receptive Republican colleagues] are living today under a tyranny to which the rule of George III and his parliament was benevolence itself. The organized working man, euphemistically so called, has taken us by the throat and has us at his mercy. He will not allow us, except on his own terms, our common rights—not even our right to live. For we

cannot live without food, and we cannot have food without railroad transportation, and this and every other public service is now being conducted at the sufferance of organized labor in the face of an impotent government and helpless people.

Then, almost as an afterthought, he added: "I turn aside for a moment to congratulate the Police Commissioner of Boston that he does not propose to allow the police service in Boston to be held up so long as he is at the head of it."

The labor representatives present, Dennis Driscoll and Councilor Moriarty, sprang from their seats to labor's defense. Driscoll called Pillsbury's speech "a threat and challenge to organized wage workers." Moriarty, to the accompaniment of some applause but more boos, condemned the police commissioner's actions and accused the Republican-dominated convention of being pro-capital and anti-labor. At this point Curtis, who was also present as a delegate, endeavored to cut off the discussion: "I do not think this is the time or the place," he told the delegates, "to discuss matters relating to the Boston Police Department, but I want it distinctly understood that because I refrain from discussing them I do not fear to discuss them at the proper time and place. Neither am I afraid that I have not taken the right stand, and I propose to stand right where I am on this issue."

Moriarty, while agreeing that the discussion should end, challenged Curtis to debate the police issue publicly elsewhere at any time and at any place, a challenge that Curtis chose to ignore. A number of the delegates hissed Moriarty; then the convention gave Curtis a standing ovation.

By now the commissioner had decided to meet the challenge head-on, placing a rush order with the City Hall printing plant for a thousand discharge and suspension blanks. He received these on August 14. Under the letterhead "City of Boston Police Department, Office of the Commissioner," the text read:

To _____

Boston Police Officer

By authority conferred on me by the Police Commissioner, you are hereby suspended until further order of said Commissioner. The cause and reasons for such suspension are as follows:

Specifications _____

This form was to be signed by Michael H. Crowley, superintendent of police. The discharge blank under the same letterhead read:

To _____
                                                    Boston Police Officer

By authority conferred on me by the Police Commissioner, I hereby discharge you from the Police Department. The cause and reasons for such discharge are as follows:

Specifications _____

This last was to be signed by Curtis himself.

In no way intimidated, the police continued with their plans for a meeting in Fay Hall in the South End the following day. On that afternoon a crowd of supporters and the curious gathered under the Dover Street elevated structure in front of the grubby two-story building that served as headquarters for the Boston Street Carmen's Union. Patrolmen kept arriving by streetcar and elevated train, all apparently in the highest of spirits. Before the meeting animated knots of uniformed men sauntered up and down the sidewalk gesticulating, laughing, talking. The issue, now finally drawn, seemed to give them a sense of relief, almost an air of jollity. Even the old-timers were putting in their appearances, veterans with twenty and thirty years' service behind them. The night men had left their beds early to attend.

That the police were about to form a union was now widely known. Nevertheless the union leaders tried to keep their deliberations private and their identities secret. A sergeant-at-arms, stationed at the hall door, scrutinized all those entering and demanded identification from those he did not know. Among those he turned back was the head of a private detective agency.

The moderates, led by Lynch, hoped to avoid or postpone any irrevocable action. But a vociferous and assertive minority had now swung over the inert majority, who found themselves carried away by the contagious enthusiasm of the militants. In both sessions, with shouts, thumping, cheers and whistles, the policemen overwhelmingly voted to accept the union charter. The Boston Social Club had become the Boston Police Union Number 16,807 of the American Federation of Labor.

While the police were voting, those gathered outside under the el structure could hear the cheers and applause echoing from behind the closed doors. Then a smiling Frank McCarthy emerged. "Well, I guess I know what you boys are here for," he told the waiting reporters, "but I can't say anything." Scarcely had the meeting adjourned than officials of the other unions began rallying their rank and file to the policemen's cause. On Saturday, August 16, a group of Boston labor leaders met at the Quincy House to discuss strategy. Although they kept the details to themselves, they let it be known that they were going to set up a "working agreement among policemen, firemen, carmen, and telephone workers," and they implied that if Curtis persisted in his course, the unions would call a sympathy strike.

On August 17 the Boston Central Labor Union (BCLU)—the coordinating body of all the AFL unions in the city—held the largest local meeting in a decade at Wells Memorial Hall on lower Washington Street. The mood was militant. A delegate introduced a carefully prepared resolution denouncing Curtis's actions as "a tyrannical assumption of autocratic authority ... foreign to the principle of government under which we live," and demanding that he revoke his amendment to Rule 35. The delegate congratulated the police for their courage in asserting their rights, promised "every atom of support that labor can bring to bear," and bade "a hearty welcome to the Policemen's Union to the ranks of organized labor."

In opening the discussion of the resolution, McCarthy called Curtis's order an attempt not only to undermine the principle of collective bargaining but to attack the American Federation of Labor, which "recognized" the right of a policeman to ownership of himself. The commissioner's "un-American" action, he told the delegates, "would end by destroying the department's morale and efficiency, since more than ninety per cent of the force had already joined the new union." Other speakers insisted repetitively that membership in the AFL in no way hindered a policeman in the discharge of his duties, and they predicted that there would be real trouble ahead if the governor and the mayor supported the commissioner. The BCLU's business manager told the delegates that "these men are working under the worst conditions of any body of men in this city," and he warned that they would walk out if even one man was discharged.

Councilor Moriarty, the last speaker, found himself in the

anomalous position of defending a body of men whom he had often previously called strikebreakers. Adopting attack as the best method of defense, he denounced Curtis's record as mayor, as collector of the port, and as a member of the Metropolitan Park Commission, giving as an example Curtis's "discharge of three hundred city laborers on Christmas Eve, when he was mayor." Labor's battle for the police, Moriarty told them, was a fight for organized labor itself. If Curtis should win his point, other employers would launch similar attacks against their workmen.

After Moriarty's speech the delegates enthusiastically and unanimously voted to accept the resolution. Already the firemen's union, which had evolved from the Russell Club, had passed a resolution supporting the police even to the extent of going on strike. The firemen's endorsement was followed that evening by the local plumbers, the boilermakers, and Hyde Park Machinists Lodge 391. The business agent of the carmen's union announced that in the event of a police strike the carmen would refuse absolutely to transport strikebreakers. Labor leaders busied themselves lining up such powerful unions as the telephone operators, the building tradesmen, and the teamsters. Boston's city council came out "strongly on the side of organized labor." The *Herald* estimated that some eighty thousand workers were prepared to strike. Under labor's smoothly united surface there were, however, fissures, lightly covered over but only waiting to become apparent. For many workmen could recall the indifference, not to say hostility, that the police had shown toward them in earlier strikes. A high-domed helmet still seemed the symbol of the enemy. Furthermore the Central Labor Union itself did not have the power to call a strike. Only the individual unions could do that, and they would not do so without the consent of their entire membership.

While the Wells Memorial Hall meeting was taking place, a reporter from the Boston *Advertiser* called Coolidge at Northampton to ask for a statement about the police situation. Coolidge replied in his customary measured manner: "I am thoroughly in sympathy with the attitude of the commissioner as I understand it.... I sincerely hope the matter will be adjusted amicably, but I have every confidence in the ability and judgment of Mr. Curtis and I intend to support him in any action he may take. Mr. Curtis is the police commissioner and I intend to allow him a free hand in the management of the department."

The crisis continued to build up like a lowering thundercloud over Boston. Two days after the Wells Hall meeting the *Herald* editorialized:

> Seldom has the feeling in this community been more tense than it is today over the conditions in the police department. No other topic of conversation approaches it ... we are at a turning of the ways. We shall take a long step toward "Russianizing" ourselves, or toward submitting to soviet rule if we, by any pretext, admit an agency of the law to become the servant of a special interest. We have entire confidence that Commissioner Curtis will stand firm. We believe the Governor will be with him. The demagogues of the municipal council see in this affair an opportunity to build up political capital for themselves. We believe the "solid right-thinking people of the state" will take this stand.

Mayor Peters was too negligible for the *Herald* to bother to mention.

It seemed another ominous sign when Superintendent Crowley cut short his vacation to return to his Pemberton Square office opposite the massive granite Suffolk County Court House. Crowley, a stocky, suave Celt, was an easy talker, well liked by his men and by the public. His ancestry had given him a face in which the map of Ireland was still traceable. He had both literally and figuratively kissed the Blarney Stone. It was said that even the dourest Yankee coming into police headquarters with a complaint, after talking with the genial superintendent would on leaving make a donation to the Police Benevolent Fund. Crowley knew the police as Curtis did not, for he had come up through the ranks. As a sergeant, through his skill in solving what became known as the Trunk Murder Mystery— a woman's body found in a trunk in a lodging house—he was in the ensuing notoriety propelled upward until he at last found himself behind the superintendent's desk. How he felt about a union he carefully kept to himself, but the patrolmen knew that in a show-down he would have to back authority, and they bore him no ill will for it. Immediately on his return Crowley called a meeting of captains and department heads. He maintained that the meeting would deal only with routine matters, but the implications were as ominous as were the new orders that kept pouring from the police department. One special order required all sergeants and lieutenants to leave their vacation addresses with their captains. The confrontation that moderates like Lynch had feared now seemed unavoidable. Years later Lynch told a priest that the AFL union was the work of a minority playing on police dissatisfactions, that originally such a union had been neither "the will nor the wish of the majority of the Social Club."

The policemen had scheduled another meeting at Fay Hall for Tuesday, August 19, at which, according to the Boston papers, they planned to elect a slate of officers and then demand the commissioner's official recognition of their union. Meanwhile several labor leaders attempted to gain the governor's support or at least his neutrality. Coolidge had shown himself sympathetic—overindulgent, in the opinion of many Bostonians—to the carmen in their recent strike, and he was well aware of the power of the labor vote. State Senator George Curran, himself a member of the seventeen-man BCLU advisory committee appointed to deal with the police situation, wrote the governor a letter attacking the commissioner as un-American, and calling his behavior a kind of "Prussianism." The commissioner's arbitrary use of power against the unionizing police, Curran told the governor, required his removal from a place of authority no less completely than the Kaiser was removed by American doughboys. He concluded: "Organized labor and the citizens of Boston call for the immediate dismissal of the Hon. Edwin U. Curtis, Police Commissioner of Boston."

Coolidge's reply was negative, indirect, nonspecific. On returning somewhat early from his vacation on August 19, he released a statement to the press that "Mr. Curtis is the police commissioner of Boston invested by law with the duty of conducting the office. I have no intention of removing him as long as he is commissioner and am going to support him."

Except for a few brief comments, Curtis kept silent. He declared that his amendment to Rule 35 was clear enough to need no elaboration. When reporters asked him if his stand was his own or whether he had consulted with others, he told them, "Like all prudent men, I have sought advice on this matter from men eminent in the legal profession." The "eminent" lawyer to whom Curtis had turned was another ingrained Yankee, Herbert Parker, member of the Harvard Class of 1878 and grandson of a Harvard president. Originally the Parkers had been Charlestown settlers but had retreated from Bunker Hill following that town's invasion by the Irish Famine refugees. They had then gone west to Lancaster in mid-Massachusetts, beyond the reach of the Celts. In spite of his Harvard connection, Parker as a young lawyer gravitated to nearby Worcester rather than to Boston thirty-five miles away. After spending five years in private practice he was appointed an assistant district attorney of Worcester County, then in a few years he advanced to First Special Justice of the Second District of Eastern Worcester. From 1895 to 1899 he served as district attorney. In 1901 he was elected to the first of three annual terms as attorney general of the Commonwealth, his sole elective office.

Attorney General Parker proved himself a skillful prosecutor whose successes gave him a political as well as a legal standing. Rigid, testy, primly self-righteous, he was nevertheless considered one of the state's leading lawyers. His own son described him as an "ultra-conservative, anti-union Republican." In 1917 he was a delegate to the Massachusetts Constitutional Convention, where he served on a number of key committees and distinguished himself by voting against every proposed constitutional change. It was Councilor Moriarty's attack on the police commissioner at the August 13 session of the convention that brought Parker and Curtis together. Parker, who regarded all unions as an unjustified restraint on trade, and a police union a crime against the Commonwealth, rushed to the aid of Curtis whom he scarcely knew and offered him his assistance in answering Moriarty's challenge. From that day began a curiously intimate relationship between the two men. Although Parker was six years older, he came in the next few weeks to regard Curtis as almost a father figure. Dropping other legal work, he became Curtis's trusted consultant. With offices at Barrister Hall, only a few hundred yards from Curtis's office, he placed himself unreservedly under the Commissioner's command. Long after the police strike, looking back on those stirring weeks when he was so close to Curtis, he wrote in his Harvard class report: "I view this service as the most inspiring of my professional life, because of my intimate association with, to me, the bravest, wisest and most faithful of all public officials with whom I have had the opportunity to serve."

Rumor, reflected in the papers, had it that Curtis and Coolidge were in constant consultation and that the governor would support the commissioner to any length. Coolidge's secretary then took pointed pains to deny that Coolidge and Curtis had even seen one another. The most that could be said—and Coolidge had said it—was that the governor had no intention of removing the commissioner. Parker nevertheless felt that the governor's statement had made it possible for the commissioner to take his stand against the police. On that same Tuesday Curtis called in reporters and broke his silence. He told them that since he had received no official notification or evidence of the men's antagonism either to him or to the rules of the police department, he would do nothing. If, however, he should receive such notification or evidence, he would of course enforce the rules of the department, according to the law. Then, more confidentially, he went on to explain that press reports of police antagonism to the department were untrue. On the contrary his relationship with the rank and file was quite cordial. He pointed out that, like O'Meara before him, he had no objection to the police forming an organization so long as it was not affiliated with an outside group. He himself had helped the men set up the new grievance committee which had granted the men almost all their requests. He had won a salary increase for the department, an increase that he had indicated would pave the way for future increases. He had established a committee to investigate the condition of the station houses and had submitted its report to the mayor with his own urgent requests for immediate action. As proof of his men's goodwill, he released two laudatory letters to him, one from the secretary of the Social Club, the other from the secretary of the grievance committee.

What Curtis failed to realize was that in spite of such rhetorical politeness the police had never considered him one of their own, as they had O'Meara and as they did Superintendent Crowley. "Useless Curtis," they nicknamed him behind his back. The belated pay raise they considered as brought about by their own militancy rather than by any action of his. They were suspicious of the grievance committee. They saw the report on the station houses buried in City Hall. Above all they were now angry and belligerent to a point beyond reason, determined on a showdown and confident that they could win. That evening they came out in open defiance of the commissioner and at their Fay Hall meeting elected a permanent slate of officers for their AFL union.

President of the new union was Patrolman John F. McInnes of Station 2, a veteran officer, well known and liked, who directed traffic at the intersection of Devonshire and Water Streets in downtown Boston. McInnes, a lean, long-nosed man with bushy eyebrows, was an impressive choice. As a young man he had served with the Seventh Cavalry in the Dakotas and in 1890 had been present at the shooting of Sitting Bull. The following year he left the army to learn the trade of bricklayer. But the Spanish-American War found him too restless to remain a civilian. He joined up in time to be with Theodore Roosevelt at San Juan Hill. In November 1898 he was mustered out, but a few months later he again enlisted. By 1906 he had risen to the rank of first lieutenant. He then quit the service for the Boston Police Department. When the United States declared war in 1917, he joined the army for the fourth time, going overseas with the AEF and returning to the police department after the armistice. In 1912 he had been elected vice-president of the Boston Social Club and later vice-president and director of the Boston Police Relief Association. When a post of the American Legion was organized in South Boston, he became its first commander. Honored and respected as he was, McInnes gave a solid standing to the nascent union. The other officers elected were:

VICE PRESIDENT:
John F. Whitten—Division Ten, Roxbury Crossing.
FINANCIAL SECRETARY:
Michael L. King—Division Nine, Dudley Street.
RECORDING SECRETARY: William P. Willis—Division Ten.
GUIDE: John Maloney—Division Four, LaGrange Street.
GUARDIAN: William Brown—Division Sixteen, Back Bay.
TRUSTEES:
James L. Butler—Division Nineteen, Mattapan.

Thomas J. Driscoll—Division Three, Joy Street.
Michael Joyce—Division Twelve, South Boston.
DELEGATES TO THE BCLU:
Stephen J. Dunleavy—Division Three.
John P. Whitten—Division Ten.
Phillip Corbett—Division Five, East Dedham Street.
Stephen Ryder, Jr.—Division Two, City Hall Ave.
James L. Butler—Division Nineteen.
William P. Willis—Division Ten.
James G. Peters—Division Eleven, Dorchester.
George E. Ferreira—Division One, Hanover Street.
Hugh Garrity—Division Two.

McInnes's first public statement was a mild one. "I decry strike talk," he said, adding that "the officers of the Union wish to state that their relations with Police Commissioner Curtis are pleasant, although there is a dispute concerning the rights of our members to organize."

Curtis learned of the meeting shortly after it adjourned. By six o'clock next morning, Wednesday, he was at his desk in Pemberton Square. At once he issued a special order summoning eight patrolmen who were leaders in organizing the union to police headquarters. The eight arrived at nine-thirty. For the next two and a half hours, with a department secretary recording the answers, Superintendent Crowley interrogated the men as to their length of service, their union membership and their roles in founding the union, and their awareness of the meaning of amended Rule 35. One by one the eight left the building, the last man at noon.

Meanwhile Curtis was conferring with a subcommittee of three members of the city council chosen at the request of Councilor Moriarty by Acting Mayor Ford—Peters still being on his yacht somewhere in Maine. The commissioner received them with stubborn amiability. After the meeting, which lasted until 1:00 p.m., the councilors released a statement summing up Curtis's position:

> The Commissioner while admitting to the right of all employees to organize and endorsing the aims and objects of labor unions in general holds that police officers are not employees in the ordinary

sense of the word, but that they are public officials of the state of Massachusetts, and in his opinion membership in a labor organization is not compatible with their duties to the people and to the state as such officials.

He further stated that the question as to whether the police officials were employees or public officials would probably be determined by the courts and if the decision were adverse to his contention, of course the rule he had promulgated would not be legal, and any man discharged for a violation would be reinstated.

Curtis felt that this was a reasonable account of his somewhat blunter view that membership in a union "unfits" a man for the proper performance of his police duties. But to avoid any misunderstanding, he told the press that he as commissioner "must not be understood as having intimated that any member of the police force who, denying the authority of the rules, abandons his duty by a strike or a walk-out would be reinstated if discharged for that reason."

After the councilors had left, Curtis met privately for two hours with three men whose identity and business he refused to make known. All he would say was that they had not come from the governor. When questioned further by a reporter he said he had not heard from Coolidge in the last six months. He now found himself as occupied as a general preparing for battle. Late that afternoon he issued General Order 119 canceling the vacation of "division commanders, lieutenants and sergeants, including the Bureaus of Criminal Investigation." All captains, lieutenants, and sergeants already on vacation were to prepare to return to duty, as were retired members of the force. Any patrolman willing to give up his vacation was invited to do so and promised that this would stand him in good stead.

It was clear now, if it had not been already, that Curtis had no intention of backing down. On their side the patrolmen were so deeply committed to affiliation with the AFL that no compromise would seem reasonable to them. That same evening more than eight hundred members of the police union returned to Fay Hall and defiantly installed the officers they had elected the night before. Two patrolmen carried McInnes triumphantly up the double flight of stairs on their shoulders. After the meeting Frank McCarthy announced somewhat reluctantly that the police union was now a fact. The union, he took pains to point out, would not and could not "in any manner interfere with the executive direction of the department." Its sole function was to "lend assistance within legal lines in protecting the economic condition of the Boston Police and establishing within the department the principle of collective bargaining in all matters affecting the working conditions of the police." He boasted that the union now had between thirteen hundred and fourteen hundred members. They and he wanted nothing more than an amicable settlement of the dispute with the commissioner. If this, however, was not reached, "the responsibility would not rest on the Police Union."

The police crisis had by now pushed aside the other news of that turbulent month to emerge on the front page of the Boston papers. "*WAR ON POLICE UNION IS ON*," the *Herald* headlines blazoned. The directors of the Boston Chamber of Commerce wrote to Curtis praising his courage and promising him their fullest support. They followed this up with a letter to Coolidge expressing the faith that the public, no less than the chamber, endorsed the commissioner's stand and urging the governor to issue a "plain" statement that unionization of the police would render them incapable of performing their duties.

On Thursday, August 21, Curtis, after meeting with the captains and division commanders, announced that "charges have been preferred against eight men for violation of Rule Thirty-five and that a hearing will be held Tuesday next." Nothing else could be learned except that these were the same eight men who had appeared at headquarters the day before. The commissioner remained isolated. Meanwhile the committee from the Boston Central Labor Union met with the governor at the State House. The committee took their by now familiar position that the controversy was not just a police affair but concerned all organized labor. Coolidge listened with silent impassivity, merely remarking afterward that he stood by his earlier statement. For the union leaders it was a rebuff. So grave did they now find the situation that they called for a special meeting of the BCLU on Sunday afternoon. Curtis was expected to suspend the eight patrolmen at once. He did not do so, but left for his summer home at Nahant. Four dragging, speculative days followed in the increasingly tense city. There were some who thought Curtis might already have come to a secret agreement with the union to make a test case in the courts of the policemen's right to unionize. Police headquarters and the union both denied this. Three years earlier patrolmen had been ordered to discontinue carrying their night sticks except on dress occasions, using instead a "pocket billy." Now Superintendent Crowley called in all night sticks, ostensibly as a routine matter but actually to arm emergency police in the event of a strike. On Friday Crowley summoned eleven more patrolmen for interrogation. Headquarters remained silent, but one of the officials there tipped off a reporter that "you'd better be around in the morning."

The hint was well placed. Next day headlines stated that Curtis would call up a volunteer police force in case of emergency. Former Police Superintendent William Pierce had emerged from retirement to "organize and equip" a volunteer force, and had already ordered five hundred badges. Within the next few days small black-margined Volunteer Police advertisements appeared on the front pages of the Boston papers asking for:

> Able-Bodied Men willing to give their services in case of the necessity for part of the day or night for the protection of persons or property in the City of Boston.
> Apply to me at Room B, Third Floor, Chamber of Commerce Building, Boston—daily except Sundays.
>
> William H. Pierce
Supt. of Police (retired)

Over the weekend rumors blazed up that the police were planning action to forestall Pierce's volunteers. In any case a strike was seen as inevitable if the commissioner found against the eight men about to stand trial. The Boston Federal Reserve Bank requested additional United States marshals, and it was reported that criminals were converging on Boston in anticipation of disorders. Meanwhile the two lawyers for the police union, Vahey and the curly-haired, pugnaciously square-jawed John P. Feeney, were preparing their arguments, relying chiefly on a wartime draft ruling that police were municipal *employees* rather than *officials*.

Sunday's meeting of the BCLU was tumultuously enthusiastic.

The three hundred delegates voted unanimously to support the police union in whatever action it might take. Speaker after speaker attacked Curtis, the city administration, Governor Coolidge, and the chamber of commerce, and promised that in spite of them all the police would win. The wispy Frank McCarthy, though warning against rash action and noting that the union officers were still working for an "amicable adjustment of the controversy," accused Curtis of trying to intimidate the police and charged that he had bullied the men called in for interrogation. McCarthy could see no justification for setting up a force of volunteers, since the police in their new union had never even mentioned the word "strike." He warned the delegates: "We have a serious situation to face if Commissioner Curtis goes through with his program, and I have no doubt that he will try, as he has the support of those higher up and the organized interests of capital. He is trying to create the impression that the ultimate direction of the affairs of the city will be by the militia, but I want to warn him and his backers that the time when a soldier takes orders to work against his brothers and sisters is past. . . . " He hoped that a break could be avoided but "any peace that comes must come with honor."

Moriarty, hoarse with anger, told the delegates to "bring victory to the police or quit." He warned them that the struggle was a class struggle, as could be clearly seen when the chamber of commerce offered its building as "a recruiting station for strike-breaking police." But he predicted that in a showdown, the other Massachusetts police would give the governor the fight of his life. Bringing up the question of whether police are employees or officials, he told the cheering delegates that "if they had been treated like officials there never would have been a thought of a union." "If one policeman is discharged," he concluded, "every organized man and woman in the city will be ready at the call to quit work and tie up the industry of the city so tight that it will take a lot of work on the part of the big interests to untie it, even after every man is reinstated in his position. . . . Mr. Curtis has thrown his hat into the ring and it is up to us to climb into the ring and kick it out."

Police leaders themselves, still hoping that the unbending Curtis would bend, were mute about what they might do if he should discharge any of the union organizers. Other unions were less reticent. The Boston plumbers, the Hyde Park mechanics, the local teamsters, the Boston typographers, the sheet metal workers—all agreed to support the Boston police by taking any action requested.

Returning to his Pemberton Square office early Monday morning, Curtis started off his week by holding a short sterile interview with Vahey and Feeney. Then he sent a set of twenty-three questions, similar to those the summoned patrolmen had already answered, to each captain, ordering him to interrogate every man in his district and to have a stenographer take down the replies. While the captains were so occupied, the police held another meeting at Fay Hall and again announced defiantly that they would fight the commissioner to a finish.

It had been customary in the police department for three captains to make up a trial board. But in the trial of the eight patrolmen, Curtis at Vahey's request agreed to act as sole judge. Vahey and Feeney wanted the full responsibility for the decision to fall on the commissioner. Curtis in turn was more than willing to take such responsibility.

The trial opened on Tuesday morning in Pemberton Square in a small headquarters room to which only the defendants, the lawyers, and a reporter from each Boston paper were admitted. It lasted a mere two hours and a quarter. Opening for the defense Feeney, a firebrand speaker with flashing eyes, denounced Rule 35 as contrary to a Massachusetts law prohibiting anyone as a condition of employment from being forced to agree not to join a labor organization. There was no legal foundation, he held, to Curtis's assertion that the police were officers and not employees of the city. He pointed out that Rule 35 was needless, since the commissioner always would have the full power to act if a policeman failed to do his duty. Membership in the AFL would no more affect a policeman's actions than would membership in the Masons, the Knights of Columbus, the Elks, or the Odd Fellows.

The resonant-voiced Vahey called Curtis's rule "the greatest invasion of a man's personal liberty and the most far-reaching attempt to restrict his freedom of action I have ever known." He saw the trial as an attack on union patriotism, even though as he pointed out, the AFL had always stood for peaceful and orderly progress as opposed to violence. Union membership, he repeated, would never hinder a policeman from doing his duty.

Curtis's secretary, James H. Devlin, defended Rule 35. Under it, as Curtis saw it, the men were free to join outside organizations, but as public officers they were not free to affiliate with a central labor organization. Devlin went on to mention that the commissioner had frequently consulted the grievance committee and that his relationship with his men had been good. As the last speaker of the day, Union President McInnes told Curtis that the first question considered at union meetings had been whether affiliation with the AFL would lessen the efficiency of the police force. The men were certain it would not. Curtis, suffering from twinges of angina, showed the strain of the two-and-a-quarter-hour hearing. Toward the end he grew increasingly testy. He announced, as McInnes concluded, that he would take the cases under advisement. There was little doubt what his decision would be. To his secretary he confided that he thought he had shown a great deal of patience.

Later that same day the chamber of commerce renewed its support of the commissioner. Stung by the charge that the chamber represented only business interests, its spokesman maintained that it represented "the whole community" and, speaking for that community, held that it was as impossible for a policeman to be affiliated with labor unions as for a judge upon the bench. "A man cannot serve two masters." A committee from the chamber visited Curtis to suggest that he engage the services of the best lawyer available. To the dismay of the members, Curtis told them that he was appointing Herbert Parker as his chief legal adviser. Realizing that the appointment of the intransigent and self-assertive Parker would undermine any hopes of a compromise, they begged the commissioner to choose someone more amenable, more sympathetic to labor. Curtly, he refused. The same day McInnes issued his union's first public statement, declaring that "the members of the Boston Policeman's Union intend to do their duty as police officers in the future as they have in the past and retain their full membership in the American Federation of Labor."

Not until Wednesday morning did a suntanned Peters return from North Haven. "I am here," he said expansively, "to do everything possible to bring about an agreeable settlement to the police situation." To Peters "everything possible" meant appointing a committee to ease the burden of decision. That afternoon he prepared a lengthy statement in which he admitted that although the issues were clear, "the merits of the question are not perhaps so clear." He praised the police and that "bulwark of patriotism and strength against bolshevism," the AFL, with whose "fundamental aims" he claimed to be entirely in sympathy. Nevertheless, he felt compelled to say that he thought Curtis was right and that policemen should not be affiliated with the AFL, since "complications might and probably would ensue." He urged the AFL and the police to relinquish their plans and promised he would do all in his power to see that justice was done them.

Peters's aim to please fell far short of the target as far as the police were concerned. They were further incensed by his claim that any additional pay increase for the police would have to be met by dropping other employees from the city's payroll. Feeney and Vahey, bristling with indignation, visited the mayor Wednesday afternoon. What they said was intended to be kept private, but an eavesdropping City Hall employee told reporters that "Mayor Peters was told just what labor men think of his endorsement of commissioner Curtis, and don't you forget it!"

Convinced that he had done all he could, that he had done all that any conscientious mayor could be expected to do, Peters prepared to return to North Haven that evening. Before leaving he announced that he was appointing a citizens' committee of thirty-four to examine the whole question of a police union and to make whatever recommendations it saw fit. "I do not think," he wrote optimistically, "the police will strike nor can I believe that the labor unions will join in a sympathetic strike, but it is plainly my duty to see that the citizens are protected and law and order maintained in any event. The public is entitled to this precaution and the public welfare demands it. With this situation in mind I have appointed a citizens' committee...."

As chairman of this committee he named the State Street investment banker James Jackson Storrow. Recognized even by his enemies as one of Boston's most exemplary citizens, Storrow was a Brahmin who had somehow transcended the provincial limitations of his city even to his appearance, for with his clipped grey moustache and oval face he looked more the New York financier or even the stereotyped Hollywood banker. For Boston he felt an inclusive affection that went beyond Beacon Hill and the Back Bay to embrace the anonymous little streets and the slums. Related to the Higginsons and the Cabots and the Lees, descendant of one of those ingeniously acquisitive Yankees who had founded the Massachusetts mill cities, he lived all his life in the Beacon Street town house of his childhood. As a Harvard undergraduate of the class of 1885, he had been captain of the crew that had beaten Yale, on graduation the second marshal of his class. From 1897 to 1909 he was an overseer of Harvard and in 1910 chief marshal of the Alumni Association, and one of the founders of the Harvard Club of Boston.

After finishing Harvard Law School in 1888, he formed his own law firm, soon numbering among his clients that most proper of Boston banking houses, Lee, Higginson & Company, with which he was intimately connected. In 1900 he abandoned the law to represent his family's interests in Lee, Higginson. Born rich, he grew to be one of the wealthiest men in New England, director of several dozen corporations. In 1910 he reorganized and became president of General Motors, then returned to his native city to head Lee, Higginson.

With Storrow's business interests went a devotion to public service that continued until his death. In 1902, backed by the high-minded Public School Association, he was elected to the Boston School Committee and later became its president and chairman. He founded the Boston Chamber of Commerce, expanded the City Club, where men of all backgrounds could meet, and gave a fortune to build playgrounds and such amenities in the slums as the West End House and the Newsboys' Club. In 1909, although a poor public speaker, he let himself be persuaded to run for mayor against the glib-tongued Honey Fitz. "Manhood against Money," was Honey Fitz's response as he conducted his usual slashing campaign, backed this time by his old enemies Curley and Lomasney. Fitzgerald spoke ten times to Storrow's one, capered on the roof of a hack to sing his theme song, "Sweet Adeline," and plastered Boston with blown-up photographs of City Hall on which was superimposed: NOT FOR SALE MR. $TORROW. Storrow countered by coining the term "Fitzgeraldism," and brought unaccustomed tears to Honey Fitz's eyes by publishing photographs of Fitzgerald with GRAFTER stamped on the forehead. In the largest vote in the city's history, Honey Fitz defeated Storrow by a mere 1402 votes and only then by juggling ballots and insinuating a straw candidate.

Dismayed but undeterred by this rejection, Storrow continued to work for the Bigger, Better, Brighter Boston of Honey Fitz's tongue-in-cheek slogan. He served as chairman of three arbitration boards, settling disputes between the Boston Elevated Company and the carmen's union. In 1915, backed by the Good Government Association and opposed by Mayor Curley, he managed to get himself elected to the city council. Whenever a mayor or governor fell back on a commission or committee to solve the insoluble, Storrow's name was the first to be considered. In 1915–1916 he served on a state cost-of-living commission. The next year he was appointed chairman of the hundred-member Massachusetts Committee on Public Safety that reorganized the National Guard and instituted the state guard after the Yankee Division had been sent overseas. As federal fuel administrator for New England during the grim winter months of 1917 and 1918, he saw to it that his region received at least the minimum amount of coal necessary for homes and industry, even using his own personal credit to cut red tape and start shipments.

For Peters it was as natural to turn to Storrow as to God, with the advantage that Storrow was more accessible. After consulting Curtis, with Storrow's assistance he enrolled a committee that he felt encompassed all interests and ethnic groups in the city, although critics would consider it weighted in favor of business. Known variously as the committee of thirty-four, the citizens' committee, and more generally as the Storrow committee, it brought together old-line Yankees like Charles F. Choate, Jr., and Charles Bancroft, Irishmen like the broker James J. Phelan and the contractor Harry Nawn, and wealthy upper-crust Jews like the merchant A. Lincoln Filene and the banker Abraham Ratshesky. Vincent Brogna represented the Italians, General Charles Cole, former commander of the Yankee Division's Fifty-second Infantry Brigade, the military. Several labor leaders were included, as well as ten bankers and six lawyers, but whatever the committee's composition, Storrow as chairman intended it to be *his* committee with himself in complete control. His goal, as he saw it, was to evolve some sort of compromise that would avoid the threatening strike while satisfying both the police and the commissioner. Suave and confident, he was sure this would be possible.

Having prepared his statement and appointed his committee, Peters left that evening for his fog-shrouded Maine island well satisfied with himself.

ON A
TUESDAY
IN SEPTEMBER

James Storrow *was* the Storrow committee. The other members, half of whom merely lent their names, were window dressing. Before the first formal committee meeting, on Thursday evening, Storrow released a mild and conciliatory statement. He spoke of his own warm affection for the police, assuring the men that he wanted to see the dispute from their "side of the fence." He praised the patriotism and wisdom of the AFL. But he held firmly that it would not be fitting for the police to join an AFL-affiliated union. "We would think it improper for a judge to join a labor union," he concluded, "so too it would be improper for a policeman who like the judge also is engaged in the administration of the law." Belonging to a union would, he felt, force a policeman to take sides in labor disputes, would cast doubt on his credibility as a witness, and would undermine the public's confidence in impartial law enforcement.

Vahey, much distressed that Storrow had apparently made up his mind in advance, immediately wrote him that he felt such a statement was made without a knowledge of all the facts. Storrow's reply was as courteous as it was open-minded: "Thank you for your letter of this morning. I am extremely anxious to see this question from both sides and it would be a great favor to me if you could arrange for me today a conference with you and Mr. Feeney and the officers of the Policemen's Union. I am anxious to hear the policeman's side of the question."

Even as Storrow was answering Vahey's letter on that Friday morning, August 29, the eleven additional patrolmen charged with violating Rule 35 appeared at police headquarters for trial. Their hearing lasted only ten minutes. Vahey, Feeney, and secretary Devlin (for Curtis) waived all debate, holding that their arguments did not differ from those of the first hearing. The young, light-hearted patrolmen, who seemed to regard the hearing almost as a joke, entered and left headquarters laughing, confident, and apparently not in the least worried. Again the commissioner postponed his findings.

At midday Friday the Storrow committee held its final meeting at the Boston City Club. Only seventeen members were present. They quickly endorsed Storrow's statement of the night before, then adopted several resolutions. First they commended the police and the AFL for past services and loyalties. Then, after this preliminary buttering-up, they set forth that they did not oppose any police organization as such but did oppose affiliation with the AFL on the grounds that this would divide the men's sole allegiance to the community they served. Finally they resolved that "the citizens committee in all friendliness urge the members of the force and the American Federation of Labor to recognize the reasonableness of this position and ask their cooperation in maintaining it."

Before adjourning, the committee reduced itself to more manageable size by appointing an eight-man executive committee, headed of course by Storrow. Following the meeting Storrow told reporters that as yet there were no plans for protecting the city in case of a police strike, since the committee's purpose was to avoid such a strike.

August drifted into September, in stagnant heat-heavy weather. Throughout Boston the ensuing days took on a hypnotic inevitability. Storrow reduced his executive committee still further to a subcommittee consisting of himself, George Brock, and James Phelan. On Saturday of that long weekend the officers of the police union met with the subcommittee in Room 28 of the Parker House. Storrow then questioned the policemen about their work, their wages and hours and was shocked by much of what he learned. That such conditions persisted beneath the smoothly efficient façade of the Boston Police Department, he had never even suspected. He found it incredible that even after the new wage scale, night patrolmen were getting only twenty-five cents an hour for an eighty-three-hour work week, day men an hourly twenty-nine cents for a seventy-three-hour week, and wagon men only twenty-one cents an hour for a ninety-eight-hour week. Afterward he said with his usual smooth precision that "perfect frankness and good nature characterized the conference, and we are trying to reach an amicable adjustment." But for all their talk on Saturday the committee and the police did not get to the crux of the matter: whether the policemen would withdraw from the AFL if their other demands as to pay and conditions were met. President McInnes and the other officers were more determined than ever to keep their union, convinced that with the backing of organized labor they were bound to win in a showdown. On Saturday night McInnes summed up his union's position: "If a struggle is inevitable, it will not be of our own seeking. But if we must strike for our rights, it will be a struggle to the finish. We hope for a victory without a struggle and such a victory would be a double victory." What he meant by "rights" he did not define, but for the first time the word "strike" came into the open.

On Sunday Storrow met at the Parker House for eight hours with McInnes, Vahey, and Feeney. At the end of their extended session they called in various reporters who had been waiting in the lobby. Vahey was the first to speak. He admitted they were at an impasse, the police insisting on affiliating with the AFL, whereas the subcommittee "questioned their right in unmistakable language to join any union or unions." Storrow interrupted him to say that he recognized the right of any laboring man to form a union and to use the strike as a weapon but, he went on to say, "my view is that the police go out armed to protect the public and to make arrests and if necessary to shoot, and I haven't been able to see so far that the state can permit such officials to undertake that duty and yet reserve the right which inheres to laboring men." Without commenting on Storrow's interjection, Vahey said he hoped that the committee would consider means of avoiding trouble. When a reporter asked him if by "trouble" he meant a strike, he hedged, declaring that "no one is committed to any plan." He did admit though that both sides had discussed many proposals for a peaceful solution. Storrow and his subcommittee recommended that the police form their own unaffiliated union. McInnes replied that this would merely be another Social Club, a club that in fifteen years had gained nothing for the force. Finally Vahey threatened that if Curtis should suspend the eighteen patrolmen, he would take the matter to court.

That evening orders came from police headquarters for all night and day men to appear at their station houses at eight Monday night. The order was the result of disturbances in the theatrical district following an actors' strike, but on that uneasy weekend it set off a flurry of rumors and speculations. One "reliable source" had it that on Monday morning the division captains would give their men the choice of either resigning from the union or resigning from the force. The *Herald* predicted dourly that "the officers will positively decline to withdraw from the union or from one without affiliation with the American Federation of Labor."

Monday, the predicted day of decision, passed off inconsequentially. Peters had hurried back from Maine to review a Labor Day parade. Tophatted, tanned, and beaming, he stood in front of City Hall with Councilor Moriarty beside him as several thousand metal trades workers paraded by, booing Curtis as they passed and giving out cheers for the policemen's union. Storrow met the mayor after the parade to give him a summary of the weekend's deliberations. Then he talked briefly with Feeney and Vahey, who were on their way to a union meeting at Fay Hall. The rest of the day he spent with his subcommittee at the Parker House. Curtis came up to the almost empty city from Nahant to talk with him late in the afternoon. The commissioner was quite willing to discuss wages, hours, and working conditions. But the question of union recognition he considered beyond discussion. Even an independent union, he felt, might interfere with his authority over his department. After the meeting Storrow told reporters that he still hoped to "find a way out." He understood now how both sides felt, and he was optimistic. Whether the police would accept the committee's "most generous offer" on wages, hours, and conditions, he could not say. Nor did he know how the city's finances could absorb another pay raise. Prudently he warned that in the end his committee's efforts might fail. "If we can't hit upon a plan in a day or two," he concluded, "I can't see what we will do."

That night at a meeting of the police union the members debated and then discarded a motion to disband the Social Club. Nevertheless it was overwhelmingly clear that the policemen wanted no more of an organization that they had come to feel was "weak-kneed" and dominated by the commissioner. For some time they had failed to pay their dues, and now even the club's president and vice-president had come over to the union.

After three days of conferences Storrow and his committee had acquired a realistic picture of the workings of the police department. But for all their sympathy with the ordinary patrolman, they could see no settlement without the men's surrender of the AFL charter, since "on no other basis could their retention as policemen be countenanced." If the men stuck to the union and went on strike, Storrow warned the leaders, his committee would do everything in its power to defeat them. By Tuesday the obstacles in the way of a settlement seemed all but insurmountable. The police were adamant in refusing to yield their AFL charter. Curtis declined to consider any union at all. Yet beneath the surface adamancy, conciliatory forces were at work. The police union council indirectly admitted this when the members argued that it was up to the Storrow committee to produce some alternate plan that would give the police the bargaining power necessary to assert their rights. Without such a plan the council could not ask the men to withdraw from the AFL. That would be like telling the patrolmen to "go back to your twenty-one-to-thirty-cents-an-hour jobs and your dirty beds or get other employment!" The union leaders now proposed that the police be allowed to keep their AFL membership until this should prove detrimental to the functioning of the department. "When that time occurs, let a rule be made and these men will obey that rule and will stay out." Storrow's countersuggestion was that the police "withdraw from the AFL and form a real organization of [their] own, safeguarded by this committee and by the mayor in such a fashion that Headquarters cannot tamper with it."

Calculating realists that they were, Feeney and Vahey had come to realize that any practical settlement would entail severing the union's AFL affiliation. They now saw the AFL charter as a bargaining counter, and this was even more apparent to them after the police of New York City and of Buffalo had given up their proposed AFL affiliation even as the District of Columbia commissioners were ordering the Washington police to sever their connection with the AFL or face discharge. The tentative plan that the lawyers drafted provided that the policemen would leave the AFL and form their own independent organization safeguarded by the committee and the mayor from any "tampering by headquarters"; grievances would be arbitrated to protect the officers of the new union from unfair treatment; in the matter of promotion, the commissioner would select candidates from the first three names on the civil service list, and if he bypassed any of those three names he would have to explain why in writing; finally, a patrolman's standing in the department would not be affected, whether or not he chose to join the union.

Vahey and Feeney submitted their plan first to the Storrow committee, then on Wednesday to the union officers, who agreed not to come to any decision until Curtis had made his. They also agreed to wait until the still-tentative plan had reached its final form before submitting it to the full body of the union. Vahey was then prepared to urge the plan's acceptance. Meanwhile the headlines of the Boston papers continued to flare with news that "NO PEACE SIGN MARKS POLICE CONTROVERSY." Police volunteers continued to appear at the Chamber of Commerce Building. Volunteering began to seem a summer adventure of sorts, and already over two hundred recruits had signed up: ex-army officers, Harvard athletes of yesterday's fame, businessmen, everyone except labor union members—who were considered unacceptable. The first to volunteer had been a sixty-three-year-old Harvard physics professor, walrus-moustached Edwin Hall, who announced loudly that the police were wrong and that he hoped his example in volunteering would be followed by hundreds of others. On August 28 he wrote to the

Herald praising Curtis for his proper and valiant stand but regretting the absence of long lines of volunteers. "Come back from your vacations, young men," Professor Hall called out to his undergraduates, "there is sport and diversion for you right here in Boston!" Seventy-five of the ablest volunteers were being trained by drill master Captain Patrick King at the castellated South Armory on Irvington Street.

Curtis had planned to announce his decision on the nineteen already-tried patrolmen Thursday morning, September 4. What Storrow now feared was that he would find the men guilty and proceed to sentence them before the compromise plan had taken final shape and before Vahey and Feeney could persuade the union members to accept it. Once Curtis had taken such action, the police would refuse to withdraw and a strike would be inevitable. Storrow, faced with this urgency, sent Curtis's close and persuasive friend, the banker Charles Bancroft, to the commissioner with a letter begging him to postpone his decision until the citizens' committee could conclude its conferences with the officials of the "Police Officers Union," conferences that he hoped and expected would find "an amicable and satisfactory solution of the present situation."

Bancroft found his entrée to the commissioner blocked by watchdog Herbert Parker, who took the letter, read it, and declined to deliver it. Whether or not Curtis read the letter, officially he never received it, and it was never answered. In any case, he was incensed that an outsider should attempt to interfere with the discipline of his department. Where his orders had been violated, he refused to be swayed. Later he might be willing to consider Storrow's compromise plan. But disobedience was not a matter of compromise. He notified Vahey and Feeney that he would deliver his judgment the following morning, Thursday, at nine-forty-five.

Dismayed but still hoping to avoid a strike, Peters—back again from Maine—hurried with the Storrow subcommittee to the State House to beg the governor to intervene. Coolidge, obviously annoyed at being injected into the police controversy, dismissed them with the curt observation that he did not consider it his duty to communicate with the commissioner. Privately Coolidge maintained he had "no direct responsibility for the conduct of police matters in Boston." A word from him to Curtis at that point would probably have led to a compromise, but as his semiofficial biographer, Claude Fuess, admitted, "that word he would not utter." In contrast to Coolidge, Mayor Peters, though uncertain of what to do, was willing to communicate with any and everybody. Early Thursday morning he sent a letter to the commissioner which Storrow, accompanied by his committee counsel, Charles Choate, personally delivered to Parker at Pemberton Square.

> I have been watching with keen interest [the mayor wrote] the conferences which have been taking place between the committee appointed by me a short time ago and the members of the Boston Police Force, looking to a solution of the problems presented by the affiliation of the police with the American Federation of Labor and impressed with the belief that a solution may be found, honorable and satisfactory to the men and consistent with the principles which must be observed in the orderly administration of the police force.
>
> With the fullest appreciation for the high responsibility that rests upon you, I must also have in mind the safety and security of the people. The importance to the public of having the question settled satisfactorily impels me to ask you to postpone action for a few days only until the development of the impending conferences may be seen. If they succeed in solving the problem without requiring you to reach a final decision, friendly discussion will have achieved the result satisfactory to all concerned.

Curtis's instant reaction was that Peters should mind his own business. He and Parker talked with Storrow briefly but refused to allow Choate in the room.

Still angry at what he felt was the Storrow committee's and Peters's unwarranted interference in police department discipline, Curtis sent for Superintendent Crowley, Vahey, Feeney, and seven officers of the police union. When they arrived at headquarters, he led Feeney and Vahey into his private office. Parker and Devlin were already there. The commissioner's frayed temper was apparent.

"What right has the mayor of Boston to send me a letter asking for a continuance?" he demanded, handing the letter to the union lawyers. Then, when they had glanced at it, he told them that he was going to make his finding now, but if they could give him any good reason for postponing the penalty, he was willing to listen to them.

"Do you mean," Feeney asked, "that you are going to make a finding of guilty today no matter who objects?" Curtis said that he was.

"Well," Feeney snapped back, "if you are going to make a finding today, I don't care when you impose the penalty. You will then have undone everything the mayor and his committee together with counsel have undertaken to do in order to adjust this matter in a friendly way to the end that Boston may have a satisfied police force. And now I want to speak plainly to you. I think that in a matter as important as this the mayor and his committee after working day and night with your knowledge and consent to settle this matter have a perfect right to ask for a postponement and you have no damn right to get upon your high horse about it."

"Mr. Feeney," Parker broke in suavely, "I don't think you understood the commissioner. He means that if counsel ask for a continuance of the entire matter, he will listen to the argument with an open mind."

"Look, Parker," Feeney told him, his face reddening, "that is not what the commissioner said. He told us he was going to make his finding anyway. He would listen to the matter of postponement of penalty only. Isn't that true, Curtis?"

Curtis said it was, and Parker broke in again, this time urging the commissioner to consider a postponement of both the finding and the penalty.

Suddenly Curtis seemed to wilt. "I'll do that," he said. "In fact, if you lawyers just ask for a postponement, I'll grant it without requiring you to give any reasons."

"Request for postponement has been made," said Feeney. "You do as you see fit with it; so far as we are concerned, we will take no sides."

"Well," said Curtis, "I will go into that hearing room and read the mayor's letter and then 'put it up to you' as to whether you object or not."

"Go ahead," said Feeney, "and I will tell you then that counsel for the police stand indifferent."

Again Parker broke in, tossing his aloof white head and scarcely concealing his contempt. "That won't do at all," he told Feeney in his irritatingly precise voice. "Your counsel must ask for the continuance."

This time Vahey rose to the challenge. "Well now we'll settle it for once and for all," he said, his voice quivering. "We won't ask for a continuance. You can do as you see fit about it. The trouble with you, Parker, is you are too damn vain, and you are vain too, Curtis.... This matter can be settled to your satisfaction and the satisfaction of all the men. But it looks to me as though you don't want to settle it. It looks to me as though you are seeking trouble."

"Well, I don't see the need of any hearing at all," said Curtis finally. Vahey replied that that was all the mayor, Storrow, and the police had been waiting to hear for the past twenty-four hours. At that point Curtis gave the mayor's letter to the press along with a statement that "having received the following letter from his honor the Mayor, and having read the same to the attorneys for the defendants and they making no objection, my finding will be postponed until Monday next at 9:15 a.m."

That same afternoon Choate on behalf of the Storrow committee gave a draft of their compromise plan to Vahey and Feeney for their suggested alterations. Even as Vahey and Feeney deliberated, a growing number of volunteers were making their way to the Chamber of Commerce Building. Over three hundred and fifty had now enrolled, "some of them superb specimens of physical manhood," according to Pierce. Already they had begun to receive training in the fundamental duties, responsibilities, and rights of a police officer. Union leaders now told reporters that the police would strike on Tuesday "if the nineteen are even reprimanded."

Another humid rumor-ridden weekend followed, one which Storrow sensed with increasing dismay would probably end in a police strike. On Saturday Vahey and Feeney returned the compromise plan with their revisions, and Storrow's executive committee voted to accept it. Storrow showed the plan to the president of the chamber of commerce, the managing editor of the *Post*, General Cole, Murray Crane, and his right-hand man, former Senate President William M. Butler, all of whom expressed their approval. He then sent his final version on to Mayor Peters. There would not be too much difficulty there. Of that he was certain. But to get the inflexible commissioner and the autocratic Parker to unbend even a little would indeed be a "delicate" task. Storrow's report to the mayor read:

The citizens committee appointed by you to consider the police situation begs to report as follows.

We recommend the following basis of settlement which we hope will commend itself to your Honor, the Police Commissioner and the members of the police force.

1. That the Boston Policemen's Union should not affiliate or be connected with any labor organization but should maintain its independence and maintain its organization.

2. That the present wages, hours and working conditions require adjustment and should be investigated by a committee of three citizens, who shall forthwith be selected by concurrent action of the mayor, the commissioner and the Policemen's Union, and their conclusions communicated to the mayor and the Police Commissioner, and that thereafter all questions arising relating to hours and wages, and physical conditions of work which the Policemen's Union desires to bring before the commissioner shall be taken up with the Police Commissioner by duly accredited officers and committees of the Boston Policemen's Union, and should any differences arise relating thereto which cannot be adjusted it shall be submitted to three citizens of Boston selected by agreement between the mayor, the Police Commissioner and the Boston Policemen's Union. The conclusions of the three citizens thus selected shall be communicated to the mayor and the Police Commissioner and to the citizens of Boston by publication. The provisions of this section shall not apply to any questions of discipline.

3. That nothing should be done to prevent or discourage any member of the Boston police force from becoming or continuing to be officers or members of the Boston Policemen's Union, and that there should be no discrimination against them or preferential treatment of them or their officers because of membership in the union.

4. That there should be no discrimination on the part of the members of the Boston Policemen's Union, or any of them against a police officer because of his refusal to join the Boston Policemen's Union or to continue a member thereof.

5. That no member of the Boston Policemen's Union should be discriminated against because of any previous affiliation with the American Federation of Labor.*

---

* Several members of his committee felt that Storrow was conceding too much to the police. One member, Colonel Robert Goodwin, resigned in protest, writing, "I am

Peters approved the plan at once and sent it on to Curtis for his "consideration, criticisms, and suggestions." There was no reply all that long Saturday. In the afternoon, still silent, the commissioner left for Nahant, while Storrow and his executive committee spent the day conferring among themselves, with Peters, and with Feeney and Vahey. So struck were they by the sense of urgency that they did not even take time for lunch but had sandwiches sent in. Hour by hour they waited for some response from the commissioner. Finally at eleven in the evening Storrow, looking worn and haggard, announced that his efforts for a peaceful settlement had failed and that he and his committee could do nothing more. "I am inclined to look for the next event at nine-thirty Monday morning," he said as he dismissed the other committee members. While the Storrow committee waited, Peters sent a special messenger to Curtis with a personal letter in which he described the compromise as offering "a speedy and satisfactory settlement of the whole question," and begged Curtis to consider it favorably. Peters's letter reached Curtis in Nahant early Sunday morning.

During the twelve days that the Storrow committee was struggling to find a way out of the police impasse, Governor Coolidge was touring the state, attending a Methodist gathering, speaking at Plymouth, and visiting Westfield for its 250th anniversary. Those concerned about a police strike found him consistently unavailable. "Governor getting tired of seeing people," Secretary Long recorded in his diary. "He is planning to visit institutions." On that hectic Saturday while Storrow and Peters and the police lawyers were conferring, Coolidge had slipped away again in his chauffeur-driven Packard Twin-six limousine that he—a nondriver —found one of the more enjoyable perquisites of office. Neither Storrow nor Peters nor the press knew where he had gone. What concerned him chiefly was to be away from Boston. First he drove to Abington on the way to Cape Cod, then doubled back north to Andover, in both places merely to attend Welcome Home gatherings for returned soldiers. He appeared his usual laconic self, quacking a few words, giving his limp handshake, and moving on,

---

firmly convinced that the stand taken by Commissioner Curtis is right and that he should have the frank and open support of every citizen who endorses his course."

but there was no trace of worry in his Vermont-granite features. At Andover he spent some time talking with General Cole. He arrived back in Boston secretly late Saturday night and left early Sunday morning for his Massasoit Street duplex in Northampton, where he could be reached only by the elect who knew the code name "Grace." On Monday he planned to motor twenty miles north to Greenfield to speak before the state convention of the American Federation of Labor. Sunday night he held a long conversation with Murray Crane.*

With the governor beyond reach on Sunday morning, two friends of Storrow's—one a lawyer, the other a businessman—begged Coolidge's intimate friend and adviser, the opulent Boston drygoods merchant Frank Waterman Stearns, to use his influence to persuade the governor to intervene. Stearns, a fretful, prissy little man known behind his back as Lord Lingerie, had an avuncular, almost a paternal, devotion to Coolidge, derived in part from their mutual attachment to Amherst College, from which he himself had graduated in 1878. With a faith transcending reason he had long held that the sandy-haired Northampton legislator with the stage-Yankee voice was destined to become President of the United States. He did not want to see his protégé burned by the police strike. "Gentlemen, I am not a lawyer," he told the two emissaries at an early morning meeting at the Copley Plaza, "but I have heard the matter discussed by eminent lawyers and have arrived at the conclusion that the compromise which you suggest—which amounts to an agreement on the part of the Police Commissioner of Boston to give the deserters a written promise to put the whole matter to arbitration—is not worth the paper on which it would be written. I do not believe that sworn officers of the law can leave a matter of this kind to arbitration."

Storrow spent all Sunday with his committee in Room 601 of the Copley Plaza waiting hopefully from morning until evening for some sign from Curtis. He waited in vain. Earlier he had sent Curtis's friend Ratshesky to Nahant only to learn that the

---

* Robert Lincoln O'Brien, the sharp-nosed editor of the *Herald*, considered that Coolidge in the police crisis was much influenced by Crane. O'Brien went so far as to call Crane the "Hamlet of the Police Strike drama."

commissioner had already left for Lancaster to visit Parker. Meanwhile the Boston Central Labor Union was holding a stormy session in the afternoon, the officers doing their best to hold down the angry and rebellious members from committing themselves to a sympathy strike before Curtis acted. Although most of those present were now convinced the police strike was inevitable, President O'Donnell managed to persuade them to leave any final decision as to what action they might take to their committee of seventeen. Just before the two o'clock meeting opened, Peters telephoned to say that the Storrow committee was still in session and that there was still hope of a peaceful settlement. Councilor Moriarty commended the delegates for not declaring their intentions until after the commissioner had acted, then launched a savage attack on the mayor. The whole problem could have been solved two weeks before, he told them, if Peters "had kept his mouth shut instead of rushing before the public saying that he had every confidence in Commissioner Curtis and supported him in any move he might make." He charged that the leaders of the chamber of commerce were the real source of the mayor's statements, and saw this as an attack against the union.

At the day's end and at the end of their rope, Storrow and his committee followed Peters's suggestion and released the text of their report to the press in time for Monday editorial comment, hoping in desperation to influence Curtis by the pressure of public opinion. Such opinion, reflected in the morning papers, showed itself all for compromise. Even the *Herald*, previously enthusiastic over Curtis's "firm, swift action" in placing the union leaders on trial, reluctantly agreed to the Storrow plan. The *Post*, the unofficial spokesman for the Roman Catholic hierarchy, called it "a wise solution" by which the police would organize within the "letter and spirit" of Curtis's regulations. Its editor was "quite sure that this way out will be endorsed by the citizens of Boston as reasonable and wise." Hearst's *American*, "the paper for people who think," most read by the working class, including the police, warmly approved. The independent *Globe*, its readers a cut above those of the Hearst paper, recognized "the fairness of the proposition of the Citizens' Committee.... For either the commissioner or the police to refuse this solution of the difficulty would be a grave mistake."

Only the *Evening Transcript* remained adamantly opposed to any such "surrender" and called the plan one of the most deplorable documents in Boston's annals.

Monday arrived as a sweltering aftermath of summer. Before the day was over the temperature would rise to the mid-90s. Early in the morning Curtis from his Pemberton Square office sent his answer to the mayor:

> The Police Commissioner begs to acknowledge receipt of your communication under date of September 6. The commissioner has given to it that careful consideration which the occasion demands. It will be obvious to your Honor that the commissioner cannot consider this communication as having relation to the present duty of the commissioner to act upon complaints now pending before him.
>
> The commissioner can discover nothing in the communication transmitted by your Honor and relating to action by him which appears to him to be either consistent with his prescribed legal duties or calculated to aid him in their performance. The commissioner approves necessary betterment in the economic condition of the police force of the City of Boston and has theretofore expressed such approval, but these are not the conditions which require his present action.
>
> The commissioner has therefore felt compelled to proceed to make his findings upon the complaints pending before him pursuant to the adjournment of such action heretofore declared.*

Beneath the stilted legalistic phraseology carefully framed by Parker, the answer was a blunt "no compromise." He would accept no solution that might impinge on his authority or "that might be

---

* In his *Commissioner's Report for 1919*, Curtis explained his refusal in detail. He held that the Storrow proposal "was not prepared by the men, and the attitude of the men in regard to it was in no way indicated." If the proposal showed a change of heart on the part of the nineteen suspended patrolmen, that change "was of importance only in the event of their being found guilty, in mitigation of the sentence to be imposed." The proposal was "fundamentally incompatible with the responsibility to the public which the law calls upon the commissioner for the government of a police force and with a sense of responsibility to the commissioner which the members of the force must feel if proper discipline and efficiency are to be maintained." Furthermore, the grievance board proposed by the plan would result in "a reversion to the state of divided responsibility, vacillating policy, and dilatory action" that the legislature had sought to eliminate when it did away with the board of commissioners.

considered as a pardon of the men on trial." It was not generally expected before the day's end that Curtis would discharge the nineteen patrolmen. At two-thirty in the afternoon the police held another union meeting at Fay Hall. Brashly confident, unintimidated by Curtis's morning statement, they were eager to accept the commissioner's challenge. When the nineteen banned patrolmen arrived they were again cheered and applauded. President McInnes himself was given a prolonged ovation. Within the sweltering hall the men removed their blue coats and sat in their shirtsleeves, mopping their foreheads. They were prepared to take a strike vote at once, but McInnes held them back, wanting no such action until after Curtis had imposed sentence. So intense was the heat that at four-fifteen the meeting was recessed for an hour.

Following the five-forty-five roll call at the various station houses the division heads read out Curtis's verdict. Contrary to expectations he had not discharged the nineteen men outright but merely suspended them, leaving at least the possibility of reinstating them later, whereas if he had discharged them outright he could not legally have taken them back. Earlier the nineteen had left for the afternoon roll call. On learning of their suspension they cleaned out their lockers, turned in their badges, revolvers, clubs, and signalbox keys. Their pay had already been stopped, and their names removed from the roster.

In front of the downtown stations sympathetic crowds had gathered ready to applaud the suspended patrolmen on their way out. When the nineteen reappeared at Fay Hall they were welcomed with cheers and clapping, their swaggering arrival bolstering the determination of the others. President McInnes issued an interim statement to the press thanking Storrow for his courteous and understanding attitude, giving a summary of his conferences with the citizens' committee, repeating the now familiar list of police grievances, and concluding that without the shelter of the AFL the police position would be hopeless and that the union "has once and for all come to stay." To the sweating, angry policemen the difference between suspension and discharge seemed negligible. The challenge had been issued from Pemberton Square, and they were ready to meet it. At nine-forty-five strike balloting began. The men had received two ballot sheets, one for a no-strike, the other for a strike vote. It was soon clear from the enormous quantity of discarded no-strike ballots littering the floor that the men were prepared to defy the commissioner. By midnight over a thousand had cast their votes, with an overwhelming majority favoring a strike. So strong was strike sentiment that McInnes and the other union officers had difficulty in keeping the men from declaring a walkout to take place at the roll call three quarters of an hour after midnight. It seemed that the 1544 patrolmen on the force, the overwhelming majority—including a number of nonunion members—would take part.*

Frank McCarthy, after a short speech to the union, telephoned BCLU President O'Donnell at Greenfield to give him a running account of what had happened. O'Donnell assured him that the other unions regarded the police struggle as their own, and said he would call a special meeting of the Central Labor Union for Wednesday or Thursday to let them register their decision on a sympathy strike. After talking to O'Donnell, McCarthy told a group of reporters that "the men of this union have been and are gentlemen and the entire issue is up to Commissioner Curtis." Some of the more impetuous patrolmen were now clamoring for a seven-forty-five morning deadline, but McInnes persuaded them to postpone it until the afternoon roll call. The voting continued through into the morning as the night men appeared after duty. In the final vote 1134 voted to strike, with two opposed. Strike headquarters were set up at Fay Hall, and the union leaders spent the rest of Tuesday preparing for the by now inevitable denouement, only a few hours away.

The Boston Police Strike would come to seem to many the climax of a year of violence. Conservatives like Senator Henry Cabot Lodge would view it as a first step toward sovietizing the country. The police themselves saw nothing political, nothing radical, in their act, nothing that would challenge the established order of which they were the guardians. They were simple men of small education. Most of them had left school at the then legal age of twelve with a grammar-school diploma. As transplanted Celts, their Catholicism was part of their group identity. To stray beyond

---

* 1117 policemen struck. 427 did not, including those ill or on vacations.

the bonds and rules of the church was unthinkable. Members of local Holy Name societies and the Knights of Columbus, they attended mass each Sunday with an unreflecting piety that the Spanish philosopher Miguel de Unamuno had called the "coal-heavers' faith." Without any preframed political theories, they bore a clan allegiance to the Democratic party that had its roots in their dislike and resentment of the entrenched Republican Brahmins, a resentment that Honey Fitz and Curley so adroitly exploited at each election. That they might be considered social revolutionaries would have moved them to profane astonishment. Nevertheless, an invisible Red thread did run through the strike, introduced by those who truly hoped that the event in Boston might bring about the decisive revolutionary situation on this side of the Atlantic for which they had been waiting ever since the October days in Petrograd. According to Ben Gitlow, one leading figure of the police union was a close sympathizer of the Communist party and collaborated with the Communists in the conduct of the strike. Gitlow wrote that

> the Communists were active in the strike. Some of the most violent episodes of the strike took place in Roxbury where the Communist Letts were concentrated. Emissaries from the Boston Communists were hurriedly dispatched to New York to report on the situation to Communist leaders and to get advice and orders on how to proceed. Communist organizers were rushed to Boston. Rank-and-file members who were footloose were directed to go to Boston to help the local comrades intensify the strike violence, to work for the calling of a general strike, and to politicalize the strike by directing it against the government.

Unofficially the American Communist party had come into being in June 1919, after Louis Fraina—who had returned to New York—had called a National Council of the Left Wing, made up of dissidents from the Socialists. These formed the nucleus of the Communist Party, U.S.A., although the party itself would not be officially proclaimed until a few days before the police strike.* As a

---

* Expelled by the executive committee of the Socialist party, the Left-Wing rebels defiantly announced that "humanity can be saved from its last excesses only by the Communist Revolution." The native-born English-speaking groups formed the

party manifesto explained: "Strikes of protest develop into general political strikes and then into revolutionary mass action for the conquest of the power of the state ... the Communist Party shall participate in mass strikes, not only to achieve the immediate purposes of the strike but to develop the revolutionary implications." When the shadow of the coming Boston police strike had grown sufficiently large, Ludwig C. A. K. Martens, for over a year the official representative of the Soviet Government in the United States, sent Fraina and John J. Ballam to Boston with eighty-five thousand dollars in funds to aid the strikers. Most of this money derived from the sale of Russian crown jewels smuggled into the United States.

Fraina and Ballam, as members of the National Council of the Left Wing, looked at the strike through the flame-colored glasses of revolutionaries. The Seattle strike had been only an overture; this in Boston would be the climax of the convulsive year, the prelude to an American October Revolution. So Fraina saw it on the way from New York, impervious to the irony of his rushing to assist those who had battered down his Lett comrades only four months previously. The police, in the stress of their struggle, were equally willing to let bygones be bygones. Short on funds and lacking experience, they were ready to accept money and directives from any source. Much of the Russian money went to pay for halls, printing, propaganda, and in some cases subsidies for the families of the striking police. Much of the advice would sharpen the edge of strike violence. But not more than a handful of the police leaders were aware of Fraina and Ballam moving with stealthy assurance behind the scenes.

Coolidge in Northampton remained unruffled by any Boston eventualities. He had planned to spend several days visiting institutions in the western part of the state. Stearns telephoned him early Monday morning at Massasoit Street, begging him to return as soon as possible, and he agreed to cut his tour short. After a leisurely breakfast he drove on to Greenfield to the American

---

Communist Labor party with a membership of about ten thousand; the semiautonomous foreign-anguage groups such as the Boston Letts, numbering some sixty thousand, withdrew into the Communist party, nine tenths of whose members were aliens. Later, under orders from Moscow, the two groups would combine.

Federation of Labor convention. His speech to the convention was short and at best lackadaisical. The delegates had expected him to make some comment on the Boston crisis, but he did not so much as mention the police or the possibility of a strike. Instead he fell back on his store of laconic platitudes, urging those present to take back to the men and women they represented the gospel "that upon all rests the responsibility of doing all that may be done to make the name America stand for mighty endeavor and strenuous effort." Hardly had he left the hall before the impatient delegates adopted a resolution condemning "the Hunnish attitude of Police Commissioner Curtis" and offering full moral and financial aid to the policemen's union.

On his way back—a three-hour drive—Coolidge stopped at Fitchburg to telephone his office for the latest news. He arrived in Boston in a belting rainstorm just as the police were settling in at their Fay Hall meeting and went directly to the two-room suite in the Adams House that he had graduated to after becoming lieutenant governor. There, sour in mood, he met at last with Storrow and Peters, who had been frantically trying to reach him since Saturday. Peters's fluttery voice turned almost contralto with excitement as he urged Coolidge to endorse the compromise plan. Coolidge refused, suggesting ironically that Peters instead call the city council together to vote whatever pay raise they felt the police should have, rearrange their work hours, and "fix up the old police stations." Finally they asked him to mobilize three or four thousand troops of the state guard. No, said Coolidge. He felt that the situation could safely be left in Curtis's hands. The commissioner did not think that a strike would amount to much; in any case the history of strikes showed that disorder did not come until after the third day, which would give them plenty of time to act.

At this point only the governor could have forced the commissioner to unbend. In hindsight the solution seems reasonable and fair to all: the police to have their unaffiliated union; the suspended patrolmen to be returned to duty; the men to call off their strike, and Curtis to agree to take no disciplinary action against the leaders; and grievances to be submitted to an impartial board. But when a group of friends called on Coolidge at the State House to warn him that unless he now spoke out he might be defeated in the

November election, he remarked that it was not necessary for him to be re-elected, and stared out the window in glum silence until his embarrassed visitors slipped away. To his stepmother in Vermont, to whom he was devoted, he wrote at about this time that he was determined to support the commissioner even at the risk of not being re-elected.

Long ago at Black River Academy John Calvin had been in bed one evening in the dormitory as several other more prankish boys pitched an old stove down the stairs. In spite of the din he stayed in bed. When next morning a master asked him if he had not heard the noise, he allowed that he had. When the master asked further why he had not done anything, he replied, "It wa'n't my stove." The impending police strike "wa'n't" his strike. As he told Crane testily on Sunday, he "didn't want to get mixed up in it." He did admit though to a reporter that he could not blame the police "for feeling as they do when they get less than a streetcar conductor." And as the strike loomed in its dark immediacy, he was nagged by the thought that he might get mixed up in it whether he wanted to or not. "E.U.," he appealed to Curtis at a private meeting just after his return from Greenfield, "we have to give in or there will be trouble." Curtis had no doubts. "If we give in now," he told the hesitant governor, "there will be no army, no police force, no government and this whole great country will fall to pieces—look what happened in Seattle!"

Monday's *Transcript* devoted a whole page to the text of Curtis's findings on suspending the nineteen patrolmen. The commissioner had felt the need of going to some length to explain the reasons and the precedents that had led him to his decision. His elaborate legal argument (prepared by Parker) was drawn from several dozen court decisions and a large number of Colonial and state statutes. Reduced to simple terms it held that the police were officers of the state and not employees. Yet, Curtis insisted, even if one granted that they were employees, Rule 35 could still legally prevent them from joining a nationally affiliated union. He concluded:

This separation and protection against the possible taint of disqualifying interest is recognized as essential to the apparent, and real, requirements of public confidence in public officials. It guards the justices of our courts, our jurymen, and all others who are to exercise authority over us. It is a salutary principle of our law. Adhering to it, I deem that I am required by the duties and obligations of my office, and in obedience to my conception, to enforce the regulation, for violation of which the accused have been brought to trial.

Exhausted in body and mind, Curtis toward the end of the afternoon collapsed at his desk. Recovering somewhat by evening, he pledged his subordinates to secrecy about his condition and returned to Nahant. Before leaving he sent a mutual friend, Arthur Chapin, vice-president of the American Trust Company, to Coolidge to sound him out as to what he would do if the police struck. Chapin reported that the governor had thought a moment and then said, "I am very friendly to Ned Curtis. I am told that he feels that enough policemen will remain loyal so that he can handle the situation, but you may tell him from me that if any emergency arises whereby it becomes necessary for me to act, I will stand back of him to the fullest extent."

Coolidge had dinner that evening with Peters, Storrow, and several members of the citizens' committee in a large private room at the Union Club. The governor declined to consider intervening. To the impotent fury of Peters and the dismay of Storrow he again refused to speak the word that would have meant compromise. It was a chilly occasion, made the more so by Peters's growing hatred for the laconic Coolidge and the governor's scarcely concealed contempt for the dilettante mayor. Nothing new was said around the table. The impasse was all too obvious. Coolidge left early and was in bed at his usual time of ten o'clock. As a precaution against what might happen, Massachusetts Adjutant General Jesse F. Stevens, Colonel R. O. Dalton in charge of state guard intelligence, and Secretary Long remained overnight at the Adams House.

That afternoon a hundred volunteer policemen had gathered in the Chamber of Commerce Building awaiting orders. Pierce took their names and telephone numbers, gave them written instructions, and told them to remain in readiness. Once they returned to be officially sworn in, they would receive night sticks, badges, and revolvers. Pierce also informed them that under Massachusetts law they could when on duty call on bystanders for help if necessary.

Anyone who refused to assist them was liable to a month's imprisonment or a fifty-dollar fine!

Within the city's restless, uneasy atmosphere preparations for disaster were being made. Hospitals cooperated with the police department to set up emergency-care stations, and their location and telephone numbers appeared in the morning papers. A fleet of fifteen ambulances was distributed strategically throughout the city. Fearful of vandalism, the larger industrial firms, banks, and stores armed their male help, many of whom had handled weapons in the army. Jordan Marsh, E. T. Slattery, Shephard's, and other department stores formed special guard detachments of their younger employees, while at the same time claiming that such preparations did not reflect any hostility toward the police but were merely intended to protect life and property. To warn off any influx of criminals, the press informed the public that bank messengers were receiving firearms instruction from Marine Corps sergeants.

On Tuesday morning Peters arrived at City Hall at an unwontedly early hour. Curtis, pale and blue-lipped, was already at his desk at Pemberton Square, his flabby cheeks sunk into his wing collar, a loaded revolver lying in front of him to protect him, he said, from any assassination attempt. Coolidge did not allow events to alter his routine. After his usual breakfast at his usual time, he strolled from the Adams House up Winter Street, across the Common, and along the mall to the State House. If he had any apprehensions, he kept them to himself. During the course of the day he received a telegram from the secretary of the Massachusetts branch of the AFL demanding that he remove Curtis as "a man who has insulted organized labor." The governor replied politically: "I have no authority over the appointment, suspension or removal of the police force of Boston. I earnestly hope circumstances will arise which will cause the police officers to be reinstated. In my judgment it would not be wise to remove Commissioner Curtis."

Peters had learned of the commissioner's findings from reporters, but he refused to comment. At midmorning he sent for Storrow and his executive committee. Storrow met the others at his State Street office before leading them, like a shepherd, to City Hall. Following an inconclusive hour in the mayor's office, he went on to the first formal meeting of the full committee of thirty-four to give

119

them a detailed account of the last ten days. After hearing Storrow, the committee unanimously endorsed his report to the mayor. By now Peters felt he could do no more. As mayor he did have the power in an emergency to call out the units of the state guard within the Boston area. Characteristically he was not aware of this. At one o'clock he bustled into Curtis's office querulously asserting that he was entitled to know what preparations state officials had made to preserve law and order in the city in case of a strike. Curtis told him that he himself could take care of any situation that might arise and that he did not need anyone else's help or advice. The commissioner remained convinced that in the final count the majority of the men would remain loyal to him. However, he did agree to meet with Peters at the governor's at five o'clock.

Even as the policemen were gathering up their belongings in the various stations, the three principal figures in the unfolding drama held a last meeting in the governor's austere Federalist office. Curtis, accompanied by a bodyguard, appeared with his revolver strapped to his side. Coolidge sat at his desk, impassive as ever, while Peters, standing by the black-marble mantel, in a voice by now verging on the falsetto, begged him to call out the state guard. "I know you are running for re-election and that you do not want trouble with labor," Peters urged him. "All right, let me take the responsibility, call out the troops at my request." Coolidge informed him of the mayor's powers within the Boston limits, then with equal irony offered to call out the state guard units in Boston if Peters did not care to exercise his own authority. Peters did not reply. Curtis at once insisted that he did not need the state guard or even the volunteers. "I am ready for anything," he told the governor. The canny Coolidge knew well that to call out the militia prematurely could be political suicide. "I am going to take the assurance of the police commissioner," he abruptly told the mayor. For Peters there was no more to say. Even his falsetto voice failed. "They frosted me out," he complained afterward to anyone who would listen to him. As soon as the other two had left, the governor dictated a letter, ostensibly for the mayor but actually for the record. Whatever the day might bring, whoever else might be exposed, he at least intended to be covered.

Replying to the suggestion laid before me by yourself and certain members of your committee, it seems to me that there has arisen a confusion which would be cleared up if each person undertakes to perform the duties imposed upon him by law.

It seems plain that the duty of issuing orders and enforcing their observance lies with the Commissioner of Police and with that no one has any authority to interfere. We must all support the commissioner in the execution of the laws....

There is no authority in the office of Governor for interference in making of orders by the Police Commissioner or in the action of the Mayor and the City Council. The foregoing suggestion is therefore made, as you will understand, in response to a request for suggestions on my part. I am unable to discover any action that I can take.

The twilight was raw, autumnal, with an overhanging mist that soon turned to rain. As the governor was dictating his letter, the first reports began to reach Colonel Dalton's office of police leaving their posts. At eleven minutes past five a bulletin came from Station 16 in the Back Bay that all but seven patrolmen had quit. Then the dispatcher at Hanover Street in the Italian district reported that Station 1 was "practically empty except for officers and that a crowd of over a thousand had gathered in front of the building." Curtis had expected that at least two thirds of his 1544 men would stay on duty, whatever their commitment to the union. He soon learned that scarcely a quarter would remain and these mostly the long-term men fearful of jeopardizing their pensions. In the end only twenty-four policemen patrolled the heart of the city instead of the usual seven hundred.

It was a tense emotional moment, for the men walked out of their station houses torn between loyalty to the department and solidarity with their fellows. Many would admit privately that they disapproved of the strike. There were few signs of disapproval from the scattered crowds outside. The sound of the Hanover Street gong summoning the patrolmen brought a long cheer from those waiting in the street. Before the roll call began Patrolman George Ferreira, one of the original nineteen suspended by Curtis, stepped forward in civilian clothes to announce to Captain Matthew Dailey: "Sir, the Boston police are on strike."

"Here, wait a minute, Ferreira," Captain Dailey told him. "You're already suspended. Get out!"

Ferreira obeyed automatically. At Fields Corner, as the men

were preparing to leave Station 11, Captain Charles Reardon spoke to them like a disappointed uncle, telling them that the action they were taking would blacken the record of the Boston Police Department. Now that they were leaving he hoped at least they would not forget that they were still police officers and that people looked up to them, and he urged them not to do anything that would hurt the dignity of the department. When he had finished, the men cheered him, both those who were quitting and those who remained behind. His words must have sunk in, for at Fields Corner only sixty of the ninety-two patrolmen struck. Patrolman John Peters, who had brought the strike notification to the station house, happened to be one of the union officers Curtis had suspended. He too spoke to the men, asking them to behave like policemen and cautioning them not to let ill feeling develop between those who struck and those who stayed. Before the strikers left the station they crowded around Captain Reardon's desk to shake his hand. Some were so moved that they could not look him in the face. Many walked away with the tears running down their cheeks, and several of the older men muttered that what they were doing was contrary to their own feelings. Frederick Claus was particularly reluctant to go out, for he was slated to be made a sergeant in December. With seven children at home, the youngest two weeks old, he hesitated, yet he did not feel he could stay on when his fellows were on strike, and he consoled himself with the thought that they would all be back at work in a few days.

Meanwhile a group of teen-age boys and their younger brothers had gathered in front of the building. A Greek fruit pedlar happened to pass by with a pushcart of oranges, and in a few seconds his cart was stripped bare. Whenever a streetcar rounded the corner, several urchins dashed off to pull the trolley from the wire. Then the whole crew began pelting the station front with oranges, mud, stones, and hunks of wood. One small boy tied a string from the station doorknob to the iron rail beside the steps. When the first policemen came out, the string broke, but the gesture seemed to please the crowd, which at once began to hoot and jeer and only grudgingly made way for the patrolmen as they inched their way down the steps with their bundles of possessions.

"Do your worst," one of the badgeless bluecoats muttered as he edged away. "No one will stop you now."

During the last hour before the walkout most of the patrolmen were occupied in turning in the public property charged to them—hat number-plates, badges, keys, revolvers, billies, and manuals—while the captains, lieutenants, and sergeants checked off each item. The strikers left carrying rubber boots, raincoats and capes, helmets and winter uniforms stuffed into boxes and bags. A few walked to waiting autos, most to the nearest el station or streetcar line, where the conductors in a gesture of solidarity allowed them to ride free.

Long before the evening roll call, throngs of the curious, the idle, the mischievous, and the sympathetic had begun to cluster before the various stations in spite of the rain. Some three hundred spectators stood in front of Charlestown's City Square station, where only one man in seventy-seven answered as Captain Michael Goff called the roll. When the patrolmen straggled out of the building, those outside applauded them. There was a very different mood at Roxbury Crossing, where a truculent crowd, egged on by Lettish agitators, pushed up to the very doors of Station 10. As one of the first striking patrolmen came down the steps carrying his belongings, an urchin picked up a handful of mud from the gutter and hurled it in his face. The man wiped off the mud without a word and walked away sadly. Now the bolder rowdies began to scoop up mud, pelting everyone who left the building, whether a striker or not. When Sergeant Patrick Byrne attempted to drive off the mud-slingers, he found himself plastered from head to foot. Some of the more daring boys attempted to tear down the station house awnings, and the door and windows were soon caked with filth. Though the remaining sergeants and patrolmen were hard put to it, they finally succeeded in breaking up the crowd. At Dudley Street an equally belligerent crowd blocked access to Station 9. Streetcars headed for the terminal were stopped, and one conductor was beaten up when he started after a boy who had dislodged the trolley. Several sergeants attempting to scatter the swirling mass were bombarded with rocks, mud, and bottles. Inside, as Captain Perley Skillings called the roll, silence greeted every name but one. Then in a burst of emotion one striker called out: "You're the best captain that the Boston Police Department ever had." The others shouted out their hoarse approval.

As might have been predicted, the most unruly scenes took place in front of the two stations in South Boston. Familiar throughout Massachusetts for its bawdy unprintable song "Southie Is My Home Town," that Celtic proletarian matrix had been recognized for two generations as the most consistently tough district of the city. Here was located the Gustin Gang—its name abbreviated from St. Augustine's, the towering brick Gothic-revival Church on Dorchester Street—the most feared gang in all Boston. Here was the spawning ground of politicians and prize-fighters, policemen and plug-uglies.

Over a thousand Southies had assembled in the rain near Station 12 to wait for the hour of decision. Some were relatives of policemen, primed for any patrolmen who dared not to strike. Others had felt the hard hand of the police and were waiting now to settle old scores. Mud, stones, bottles, eggs, and ripe tomatoes filled the air as the first strikers walked out the door onto East Fourth Street. One patrolman had his helmet knocked off. The station house was soon splattered with mud and garbage, and many of the windows were smashed. The Gusties began shouting for Patrolman Florence O'Reagan, an amateur boxer who had built up a reputation for knocking out malefactors with his bare fists. Fortunately for him, he was still away on vacation. A squad of Metropolitan Park police dispatched to aid the loyal patrolmen could not control the surging crowd. Four sergeants and the ten patrolmen who had remained on duty were forced to retreat into the station under a barrage of stones after a vain attempt at clearing the steps. An even larger and equally unruly crowd gathered in front of Station 6 on D Street. Some of the departing patrolmen were in civilian clothes, some in their badgeless uniforms. A few even wore their numberless helmets. As one of the policemen headed down the steps, his arms encumbered by his possessions, a young man in a tweed cap pushed forward to face him. "I waited eleven years to get you," he shouted. "You're not a cop now." And he punched him in the jaw. The policeman staggered, dropping his bundles. No one moved to help him. The spectators jeered.

Other malcontents elsewhere found the strike a heaven-sent

chance to get even with authority. One striker leaving Station 2 carrying a pair of rubber boots and an extra uniform was confronted by a heavy-built truck driver who shoved his way through the crowd, bawling, "Give me a traffic ticket the other day, would you?" then struck the bluecoat in the face. The policeman winced but kept on going.

Yet for the most part those who had clustered before the stations showed themselves well disposed to the striking police. The crowd in front of Station 14, Brighton, waited with noisy approval. Captain Forest Hall had ordered his men there to answer Yes or No as to whether they were going on duty. There were only three Yeses. After the roll call Patrolman Edwin Lavequist stepped from the ranks to announce that the strike was on. Then he conveyed his good wishes to the officers and proposed three cheers for Captain Hall. After the strikers had left, Hall turned to the three remaining patrolmen. "Well," he said shaking his head, "this is something I never would have believed could happen in the police department."

At Station 2, near City Hall Avenue and close to police headquarters, an odd consortium of sympathizers and mischief-makers wedged into that alley between School Street and Court Square. A number of toughs idled in front of the steps, waiting for the Harvard volunteers who were rumored to be on their way. As soon as the first strikers emerged, truckers sounded their horns and teamsters shouted approval; young swaggerers began shooting craps beneath the station windows, while others crowded up the steps jeering and shouting, and still others climbed lampposts or clambered onto the window sills of nearby buildings. Captain Jeremiah Sullivan twice appeared in the doorway to beg the crowd to be orderly. Union President McInnes, out of uniform, circulated through the throng, trying to restrain the mischief-makers while speaking an encouraging word to each emergent patrolman. Standing near McInnes, Mae Matthew, secretary of the telephone union, declared loudly, that "the girls will back up the police and will go out, if necessary, to help them win." Vahey, passing confidently by, was warmly applauded. Eighty-six of the 128 police in Station 2 struck. At Joy Street station on the far side of Beacon Hill the percentage was even higher, only sixteen being left behind out of a hundred. As the men headed down the hill, the unionized firemen in the firehouse on the other side of Cambridge Street let loose with sirens and whistles. The traffic officers, on quitting their downtown posts, marched in platoon formation to the LaGrange Street station, calling out to each patrolman they passed to join them. They were trailed by bumptious hangers-on who cheered each additional recruit. Ninety-five of the 120 LaGrange Street men quit. Most of them had left the station when Patrolman James Long arrived several hours after the roll call, having only just received orders to return to duty on getting back from his vacation late that afternoon. Only a dozen patrolmen remained, all older men with service stripes running halfway up their arms. One of them, Joseph Ray, a giant of a man whose beat was in the South station, sidled up to Long. "I don't know what to do," he said in great distress. "You just stay exactly where you are," Long told him. "You're too close to your pension. Let us younger men go."

Long stepped to the desk and saluted. Captain James Canney looked at him sharply and asked him what he was going to do. "I'll do what I think you would do if you were my age," Long told him. "What's that?" Canney asked. For answer Long handed over his keys, badge, and revolver. "I don't know but what you're right," the captain said slowly. Only the City Hall police detail stood solidly against the strike. The twelve patrolmen there, all with years of service, had charge of guarding the mayor and the collector's and the treasurer's office, escorting paymasters, and patrolling City Hall outside office hours. They looked on themselves and were looked on by others as an elite contingent. Nor had they forgotten the proximity of their pensions.

At the suburban stations there were neither crowds nor confusion. In Mattapan only a few children waited outside Station 19. Many of the men there had tears in their eyes as they shook hands and said goodbye to Captain James Watkins, among them three "five-stripers." (Policemen received a stripe for each five years of service.) One patrolman in going out handed his helmet to a small boy. The steps of Hyde Park's Station 18 and the West Roxbury station were deserted at roll call, although only a handful of nonstrikers remained in both stations. At Station 13 in primly suburban Jamaica Plain small boys shouted to one another, "Come on out and steal apples—no more cops!" as the policemen walked out. A little girl paraded up and down in front of the station house wearing a policeman's helmet. In the equally quiescent Back Bay the patrolmen whiled away the minutes before five-forty-five singing "Hail, Hail, the Gang's All Here," and "Till We Meet Again." When the roll call bell rang, they burst out into the chorus of "Farewell, Farewell, My Own True Love." Meanwhile strikers made efforts to picket each station. McInnes had warned them not to interfere with any loyal patrolmen or volunteers.

Most of the striking policemen after returning home with their belongings and changing into ordinary street clothes, made their way to strike headquarters at Fay Hall. Councilor Moriarty and Frank McCarthy were already there. McInnes appeared later after a tour of the nineteen stations. Earlier McCarthy had telephoned O'Donnell at Greenfield and extracted a promise from the Central Labor Union president to call a special meeting on Wednesday or Thursday to give the member unions time to back the police. O'Donnell reassured McCarthy that the unions were determined to make the policemen's fight their own. Peter McHugh of the Lagrange Street station was the first striker to arrive at the Hall, showing up at six-fourteen. By eight o'clock the men were pouring in by streetcar and elevated train and private auto.

Governor Coolidge had placed 100 of the 183 state-controlled Metropolitan Park police in the Boston area at Curtis's disposal for the duration of the emergency. Fifty-eight of these now refused to do Boston police street duty and were at once suspended. Defiantly they marched in a body to Fay Hall in their grey uniforms but minus their hat shields and badges. A number of policemen from other Massachusetts towns and cities were already there to show their solidarity. The striking policemen, their spirits undampened by the rain, had no worries or premonitions about what the night might bring.

Shortly after finishing his letter to the mayor, Coolidge left the State House by the rear entrance, where his car and driver were waiting for him in the arched and covered roadway. He then drove to the Hotel Touraine in the Back Bay for a leisurely if uncommunicative dinner with Attorney General Henry Wyman, Colonel Dalton, and Frank Stearns. Although an excited messenger arrived from City Hall to inform the governor as he was eating that hundreds of policemen were "walking off," the governor never so much as mentioned the strike during the meal. At that point Commissioner Curtis feared there would be conflict if he sent even token volunteers to the station houses while the regulars were still there. In any case he felt the volunteers were too hard to reach, too scattered to be mustered sooner than the following morning. This was why, he explained later, he did not have them ready for duty when the police walked out.

For the rest of the afternoon and early evening Peters continued bustling about in a frenzy of ineffectuality. As he now knew, the General Acts of Massachusetts, Chapter 327, Part 1, Section 26, gave him the right to call out the local state guard "in case of a tumult, riot or mob," or when such "tumult, riot or mob is threatened." But how could one know whether a tumult, riot, or mob is threatened until after the event? So sternly convincing had been Curtis's assurance of having everything under control that the mayor could not bring himself to affront his Democractic supporters, his labor half-friends, and the loudmouths in the city council by rashly calling out the guard. Curtis had informed him that under Section 20, Chapter 26, of the Revised Laws of Massachusetts, he could in an emergency borrow policemen from other towns. Toward sundown he telephoned the police chiefs of adjacent Newton, Brookline, and Milton. All very politely—and quite legally—turned him down.

After a messenger had brought him a copy of the governor's letter, Peters penned a plaintive reply: "I had hoped that you would consider that the recommendations of the Citizens' Committee pointed a way toward a practical solution of the problem."

"I am sorry that you have not viewed them in that light and that no countersuggestion has been presented."

When reporters, apprised of Chapter 327, Section 26, asked him what he would do in case of a riot, he had replied that he would make his plans when the emergency occurred. "Police Commissioner Curtis," he told them, "assured me that he was in a position to give the people adequate protection. Governor Coolidge said he was fully prepared to render support to the Police Commissioner in any measures which might be instituted by the Police Commissioner. I am relying on them." Curtis and Coolidge, as he could now see, were hand in glove. As the hours wore on, the mayor grew more and more convinced that they were using the whole police crisis to destroy him politically. Even as the mobs gathered, Peters could think of nothing more to do than to prepare another press release. As if he were talking to give himself courage, he repeated that he had been trying to improve the hours and working conditions of the police, that he had given them a $200 raise in the spring. "To impute in any manner that I have not given the men what they wish is a direct misrepresentation of the facts," he declared plaintively, adding in an even more plaintive conclusion, "I am by law deprived of any control of the working hours of the patrolmen and I repeat that the only request for an increase in salary submitted by the men has been granted." Then for the rest of the evening he went out of sight as completely as had the governor over the weekend.

That same evening the motor corps and the First (and only) Cavalry Troop of the state guard were holding their regular weekly drill in the fortress-like brick building that was the Commonwealth Armory. Peters, informed earlier of the drill, still could not make up his mind about calling out the guard. Aimlessly he had his chauffeur drive him through the night and aimlessly he meditated. Why should he take the blame for the unreasonableness of the governor and the commissioner? The lurking question remained unanswered. Shortly before the end of the drill period the mayor from some remote way point finally telephoned the armory to request that the guardsmen be held in readiness after the drill.

Coolidge had gone from the Touraine to his suite in the Adams House. There he sat for several hours with secretary Long, Adjutant General Stevens, and Colonel Dalton. A wire had been installed so that the governor could be reached privately at any time. When he learned that Peters without authorization was attempting to hold the cavalry and the motor corps in readiness, he stood up in anger, ordered Long to have his car brought round, and set out with Stevens for the armory.

With the perplexed and silent adjutant general just behind him, Coolidge strode through the armory arch. Fifty or so troopers standing about on the lower floor with their equipment in readiness stared in surprise as the irate governor quacked at their executive officer, Major Dana Gallup, "Who told you people to stay here? Go on home." With that he stalked petulantly upstairs to the orderly room, followed by Gallup and Curtis.

Then occurred one of the dramatic minor episodes of the strike. Peters, increasingly panic-stricken at the surge of events, had again set out in pursuit of Coolidge. Ten minutes after the latter arrived, the rumpled and excited mayor burst through the armory door demanding to see the governor at the very moment that Coolidge was coming downstairs. The two men met each other face to face on the stairway, Peters stammering high-pitched accusations until Coolidge cut him short with a waspish, "You have no business here!" At that, Peters made a rush for him, swinging his arms wildly and somehow landing his fist squarely in the governor's left eye. Coolidge did not attempt to strike back nor did he make any move to retreat, but merely leaned against the balustrade with his hand to his face. Troopers seized the gesticulating mayor.*

Those, at least, who saw the governor close to in the next few days were aware of a certain discoloration around his eye. It did not seem to discommode him greatly. From the armory he drove back directly to the Adams House. Leaving word with Long that he was not to be disturbed, he slept soundly through a night of rioting.

* I am grateful to the late Lawrence Wogan for this unrecorded incident that he witnessed from a few feet away as a young trooper.

THE RIOTS

If shortly after the strike began Governor Coolidge had bothered to look out across Boston Common from the oval windows of his office before leaving for dinner at the Touraine, he would have seen mushroom rings of crapshooters springing up on the slope of the Frog Pond under the shadow of the State House. Boston's policeman sedately patrolling his beat was gone, and in that astonishing moment of relinquished authority, the first thing that came to mind for the city's mindless twilight figures—the streetcorner hangers-on, the floaters, the pool-room johnnies—was to start an open-air dice game. As the dusk fell, several score games were in progress on Boston Common, with stakes ranging from a quarter to fifty dollars. After the traffic police had left their posts on Tremont and Park Streets, the biggest game broke out on Brimstone Corner—so-called for the hell-fire preaching emanating from the Park Street Congregational Church opposite. There, by the Neptune fountain, as new players kept joining in, stakes rose to several hundred dollars. A spontaneous announcer barked out a roll-by-roll account of the game to the growing crowd, and the winners were cheered and in some cases lifted up on their friends' shoulders. One winner walking triumphantly up the mall with three hundred dollars in his pocket had not gone fifty yards before he was set on by three sharp-eyed, quick-fisted bystanders who knocked him down and grabbed his winnings.

For all the boisterous crapshooting there was at first little real violence. A few more players were robbed. The occasional pedestrian belatedly wearing a straw hat had it knocked into the gutter. Small boys shinnied up poles to the red fire boxes and rang in false alarms. Yet commuters hurrying into the Park or Boylston Street subway entrances were unmolested. The evening migration to the suburbs continued as usual. After the rush hour, traffic moved freely in spite of the absence of directing patrolmen, although some drivers began to show a certain sportive urge to violate minor regulations on signaling and turning. A few young rowdies made a game of snatching off spare tires from the rear of parked cars and using them as hoops. Throngs wandered aimlessly in the dampness of those first hours through the twisted streets of the central city, ambling past Faneuil Hall and the Old State House, drawn without any real positive intent toward Scollay Square. That half-world honky-tonk district of burlesque theaters, bars,* clip joints, and all-night cafés, interlaced with tattoo parlors and photo studios and flophouses, had long been a magnet for the sailors of all nations as well as for local drifters and derelicts and petty gangsters. If trouble was to start, Scollay Square with its numerous side alleys would be the apt place for it.

At eight o'clock on Howard Street just off the square, four non-striking policemen found themselves forced up against a wall by a crew of toughs, who melted away, however, when the police drew their clubs. By ten o'clock the crowds were still growing, in Scollay Square, Adams Square, Haymarket Square, the crossroads of city traffic. Mist-shrouded figures shuffled along, men and a few women, curious, unhurried, talking in low tones. Then a more cohesive group headed down from Scollay Square toward Washington

---

* The wartime prohibition act had not reached down to the level of Boston's bars. These would survive for a few more months until the National Prohibition Amendment went into effect on January 16, 1920.

Street, passing Young's Hotel, edging through City Hall Avenue past Ben Franklin's pigeon-splattered statue and the grey incongruous Second-Empire City Hall to the lower end of School Street. A gigantic whisper seemed to emanate from the amorphous crowd. One spectator thought it was like the tense few minutes before a funeral. Restlessly the vague throngs trudged through the rain and darkness, waiting only for that unifying act of violence that would turn them into a mob.

Then it happened: a paving brick thrown through a cigar store front; the crash and tinkle of glass; quick eager hands reaching through jagged window frames. Those nearest the displays began to snatch at pipes and cigars and cigarettes, while others more determined battered down the locked door. Within minutes the store was stripped clean. A looter cried out as he sliced his hand open on a glass sliver. A woman screamed. Their cries were like a signal. The mob was off.

It seemed as if the brick had shattered the surface of a pond, sending the ripples circling outward. All along Court Street and beyond, the store windows disintegrated: Sal Myer's Gents' Furnishings, the Princeton Clothing Company, Lewis Shoes, Peter Rabbit Hats. Men exchanged straw for winter hats, discarded old coats for new ones, strutted along the sidewalk with armfuls of shirts, neckties, socks, handkerchiefs, shoes. Some even sat down on the curb to try on their acquired footwear, swapping or throwing away those that did not fit. Soon the streets were littered with discarded shoes, hats, and clothing. Here and there fist fights broke out over the booty. But by and large the mob remained good-natured, with three or four onlookers to every active looter. It would not remain that way. The mass soon began to shape itself into more purposeful groups, with self-appointed leaders taking over as if they had sprung out of the ground. These smaller mobs expanded, contracted—retreating when faced with too much resistance—re-formed, and moved on to loot and plunder. The wet dark huddle of streets re-echoed to the sound of running feet, jeering laughter, hysterical cries, and occasional pistol shots. Bands of hard-paced bruisers stomped along the sidewalks between Scollay Square, Washington Street, and Faneuil Hall, breaking the straw hats of those men rash enough still to be wearing them, elbowing the more harmless pedestrians into the gutter, stopping here and there to despoil or ransack a fruit stand or smash any remaining windows. Each band seemed to have its uniformed quota of soldiers and sailors.

A little after ten a phalanx of plug-uglies suddenly charged out of Scollay Square down Hanover Street, gathering adherents as they swept along, bursting through the doors of Waldron's Casino, where a burlesque act was going on, ripping posters and hangings from the walls, and after jeering and hooting at the frightened actors, swaggering away. Coleman & Keating's liquor store on the next corner limbered up their spirits. After sacking that establishment they continued along the street, hurling bottles through windows as they went. About to wreck the premises of wholesale provision dealer Arthur E. Dorr, they were driven off by the solitary watchman, James Burns, a former policeman, who leveled his revolver and sent them scurrying across the street. By the time they reached Faneuil Hall two hundred had swelled to almost a thousand, some with weapons, almost all carrying stones. There they were confronted by three sergeants and three plain-clothes men. Pushing forward, they began to chant "Kill the cops! Kill the scabs!" As the mob edged closer, the six police drew their revolvers and fired over the heads of the vanguard, then charged in with clubs swinging. The swirling mass gave way, started to break up. Then a paving brick hurtled through the window of the Howard Jewelry Company. The noise of the shattering glass seemed to inflame the rioters. There were shouts of "To hell with the police." Stones and bottles flew through the air, plate-glass windows collapsed like ninepins. Again the sergeants and the plain-clothes men brandished their sticks and started swinging, but this time the mob refused to yield. Finally the police leveled their revolvers at the turbulent figures, and a hoarse-voiced sergeant warned that he would shoot to kill. At the sight of the glinting revolver barrels pointing directly at them, the rioters broke, the foremost almost sprawling on the ground in their panicky efforts to get away.

Somewhere in the dank higgledy-piggledy of North End streets, the remnants of the mob regrouped and started out again for the core city, avoiding Faneuil Hall this time to march directly on Washington Street. Two sailors and several older men took the lead as they advanced toward the shopping center. Joyce Brothers' clothing store, the Walk-Over Shoe Company, Jackson the Furrier and Hatter, Posner's Gents' Furnishings, all were wrecked and pillaged in rapid succession. Five patrolmen and a sergeant from the Court Square station stood by helplessly. Heaving shoulders burst down doors for the avariciously eager to swarm into the interiors. Shoe and clothing stores, cigar stores and small jewelry concerns were the chief targets, but more calculating individuals headed for the hardware and sporting-goods stores with their stocks of weapons and ammunition. Crowds of hangers-on followed in the wake of the mob to enjoy the pillaging. The looters—many of them bloodied from glass cuts—steered clear of the large brightly lighted department stores like Filene's and White's and Chandler's, where guards with rifles waited at the ready behind drawn curtains. When the mob reached Jordan Marsh's on Summer Street, there was a pause followed by a burst of gunfire from the guards in the interior, at which the rioters retreated in a panic. As a background accompaniment to the shouts, the crash of glass, and the sporadic shots came the steady insistent clang of fire apparatus responding to false alarms. During the height of the looting two taxis cruised down Washington Street, stopping at advantageous points to load up with merchandise and jewelry. Men waving pistols stood on the running boards. With the appearance of several sergeants from LaGrange Street, the taxis drove off. Directly in front of the pillaged Washington Street entrance to Macullar, Parker's, Boston's foremost clothier and tailor, two sailors beat up a pedestrian and took his watch and money in view of some hundred spectators who stood round urging the sailors to "go to it!" "Well, I'm damned!" a Hearst cub reporter muttered to himself. "From now on I'm a conservative!" Judge Frank Deland, passing by, thought the French Revolution had come to his city.

In other parts of Boston, mob action and violence were more sporadic. A menacing group on Court Street melted away when faced on one side by a dozen Metropolitan Park police with drawn clubs and on the other side by Superintendent Crowley with a squad of plain-clothes men. Crowley kept speeding from one part of the city to the other, wherever trouble seemed to be brewing, brandishing a revolver and occasionally making an arrest in person.

The skeletal police force managed to make 129 token arrests in all. Five rioters were shot. One of them, twenty-one-year-old John W. Scalizy of Brookline, was shot in the head while running with an armful of clothing from a Huntington Avenue haberdasher's. He was taken to the City Hospital and his name placed on the danger list. Police opened fire directly on the plunderers in the Studio Jewelry Company at Temple Place. No one was injured, but one man was arrested. Across the street on the Common, a mob defied a police sergeant's order to disperse, in spite of warning shots. The mob then moved down Tremont Street breaking windows and looting, followed by police in a patrol wagon. Policemen again opened fire but the looting continued—Chamberlain's Hat Store, the United Cigar Store, scattered clothing and jewelry shops. Looters entering the rear of Kabatznick's Art Shop on Boylston Street, in a rage at not finding money or valuables, tore oil paintings from their frames, threw pictures and prints on the floor, and then trampled on them. Several dozen roisterers burst into Plakias's Restaurant near Dover Street, grabbing up the pies and sandwiches and rolls on display and bombarding the countermen with them. When the manager drew a revolver, they rushed out, jeering and hurling coffee mugs through the glass counters. At Mechanic's Building, where a boxing match was going on, an uptown crowd broke through the side and back doors and several hundred managed to crash the gate.

In the LaGrange Street station Jim Long, after gathering his possessions together, went across the street to a cafeteria for a cup of coffee. He was still there when the rioting started and the window-smashing mob swept past. Cautiously he followed, walking over his old beat—Tremont Street to Avery Street, then through Avery to Washington Street, and from Washington to Stuart. In spite of the rain, clusters of men were rolling dice on every corner. There didn't seem to be a single window intact. Discarded shoes were scattered everywhere. As he walked he could hear the glass crunch under his feet.

All evening the Haymarket Square Relief Station received a steady stream of the cut and battered. One of the Washington Street ringleaders, a sailor from the U.S.S. *Hingham*, was treated for a two-inch scalp wound. Several minutes after he was released, three sergeants arrived looking for him. In or with the mob there was relative safety for the individual. But the unwary who were walking alone often found themselves waylaid and robbed. Women venturing out by themselves did so at their peril. One woman going along Atlantic Avenue near the front of State Street was seized by a group of young men, knocked to the ground, and gang-shagged. Farther down in the North End other women were forced into doorways and violated within sight of hundreds. In Chair Alley off Fulton Street a young woman was beaten and raped but managed afterward to stagger into a bar bruised and bleeding and with several teeth missing. Ironically, she happened to be a prostitute.

Throughout the city tough, restive adolescents itching but not quite daring to challenge authority at last had their chance. In Roxbury a gang stole a buggy, ran it onto the sidewalk in front of the Roxbury Crossing station, and set it afire. In Dorchester at Dorchester Avenue and Eliot Street, another gang piled boxes, barrels, and old mattresses on the car tracks, then smashed all the windows of the streetcars as they came to a halt. The most concentrated violence occurred in South Boston, where roisterers stormed and pillaged and destroyed, not so much for loot as just for the delight in violence.

Disorder was not scattered but general. On Broadway, South Boston's main artery, all the grocery stores were ransacked and the contents flung in the street, making the road look more like a dump than a spacious boulevard, its surface inches deep in sugar, flour, eggs, squashed oranges and bananas, cans of fruit and vegetables, and even smoked hams. From the waterfront to Andrew Square there was scarcely a whole window. The few remaining police stood by powerless, even when pillagers and window-smashers came within a few feet of them. As soon as a streetcar appeared, urchins yanked the trolley cord and as the car lurched to a stop broke every window and then stoned the passengers struggling to get out. Shots echoed. A motorman was shot through the head. Young boys and girls hauled crates of eggs from the Mohican Market and tossed them at random. At the lower end of West Broadway a gang headed up the wide street, gathering strength as it went and smashing and looting every shop in passing. Superintendent Crowley, pausing in one of his dashes about the city, stood on the corner of Broadway and C Street. Opposite him, beyond the pavement ankle deep in debris, he could see a crap game going on and could hear the howls of the mob as eggs and stones flew through the air and glass crashed on all sides. "If anyone had told me," he remarked to a police inspector standing next to him, "I never would have believed it."

At the height of the rioting some ten thousand persons were milling up and down Broadway. Throughout South Boston, as the aimless destruction spread, the store fronts disintegrated: Connor's and O'Keefe's, the Irish-American grocery chains; Wallenheim's bakery; Louis Alphas's fruit store and spa; the Budnick Creamery; bicycle shops, pawn shops, tailors, cleaners, haberdashers. In the Bay View section the saloons and bars fell an easy prey, raiders bursting in, grabbing whatever bottles they could lay hands on, and tossing the glasses out into the street.

Near St. Augustine's a squad of loyal Metropolitan Park police was cornered by one of the larger street gangs and stoned. After one patrolman dropped to the ground, his forehead split open, the others drew their clubs and revolvers. Still the crowd did not budge but began to shout, "Kill them! Kill the dirty sons of bitches!" Picking up their wounded comrade, the police began a slow retreat. Those inhabitants who were not on the streets seemed to be hanging out the windows of the massed three-deckers cheering the others on. At Andrew Square the several dozen small proprietors found their premises stripped bare even to the gas and electric fixtures. The unwary driver of a fruit wagon was stoned, his fruit dumped into the street, and his horse lashed until it bolted. Parked cars were overturned. More false alarms added to the din, unionized firemen being pelted as they attempted to get their apparatus through the clogged streets. Even the mail trucks were brought to a stop and spattered with mud and egg yolk. During the height of the violence, patrons of the Waldorf Lunch on Broadway knocked out the manager when he tried to get them to pay their checks, then dashed into the street, stripping the counters of cakes and pies as they left.

Crowley, egg-smeared, waving his revolver, led a band of reserves and some fifty park police in repeated sallies to clear Broadway. By midnight he and his outmanned force had managed to separate the spectators from the rioters and drive the latter into the side streets and alleys, where they hung on, sullen and threatening, yet not quite prepared to meet the challenge of live bullets. The revels now seemed over for the night, and gradually the rioters broke away, heading for their homes in the ubiquitous three-deckers that were themselves almost the symbol of South Boston.

By one-thirty in the morning the core city was beginning to quiet down, the mob losing its coherence in a crowd that thinned out as more and more individuals wandered away through the littered streets, either out of weariness or conviction that the show was over. Crowley had ordered the street lights to be kept on all night, and the frayed city in the early morning hours looked disjointedly empty under the still-falling rain.

Even as the mob ransacked the streets, Mayor Peters was preparing another press release in which he defensively insisted that he was not to blame, that he had given the police a $200 increase in the spring as soon as additional revenues had been available. "To impute in any manner that I have not given the men what they wish is a direct misrepresentation of the facts," he concluded in a mixture of self-righteousness and self-pity. "I am by law deprived of any control of the working hours of the patrolmen and I repeat that the only request for an increase of salary by the men had been granted." Then he disappeared. No one knew where he was. No one could find out. Actually, he had his chauffeur drive him aimlessly through the tranquil outer suburbs. Not until after one in the morning did he return to his Jamaica Plain home. At half past two his secretary arrived breathlessly on the doorstep to tell him of the downtown tumult and to beg him to call out the local state guard. Peters telephoned General Cole and asked him to arrange a conference of state guard officers first thing in the morning. Then, after listening to several disheartening telephone reports about the rioting, he went to bed.

Wednesday morning was lowering, with the threat of showers, the Custom House tower blocked out by mist. Shortly after eight o'clock the mayor's high-pitched voice could be heard in the corridors of City Hall. Striding into his office, gesticulating nervously, his tufted eyebrows twitching like porcupine quills, he was now resolved to show himself to his shaken and apprehensive advisers as a model of decisive action. Curtis, his confidence of the day before dissolved overnight, had already written him that he was of the opinion that "tumult, riot or mob is threatened and that the usual police provisions are inadequate to preserve order and to afford protection to persons and property." Masking his humiliation behind icily formal language, the commissioner "respectfully" suggested that "if the facts which I call to your Honor's attention appear to your Honor to exist you will exercise the powers and the authority specified by the statute." For Peters it was a moment of triumph. The man who had denigrated him was now begging for help. At once he consulted with Colonel Thomas Sullivan of the state guard—who also happened to be his public-works commissioner—and his corporation counsel and Harvard classmate, Alexander Whiteside, and the now supernumerary members of the Citizens' Committee. Then he issued an order calling out the state guard within the Boston area: the Tenth Regiment under command of Colonel Sullivan, the First Cavalry Troop, the First Motor Corps, and the Ambulance Corps.

The Massachusetts State Guard had been formed as a militia organization in 1917 after the National Guard Yankee Division was called into federal service. Made up of underage enthusiasts, the physically unfit, and the overaged who saw in domestic military service a recompense of sorts for the war they had missed, the state guard was officered for the most part by old-line Yankees and commanded by Brigadier General Samuel Parker, lawyer, Harvard graduate, and amateur soldier. Parker had served eighteen years in the state militia, was inspector on the staff of three governors, and had retired as inspector general until called back to the state guard. A gentleman farmer, whose family fortune had been woven in Massachusetts textile mills, his long-jawed face could have matched Uncle Sam's if the latter's chin whiskers had been shaved off. Once a week for two and a half years, his five thousand Massachusetts guardsmen, from the pustular to the pot-bellied, had been donning their makeshift uniforms—some khaki, some olive-drab—to march and countermarch in the empty armories, to learn at least the elements of close-order drill, rifle, and bayonet practice for the unlikely emergency that had now arrived. Many of the officers had served in the Spanish-American War. Peters ordered the Boston guard to mobilize by five that afternoon. At the same time he sent a letter to the governor asking for three thousand additional guardsmen.

The mayor topped off his morning of belated zeal by taking over the police department, something he could do—as corporation counsel Whiteside pointed out to him—under the provision of Section 6, Chapter 323, of the Acts of 1885, which allowed the mayor to assume control of the police whenever "tumult, riot, and violent disturbances of public order have occurred within the limits of the City of Boston." Placing General Cole in command at Pemberton Square, he dispatched a unit to Curtis "to execute all orders promulgated by me for the suppression of tumult and the restoration of public order."

Curtis, a civil servant far more familiar with the acts than was the superficial mayor, marked his chagrin in his brief reply: "Sir—Your note of September 10 notifying me that you assume control for the time being of the City of Boston is received. I respectfully wait your action."

Beaming and satisfied that he had put both the governor and the commissioner in their place, Peters went out to lunch. To his enormous gratification, a small group of spectators applauded him as he left City Hall. All day Tuesday, volunteers had been coming in increasing numbers to the temporary office ex-Superintendent Pierce had set up next to the Chamber of Commerce reading room. Seated at a massive desk, flanked by two retired officers, he interviewed each applicant, meanwhile scanning long lists of names and mysterious printed sheets which his clerks from time to time took from his blotter and mailed off in double-sealed envelopes. Many of the trimly tailored volunteers looked as if they had just strolled over from the Somerset or Union club, men for the most part in their solid early middle age, brokers, bankers, lawyers, established businessmen. Conspicuous among them were old Harvard athletes whose names had made the headlines in other years: Huntington "Tack" Hardwick, 1914's legendary halfback; John Richardson, Jr., captain of the crew that had beaten Yale ten years before; Bartlett Hayes, no-hit pitcher of 1898; and scores of other football, baseball, crew, and track stars. Pierce proudly released to the press the names of such distinguished volunteers. He felt honored by the presence of General Francis Peabody, whom Curtis had defeated for mayor twenty-four years before and who since then, without ever having seen active service, had become a brigadier general in the National Guard, a title he nursed in his retirement. As a counterbalance, the navy was represented in the person of retired Admiral Francis Bowles. Former officers of the Yankee Division far outnumbered the enlisted men. No one could miss the *Social Register* tone of the recruits any more than one could miss the presence of Godfrey Lowell Cabot, cousin and classmate of Harvard's president, A. Lawrence Lowell, with a brace of pistols strapped on and wearing a naval cape.

Once again, if briefly, the old Bostonians were achieving physical control of their city. Yet though Back Bay and Beacon Hill seemed to predominate among the volunteers, all walks of life were represented, including a few odd walks. An Oklahoma rancher staying at the Parker House appeared before Pierce wearing a sombrero and high-heeled cowboy boots to announce with loud casualness that he was joining up because he wanted some excitement. Laurence Davis, a Red Cross worker just back from overseas, offered his services, although he had only one arm. The oddly named Patsy Soldier, a naturalized Italian recently discharged after twenty-seven months in the army and still wearing his army uniform, arrived and told Pierce in somewhat broken English: "I want to be a cop. I had one job for eighteen a week. I look for work all around, no luck." Helen Coran, a tall brunette wearing a fur boa, was the sole woman volunteer.

On Tuesday afternoon Louis Frothingham, in his twin role of Harvard man and volunteer policeman, sent a telegram to Harvard's president asking what the college was prepared to do in the event of a strike. President Lowell replied: "In accordance with the traditions of public service the University desires in time of crisis to help in any way it can to maintain order and support the laws of the commonwealth. I therefore urge all students who can do so to prepare themselves for such service as the governor of the commonwealth may call upon them to render."

The college's fall term would not open for another week, but some summer-school students were still there and others, including the members of the football squad, had arrived early. A hastily formed Harvard emergency committee of three acting deans and two seniors, after posting calls for volunteers on the various bulletin boards, opened an all-night recruiting office at University Hall. On Wednesday morning every student found an announcement from the emergency committee tacked under his door, TO ALL HARVARD MEN, containing Lowell's statement and an appeal for any man who could offer his personal services or who could furnish a motor car or motorcycle with or without sidecar to report at once to University 2.

On learning of this, one labor-minded alumnus telephoned University Hall to ask with asperity when Harvard had become a training ground for strikebreakers. Indignantly the committee replied: "We want it understood that the Harvard students are not going into this matter merely for the sake of defeating the policemen. It is not as strike-breakers that the undergraduates are offering their services. They are enrolling solely to protect life and property."

By midnight Tuesday at least fifty undergraduates had enrolled. The following morning as the news of the rioting spread, there was a rush to join. Harvard head coach Bob Fisher dismissed his 125-man football squad, telling them "to hell with football, if men are needed to protect Boston." Carloads of students left for Boston, buoyed up by Professor Hall's promise of "sport and diversion," among them pudgy Bill Hoffman from Tuxedo Park, New York, a cousin of the Roosevelts, who crammed his Stanley-steamer touring car with like-minded Harvard friends and set off across the river with boisterous enthusiasm. Over one hundred fifty eager undergraduates arrived at the Chamber of Commerce Building before noon, causing the Boston *Globe* later to remark that "some of the students in times past had considerable experience with the police but until now few of them had experience as policemen."

Undaunted by the weather, the first volunteer patrolmen reported at eight o'clock to their assigned stations, drawing badges, revolvers, and the old-fashioned night sticks. Station 2, so conveniently located between the State House and the financial district, became the most sought-after post, attracting the elite and the adventurous. Smiling, self-assured, dressed in trench-coats copied from the wartime British officers, they gathered in front of Captain Sullivan's desk. The captain instructed them as he handed out cartridges: "See? These are what they call riot pills!" General Peabody in a rakish tweed golf cap saluted smartly on receiving his ammunition, as did George von L. Meyer, the son of the late ex-secretary of the navy, and Francis Lee Higginson, the Boston banker of bankers. When Peabody left the station, Sullivan assigned a loyal patrolman to show him his beat. Smoking a large cigar, a billy protruding from his pocket, the general followed the patrolman across the street and received his first lesson in how to ring up from a box. So interested was Peabody in the mechanism that he insisted on trying it himself. Farther on, just beyond City Hall, he met Admiral Bowles, also sporting a badge and billy, and they stopped to shake hands. "Watch us tonight," said the Admiral. "I've got the greatest crowd of fellows you ever saw. Young, brawny college fellows—athletes!"

More cautious citizens flocked to police headquarters for pistol permits—several thousand were issued in the course of the day—while in the financial district the insurance companies did a land-office business in riot, fire, and theft insurance. One group of volunteers sounded a note that in the next few days would echo across the country. Placing an advertisement on the front page of each Boston paper, they urged others to join them. They themselves bore no hostility, they said, to the striking policemen, but had obeyed a call of duty, since "in the absence of its appointed and sworn defenders, means must be adopted for the protection of life and property.... We are convinced that the real issue now is whether organized, properly constituted democratic government representing all the people, shall be sustained and perpetuated, or whether any element, no matter what, shall assume control of the destinies not merely of our city, but inevitably, of the republic itself."

"A night of disgrace," a *Herald* editorial writer called it the previous evening, and went on to say: "Somebody blundered. Boston should not have been left defenseless last night ... it was a sickening scene and no hand was available to arrest the unlawfulness."

Wednesday brought no renewed violence, but there was a sense of menace in the air, of unknown forces gathering strength. Although those arrested the night before were promptly tried and sentenced in the municipal courts, they were only a token number, and it was obvious that the city was still not under control. Volunteers leaving Station 2 had to make their way through a hostile group of spectators who shouted "Scab!" and occasionally spat at them. Led out to their beat by an instructing sergeant, they were preceded and followed by jeering street urchins. The devastated streets, the smashed windows now being hastily boarded up, and the barbed wire being strung across the damaged entrances gave the city "a wide-open look," like that of some western mining town. Sightseers and idlers remained thickest in and around Scollay Square. Near the Old Howard with its leggy display of the Crackerjack Burlesquers, some thirty young men started a crap game in the middle of the street, waving their dollar bills with bravado as they rolled the dice. Rolling dice seemed to have become the preoccupation of Boston's anonymous citizenry. From the Common across the Public Gardens to Copley Square, and even on the steps of the Public Library and at the doors of Trinity Church, ribald games were in progress. A marathon crap game drew the most eager and determined gamblers to the corner of Avery and Washington Streets. Avery Street remained completely blocked off by the fluctuating ring of men in the center of the road, shaking the dice to the cries of "Fifty cents to open! Who'll shoot?" Spectators jammed both sidewalks until it became impossible to pass. Even a few women took part in the game. But there were noticeably fewer women on the Boston streets. Crowley begged the curiosity-seekers to stay home. The *Globe* gave a front-page warning that "there is no such thing now as 'an innocent bystander.'"

Nevertheless, the life of the city went on much as usual. The larger department stores opened, their armed guards keeping a finger on the trigger and a wary eye on the shoppers. Festoons of barbed wire partially blocked the bank entrances, but the banks remained open, as did the Boston Stock Exchange. In the upper window of Iver Johnson's (the lower windows had been smashed) an ex-soldier salesman, Alan Flynn, sat with a shotgun across his lap and noticed how the pedestrians scattered to the other side of the street as soon as they saw him. Most of the restaurants and cafeterias stayed open except for Walton's Lunch, whose employees were already on strike. To children's disappointment, none of the Boston schools closed. Other events took their scheduled course. Waldron's Casino's *Hip-Hip-Hooray* and the Old Howard's *Crackerjack Burlesquers*, and B. F. Keith's with its vaudeville turns prepared to open their doors as did the legitimate theaters. At the Colonial the brand new musical *Hitchy Koo, 1919*, starring Raymond Hitchcock, advertised itself as "a national necessity." Henry Jewett continued to appeal to his proper Anglophile audiences with the old London hit *Clothes and the Woman*. On the screen the Modern & Beacon was showing Billie Burke as *The Misleading Widow*. However, a mass meeting against the League of Nations scheduled that evening at Symphony Hall and sponsored by William Randolph Hearst, with Senator James Reed of Missouri the principal speaker, was canceled. The Roxbury Historical Society could see no reason for canceling its monthly meeting and heard Charles F. Read, clerk of the Bostonian Society, speak on "A Boy's Memories of the Civil War and the Assassination of Abraham Lincoln."

Within range of Boston, William Jennings Bryan, under the auspices of the Anti-Saloon League, continued his tour of the state, making his passionate defense of Prohibition, "Work Accomplished and the Task Before Us." In Greenfield the delegates at the AFL convention turned from the affairs of the Boston police union to the fiery Eamon de Valera, just over from Ireland, whose speech impelled them to vote for recognition of the Irish Republic. Beyond the boundaries of Massachusetts, Belgium's Cardinal Mercier arriving in New York warned Americans that the Germans were plotting a war of revenge. Even as the cardinal spoke, General Pershing, his four stars a-glitter, led a triumphant parade of the returning First Division down Fifth Avenue. But beyond all the other news, the Boston Police Strike dominated the country's headlines from the *New York Times* to the *Times* of Los Angeles.

While the volunteers, the "subs" as they were now labeled in the press, were patrolling the streets with varying degrees of confidence and efficiency, the striking policemen were holding another meeting at Fay Hall. Their mood was jubilant. The riots of the night before, they were convinced, had taught the public what it meant to be without police protection, a lesson that would hasten a settlement. While waiting for the meeting to be called to order, they bellowed out "Hail, Hail, the Gang's All Here" in cheerful if monotonous refrain. McInnes exuded confidence as he spoke to them. He said that no settlement proposals had yet been made and added defiantly that any such must come "through the regularly established channels of organized labor." Almost as an aside he expressed regret for the disorders of the previous night. He added that Vahey was holding a conference with the business agent of the Boston Street Carmen's Union and hoped for a sympathy strike. Both the firemen's union and the Metropolitan Park police had pledged their support.

At the close pickets were assigned for duty, twenty to each station, to work in four-hour shifts of five men. Following the meeting the striking policemen gathered together on the playground behind the fire department headquarters to pose for the Pathé newsreel cameras.

Those unlucky enough to have been taken into custody during Tuesday's melee—some fifty in all—were being brought before the municipal court in Pemberton Square and the South Boston district court, to be charged with breaking and entering, larceny, and so forth. At Pemberton Square there was a flurried attempt by onlookers to rescue the prisoners that was quickly broken up by Sheriff Keliher. In South Boston, Judge Edward Logan, who had commanded the Yankee Division's 101st Infantry until a few weeks before the Armistice, when he was relieved because of "inertia," showed no inertia in sentencing the rioters brought before him. Six months in the house of correction, Judge Logan felt, would serve as an example to show that South Boston authority was not to be trifled with. In the municipal court, Charles Hayes, convicted of assaulting Sergeant James Laffey of Station 2, was given a year.

Coolidge in the Adams House woke at his usual hour. Not until then did he learn of the disorders of the night before. Outwardly unperturbed, he took his customary breakfast of prunes and oatmeal and then his walk along Washington Street and up West Street, across Tremont Street and the Common to the State House. The governor's walk had by this time become a rite of passage. "It was as good as a show to watch him cross Tremont Street," a *Globe* reporter recalled. "The traffic was thick, of course, and sometimes Coolidge came to the street before the traffic cop was out in the morning. He always stopped, glanced, bird-like, up and down the street, measured the distance to the nearest car, and if he thought he could make it, he started across. If that car brushed his coattails he would not run. He had calculated the distance and the time. He had faith in his calculation. And evidently he considered it the driver's fault if he went faster than the Coolidge calculation provided. Having escaped, he did not exult."

On that hung-over Wednesday morning, accompanied by his bodyguard, state policeman Edward Horrigan, Coolidge passed the debris, the boarded windows and barbed wire, and a hardy band of crapshooters still rolling dice on Brimstone Corner. The wise old owl observed but said nothing, nor did he say any more when he was finally seated behind his vast glass-topped mahogany desk with the picture of his mother on it. Under the shadowed portraits of John Hancock and Samuel Adams, he conferred briefly with Secretary Long before calling in reporters. Peters, in his latest press release, had accused the governor of trying to shift the blame for the rioting from the commissioner to the mayor. "I made no such statement," Coolidge told the reporters testily. "When Mayor Peters and Commissioner Curtis were in conference with me yesterday, I told the mayor that he had the authority under the law to call out units of the state guard and that I of course could call out those units and other units in the state. I further said to him that if he did not care to exercise his authority in the first instance, I would on his request call out the troops if he should request me to do so. He did not make such a request. I stand ready to continue fully to support the mayor and the commissioner as I already have done."

There was no sign of emotion in the governor's face. Yet for all his outward impassivity, he was deeply troubled. After the reporters had left, he sent for his car and had his chauffeur take him as inconspicuously as possible across the Charles River to Watertown. Accompanied by an old Northampton acquaintance he drove to a time-worn, neglected cemetery surrounded by encroaching warehouses and factories on the road to Watertown Square. There, moving surefootedly among the slate stones, he made his way to one marking the grave of John Coolidge of Cambridge, England, who had died in 1691 and was buried with his wife, Mary. Coolidge stood by the grave in enigmatic silence for several minutes, finally remarking, "These are my first ancestors in this country." Then, as if he had gathered strength from this contact with the dust eight generations removed from him, he turned abruptly away.

The mayor's precept for the mobilization of the state guard within the Boston area reached Adjutant General Stevens's office at midmorning. In an accompanying letter to the governor, Peters asked for the three thousand additional troops. Coolidge at once complied, calling up the Eleventh, Twelfth, and Fifteenth regiments plus a machine-gun company and placing this force under Brigadier General Parker's command. Following General Cole's advice that it would be more effective to display the troops in force than to have them come straggling in, Peters requested mobilization for five o'clock that afternoon. Later he conferred with General Parker, who had moved with his staff from the South Armory to the third floor of police headquarters, then he formally asked the governor for additional troops. "You are at liberty to call on me," Coolidge replied, as he ordered up the Fourteenth and Twentieth regiments, the last of the state's guard units. The mayor's morning confidence oozed away in the ensuing hours, to be succeeded by a postprandial depression. Would even the full muster of the state guard be enough to protect his city from renewed violence?

Midafternoon found him telephoning Assistant Secretary of the Navy Franklin Delano Roosevelt begging for a provost guard from the Charlestown Navy Yard to help in preserving order. Then still smarting from Coolidge's noncommittal aloofness, he prepared another press release defending his seemingly passive role in the disorders of the night before:

> I have only now had opportunity to consider the statement issued a few hours ago by Governor Coolidge, in which he tries to place on me the responsibility for the distressing disturbances which occurred last night. I think I am entitled to state the facts.
>
> Until riot, tumult or disturbance actually takes place, the only person who has authority to police the city is the Police Commissioner and he is appointed by the Governor. The Committee of thirty-four appointed by me and myself have made every human effort to avoid the strike of the policemen, but received no cooperation from the Police Commissioner and no help or practical suggestions from the Governor.

Furthermore in a recent communication from the Governor, he states so plainly that no one has any authority to interfere with the Police Comissioner, that I should have hesitated to take control of a situation which the Commissioner assured me was under control, even had I had the power.

I had no alternative but to give the Police Commissioner a chance to demonstrate that he had adequately provided for the situation. The disorders of last night have demonstrated that he misjudged it....

After this appeared in the early editions of the afternoon papers, rage fissured Coolidge's granite features, and for once he became voluble to the point of profanity. When a deeply distressed Curtis appeared at his office to say that he would resign rather than continue at police headquarters as a supernumerary under Peters, the governor assured him that he could count on his, Coolidge's, backing. As Coolidge later wrote in his autobiography: "If he [Curtis] was to be superseded, I thought the men he had discharged might be taken back and the cause lost. Certainly they and the rest of the policemen's union must have rejoiced at his discomfort." Both the governor and the commissioner felt that the mayor might be induced to submit the strikers' grievances to arbitration. Curtis had already determined that, so far as it was in his power, none of the striking policemen would ever wear uniforms again.

While mayor and governor bickered and the state guard units prepared to mobilize, Boston continued to simmer, with always the latent threat that the city might boil over. Women had their handbags snatched on Washington Street. Near the Old South Meeting House, a pedestrian was jumped by two pickpockets but managed to shake them off and escape into a store, from where he was rescued by a sergeant and two patrolmen. One Harvard volunteer directing traffic in front of the Ames Building was forced against a car by a belligerent teamster and then knocked down and kicked by several bystanders. A truck loaded with thirty-nine cases of shoes belonging to the McElwain Shoe Company and valued at over ten thousand dollars was quietly driven away to oblivion. Across the Charles River the Harvard Yard was being patrolled by university police and ROTC students, and only one gate was left open.

In South Boston hordes of boys between five and eighteen roamed the streets, bent on mischief. Law-abiding Southies, under the leadership of former Lieutenant Governor Edward Barry, hastily formed a South Boston Vigilance Committee. A large crowd gathered in front of Station 6, following a rumor that volunteers were going out from there on duty. So threatening was the crowd that Captain Daniel Murphy kept his thirty Harvard subs inside for fear that they would be torn apart. As it was, the station house was bombarded with stones, tin cans, and bottles. Picketing strikers made no effort to stop the disorder.

Scollay Square, not a square at all but an irregular quadrangle below the Pemberton Square Courthouse, where eight streets meet, remained the focus of disorder, and those volunteers—mostly Harvard graduates and undergraduates—who went on duty there had a rough day of it. From early morning a restless mass roamed back and forth across the square between Sudbury and Court Streets with an insistent aimlessness, blocking traffic, hooting and pelting the dozen or so volunteers and the few loyal sergeants and patrolmen with stones and potatoes, while individuals occasionally darted closer to fling mud in their faces. One small boy snatched a night stick from a volunteer, then darted away, the crowd opening up to let him through but closing in again so that the enraged volunteer could not follow. A passing coal wagon had its contents dumped, and soon coal lumps were arching through the air. Arthur Morse, a suburban lawyer-volunteer, was struck in the eye with a piece of coal. Another volunteer had his cheek laid open. From time to time a sergeant or a sub would brandish his pistol and threaten to shoot, and the crowd would then scatter, laughing and jeering, only to surge back as soon as he had put his weapon away. Some of the brawnier and more pugnacious volunteers would occasionally wade into the crowd with their night sticks, where they managed to knock several of their tormentors unconscious. With each hour the crowd grew more and more uncontrollable. A passing United States mail truck was stopped and rocked back and forth, and only the most concerted efforts of Captain Sullivan and his sergeants prevented it from being tipped over.

Even as Sullivan was straining to rescue the mail truck, former Mayor James Michael Curley was making an impromptu speech on Washington Street just the other side of City Hall. Always ready to fish in politically troubled waters, and mindful of the next municipal election two years away in which he had already selected himself as the leading candidate, Curley had had his chauffeur drive him in town from Jamaica Plain. Standing on the running board of his car at the corner of Washington and Bromfield Streets, he denounced Mayor Peters to a hastily collected audience, pointing out to his listeners in his sonorously theatrical voice that during the crucial August days Peters had been sailing in Maine and adding that anyone getting as large a salary as the mayor's ought to stay on the job and earn it. Then, as if to underline his contempt for Peters, he ordered his chauffeur to drive the wrong way down one-way Washington Street.

By late afternoon at least five thousand malcontents and troublemakers had wedged themselves into Scollay Square, bringing all traffic to a halt. Captain Sullivan fed additional volunteers into the area as the tension grew, until there were twenty of them, the most conspicuous being the tall and rangy Tack Hardwick. In an effort to split the crowd, Hardwick and the one-armed Laurence Davis finally led several Harvard undergraduates in an ostensible retreat down Brattle Street. A segment of toughs immediately started after them, yelping like hounds on the trail of a fox. Every block or so Hardwick's little group turned on their pursuers with drawn revolvers. Pausing at a safe distance the gang hurled stones and coal, then pressed on as Hardwick's cohort continued its retreat. Where Cornhill meets Washington Street, the augmented gang closed in on them viciously. Two of the volunteers were downed in a doorway and then stomped; two others were forced against a wall, and pummeled and bludgeoned, their night sticks and revolvers seized. Hardwick, bloody-faced, tried to fight his way out with his fists. Hearing the shrieks and the uproar from Washington Street's Newspaper Row, sergeants Berry and Flynn of Station 2 dashed to the rescue as did Superintendent Crowley, who was on the point of leading a fresh detail into the square. Even they might not have been able to reach the beleaguered volunteers. But at this moment, as opportunely as at the climax of a Victorian melodrama, the First Troop of Cavalry, led by Captain Frederick Hunneman, cantered down Pemberton Hill from the Court House. After reporting quickly at headquarters, Captain Hunneman wheeled his troop in line facing the expanse of Scollay Square. There was a moment of silence, then a sharp command, and with pennons flying and sabres flashing in the wan afternoon light, the clink of chain bits and the clatter of hooves, the troopers charged. The crowd wavered and broke, then panicked. Oddly enough there were even a few cheers as the cavalry trotted by. Dividing, the troop formed platoon fronts, one platoon forcing a segment of the crowd toward Howard Street, the other driving the rest down Court Street, Cornhill, and Brattle Street. Hardwick's battered subs on Cornhill were rescued just in time.

The cavalry troop was not the first state guard unit to appear in the city, for shortly before its arrival two squads of infantry had marched across the square, the crowd making way for them, and had disappeared down Tremont Street. By now the guard's regiments and detachments were beginning to move into Boston from every section of the state. Mobilization had been swift and efficient, carefully planned well in advance, though hardly ready for the five o'clock deadline. Over the weekend the chief quartermaster of Massachusetts, scenting trouble, had ordered up cots, blankets, mess kits, and cooking utensils for the Tenth Regiment, and this equipment had arrived at the Commonwealth Armory Monday night. Tuesday morning Adjutant General Stevens ordered supplies for two more regiments and made arrangements for transporting, quartering, and feeding them. The East Armory on East Newton Street, with its kitchen capable of feeding three thousand men at once, was designated as mess headquarters, and Wednesday morning the commissary provisioned and staffed it. Other city armories were assigned as barracks for the incoming guardsmen.

From three o'clock on, summoned by fire whistles and alarm signals, the separate guard companies across Massachusetts mustered in the whimsically machicolated mock-medieval fortresses they called armories. Former guardsmen hastened to rejoin and were sworn in at once. The Tenth Regiment, all its units located within Boston's boundaries, was the first to respond. Companies came from Roxbury, Dorchester, West Roxbury, Charlestown, Jamaica Plain, Roslindale, Brighton, and East Boston. By six-thirty the Tenth was completely mobilized at the East Armory, except for Company L from Allston and Brighton, which was quartered at

Brighton's Commonwealth Armory. Beaming Colonel Sullivan, in full uniform and wearing the ribbons of the Spanish-American War and of the Society of Santiago de Cuba, looked ten years younger than he had as public-works commissioner. He felt prepared for anything as he ordered fifty rounds of ammunition issued to his men for their Springfield rifles.

The Eleventh Regiment—from Marlboro, Southboro, Newton, Clinton, Lowell, Westford, Concord, Haverhill, Lawrence, and Framingham—assembled with dispatch at the South Armory from this wide-ranging arc. Three companies arrived at the North Station from Lowell at five in the afternoon and marched through the business district to the armory with fixed bayonets: an impressive sight, as they themselves thought. The thirty-nine men of Framingham's Company E were reinforced by eleven sudden recruits that included five AEF veterans. Company M's thirty-three guardsmen from Clinton marched to the Union Station at four-thirty to find a thousand of their townsmen waiting to give them a send-off.

Newton's Company A received its call at two o'clock. Captain Henry Crowell at once notified First Sergeant John Perry to put the alarm list in operation. Special operators, as previously arranged, sent out the call from the West Newton switchboard. The armory doors were opened and within the hour the first guardsmen in their piecemeal uniforms came straggling in. They found sandwiches and coffee ready in the hallway, and the captain urged them to "snack up," since there was trouble in Boston and it was going to get worse. Ripples of excitement ran through the armory, as through all the small Massachusetts armories, a sense of anticipation that recruits commonly feel before soldiering becomes too boring or too dangerous. The news spread across Newton. Eighteen former members of Company A showed up for the "sport and diversion." At four o'clock the bugler sounded assembly. The three officers and forty-eight enlisted men—including a machine-gun unit—fell in on the floor of the armory, then marched to the West Newton Station to entrain for Boston. In Boston they detrained across the street from the South Armory, where they went immediately. Inside the armory they found a bustling confusion of units arriving from all points of the Massachusetts compass. No sooner did they set down their baggage in one area than they were ordered to take it to another. Seven minutes after Company A's arrival, twenty of its guardsmen and a lieutenant were sent off by truck to Station 10 at Roxbury Crossing, with only the chance of grabbing a sandwich as the men left. En route they decided to call themselves the "Flying Twenty." Within five minutes the rest of the company, consolidated with skeletal companies from Taunton, Fall River, Concord, Clinton, and Lowell, and under command of Captain Crowell, was dispatched to Station 9, Dudley Street. "Jesus," said Police Captain Skillings as he looked over his raw but eager recruits, "I didn't expect to see any of you before midnight!"

The companies of the Twelfth Regiment, from Somerville, Waltham, Stoneham, Cambridge, Medford, Wakefield, and Arlington, assembled at the Cambridge Armory. Among them was the youngest guardsman in the state, sixteen-year-old Private Jack Hesketh of Company G. At six-thirty, eight companies were sent to the Joy Street station on the far side of Beacon Hill. Sergeant Augustus Hermann was out of town when the call came and did not get to the armory until after dark. Two truckloads of the latecomers were then ordered to South Boston. When the drivers heard their destination they at first refused to go there, and it took a considerable amount of soldierly persuasion to make them.

Most of the Fourteenth Regiment was made up of guardsmen from Quincy and the towns along the South Shore. They mobilized at the Quincy Armory and came to the Commonwealth Armory by train. Two companies from more distant Brockton, West Bridgewater, and Taunton followed by truck.

From the North Shore, from Everett, Winthrop, Chelsea, Lynn, Salem, Gloucester, Rockport, Beverly, fire alarms and sirens summoned the men of the Fifteenth Regiment. The Guardsmen of Company F rode in from Beverly in their own truck. Companies B and C left Lynn at six o'clock in ten jitney buses for the Charlestown Armory, a crowd cheering them as they left. The Danvers and Salem companies commandeered streetcars.

In the western part of the state the mobilization went more slowly, the Twentieth Regiment guardsmen from Springfield not being called out until after dark. Harry Cross, a seventeen-year-old journeyman electrician of Company G got his order to report only

after he had come home from work. He managed to join the rest of
his company at the Howard Street armory before they left by train
for Boston. It was midnight before they arrived. They were sent in
great haste to the Commonwealth Armory. There the haste
stopped. The men were given a supper of frankfurters and beans.
No orders followed. There was nothing left for the men to do but
to bed down in the earth of the drill shed on their overcoat rolls
until morning.

While the state guard units were converging on Boston and
being funneled off to the nineteen police stations according to
need, more Yankee Division veterans in search of excitement and
wearing their old uniforms flocked to the East Armory. They were
mustered into service at once. A number of ex-cavalry and artillery
officers reported directly to the police department and were given
badges and night sticks and told they were now mounted police.
The First Corps Cadet Armory on Columbus Avenue became the
headquarters of the Motor Transport Corps, consisting of three
trucks, three motorcycles, a dozen touring cars, and some sixty
commercial vehicles that Lieutenant Colonel John Decrow was in
the process of requisitioning. The Ambulance Corps drivers, also
stationed at the Cadet Armory, were warned to exercise patience
and tact with the public and to avoid provocation. The several
machine-gun companies arriving in Boston were issued with Winchester riot guns, and a machine gun was installed at each police
station. Every company commander received a map of the city
showing the general defense scheme. By evening the city's armories
were humming like militant beehives, and Boston itself with its
various strongpoints had come to resemble a besieged fortress. At
six o'clock an urgent call came to the Pemberton Square headquarters for a hundred guardsmen to be sent immediately to South
Boston.

The Boston mob as it developed Wednesday night, though
smaller, was harder and more menacing than the night before,
since many of its members were armed, and it was reinforced by
professional criminals who had been heading toward the city all
the afternoon. Striking policemen mingled in the throng, urging on
the more violent. At the sight of the guard columns, bayonets fixed,
and in the highest spirits, many of the policemen felt their earlier

self-assurance evaporate. Now they struck back desperately. The Roxbury Letts were also circulating in the darkness with revolutionary zeal, having been directed to Scollay Square with their transient New York comrades by Fraina and Ballam to intensify the disorder that they hoped would lead to a breakdown of all civil government.

In the fifteen minutes following their charge over the cobbles of Scollay Square, the First Cavalry had cleared the now-sodden quadrangle of all except those who had business there. For a while it seemed that the troopers were in unchallengeable control. Traffic began to move along unimpeded. Volunteers leaving Station 2 were no longer subject to a barrage of boos punctuated by debris. But, gradually, detached gangs of several hundred surly drifters congregating in the feeder streets leading into the square—Sudbury, Hanover, Howard, Brattle, and Court Streets and Cornhill—began filtering back into Scollay Square itself. The troopers, though aided by guardsmen with bayonets, volunteers with revolvers and billies, and a contingent of hardened 101st Infantry veterans wearing steel helmets and their old YD uniforms, could not keep the cobbled quadrangle open. By seven-thirty a restive, ugly crowd of some ten thousand was wedged into that narrow space. Remaining windows in and near the square were soon smashed—the Market Men's Shop, Woolworth's, the Alpha Lunch. No guardsmen were agile enough to stop the small boys who climbed up building fronts, onto wagons, and on the roof of the subway entrance, where they flung down coal, stones, and chunks of wood. Older roisterers were making their way to the tops of buildings to bombard the troopers with bricks and bottles. John McTiernan, a striking patrolman from the Joy Street station with a few drinks under his belt, threatened to beat up a police sergeant who told him to clear out of the square. As soon as the sergeant's back was turned, McTiernan hit him with a lump of mud, then swaggered down Howard Street with two other strikers, McKinnon from his own station and Conlan from Station 1. All three had stones in their pockets. When a guardsman passed, McTiernan tossed a bottle he had just drained and struck the soldier on the head. The man leaned against a wall, stunned and bleeding. Not far from the three, Patrolman Kuhlman of Station 12 aimed a rock at another sergeant. McTiernan continued on his belligerent way until he came across a volunteer, John McLaughlin, Jr., of Winchester, sitting in a car, and threatened to pull him from his seat. When the nervous young man drew his revolver, McTiernan laughed in his face and dared him to shoot. A crowd surrounded them. Told of this confrontation just round the corner, Captain Sullivan sent out a special detail to bring McTiernan in, and booked him on a drunkenness charge. The other strikers continued to stir up trouble unimpeded. Carousing sailors beat up civilians and smashed windows until a contingent of marines subdued them with their fists.

From the windows of the Crawford House overlooking the square, the patrons of that once elegant but now seedy establishment watched as troopers charged again and again, sometimes collapsing under the rain of stones and brickbats from the rooftops in their vain efforts to break up the swirling crowd. Guardsmen kicked in the doors of houses and charged upstairs. Occasionally pistol shots rang out, often a succession of them. Arthur McGill, thirty-one, of the South End, who was standing near the patrol box on Howard Street, slumped to the ground dead with a bullet in his chest. A young woman, Gertrude Lewis of Townsend Street, Roxbury, was shot at the same time in the right arm. No one knew, no one was ever to know who fired the shots, but McGill's was the first death in the strike.

Bill Hoffman and his sub friends had had a rough if exciting afternoon. Several times they had been jostled and knocked to the ground, but each time by flourishing their revolvers they had forced the troublemakers back. A few bruises were in any case no worse than those from a football scrimmage. But in the evening he and two friends found themselves cornered in a doorway near the Old Howard by a gang who had been "laying for the Harvard guys." Even the menace of drawn revolvers failed to intimidate their adversaries. When the boldest started to climb the steps after him, Hoffman fired in the air. There was a tinkle of glass followed by a woman's cry, then shouts of "Baby killers!" Hands reached out of the shadows and snatched away his revolver. Then the enraged wolfish faces closed in; fists beat down on the panic-stricken students. Hoffman felt a jarring blow on the head; the street itself seemed to reel toward him.

Not until after ten was Scollay Square finally cleared through the sporadic but increasingly coordinated efforts of troopers, guardsmen, shaken but undaunted subs, and a provost guard from the Charlestown Navy Yard. The mob showed more fear of the horses than of anything else. With its cohesiveness finally broken, the disordered remnants streamed down Cornhill and State Street to the Old State House, breaking windows routinely in passing. Iver Johnson's remaining plate glass caved in; more persistent looters smashed their way into Burnham's Book Store, the Conclave Phonograph Company, American Wallpaper Distributors, and H. Goldthwaite, a dealer in surgical supplies. As the mob members retreated they found a convenient shelter in the subway entrance under the Old State House. Several of them with gleeful malice set the trash baskets on fire. Winkled out by the horsemen and driven further along Washington Street, they came face to face with a line of guardsmen at Summer Street and were diverted down Franklin Street. One recalcitrant was struck over the head with a revolver butt by a guard lieutenant and went sprawling on the cobbles. Troopers then harried the others beyond State Street into Adams Square, where what was left of the mob resolved into footsore and damply dispirited individuals.

With Scollay Square at last permanently cleared, General Parker now put his master plan into effect, cordoning off downtown Boston by degrees into controllable sections. The feed-in streets to Scollay Square were barred to pedestrians and traffic alike. Patrols and pickets kept the whole length of Washington Street as far as Chinatown a forbidden section into which no outsiders were allowed to make their way. All the little streets running from Tremont Street and the Common to Washington Street were closed. Guardsmen engaged in sharp if brief battles with skulkers on West, Summer, and Bromfield Streets. Avery Street was blocked off at both ends. The several hundred crapshooters and onlookers wedged into that narrow street faced the militia with defiance. "Let's go!" one of them shouted. At that a squad of guardsmen advanced with bayonets, and the crowd wilted.

Troopers rode the sidewalks on Newspaper Row, forcing pedestrians away from buildings and windows. The first detachment of cavalry to clear Washington Street was made up of volunteers, gentlemen-riders such as Richard Russell from the North Shore, the young partner of Mayor Peters's corporation counsel, who only a few months before had been discharged from the army after serving overseas as an artillery officer. With several other former officers, all of them wearing their old uniforms, he had joined up at the Chamber of Commerce Building and enrolled as a mounted policeman. His first assignment came Wednesday night, when he and three others were given police horses, ordered to clear Washington Street, and instructed to back their horses into any rioters who tried to hide in doorways. Starting from the foot of Court Street the amateur policemen edged their horses down Washington Street. From upper windows china and bottles were aimed at them but none hit. Scattered gangs along littered Washington Street showed little or no opposition, taking to their heels as the horses edged toward them. Those in doorways seemed terrified of the horses' flanks. Guardsmen, following the horsemen, took up positions twenty feet apart, the whole length of the sealed street. Once the bounds were set, downtown Boston grew as quiet as on any ordinary evening.

In South Boston, as in Scollay Square, the turbulence lurking just below the surface continued to break out in intermittent violence. All Wednesday afternoon the Gustins and lesser street gangs were out in strength, stoning passing cars, smashing windows, waiting only for the darkness to resume the mass pillaging of the night before. By early evening when trucks carrying the first detachment of the Tenth Regiment's three hundred fifty men pulled up on Broadway near Station 6, the few exhausted police were beginning to lose control. As the guardsmen in their floppy felt hats dismounted, a derisive howl went up from the sullenly bellicose crowd gathered there. Quickly the guardsmen formed a line across Broadway. Showers of stones, sticks, vegetables, and tin cans met them. Twice as many bystanders had gathered as on Tuesday night, sympathetic to the roistering gang but for the most part content to cheer the rioters. Violence was confined to the gangs and to furtive adolescents hurling missiles from the shadows. Nevertheless, the sight of uniformed men with rifles, bayonets, and riot guns posted at intervals along Broadway had a temporarily sobering effect. Occasionally a more pugnacious group would taunt or challenge the patrols but would break away sharply if the guardsmen lunged with their bayonets. Beyond Broadway the rest of Southie remained calm. Station 12 seemed the quietest place in the district. Patrols in the City Point area encountered no incidents at all.

Trouble broke out just after eight o'clock near Station 6, where the crowd was thickest, when three off-duty volunteers left the station and headed for the car stop on Broadway. With shouts of "Strikebreakers!" a mob of at least a hundred started after them. The volunteers broke into a run but were soon cornered. Just as the mob ringleaders were closing in, Monsignor George Patterson of St. Vincent's Church thrust himself between them and the unarmed volunteers, begging the mob—a number of whom he recognized as his own parishioners—to stop the senseless violence. But for once a priest's voice had little effect in that Catholic community. The three were rescued only after a state guard officer forced his way through the crowd, automatic in hand, and with the aid of several guardsmen led the volunteers back to the safety of the station.

An hour later small bands of young men began racing through the streets, hurling stones and bricks through store windows, though there was nothing like Tuesday's systematic demolitions. At the renewed sound of shattering glass, the crowd yelled approval. Half a dozen alley boys on Broadway took to throwing stones at the windows of Stephen Burdick's jewelry store. Burdick rushed out into the street pretending to draw a pistol from his hip pocket, and at this gesture the stone-throwers retreated. He went back to his store, turned off the lights, locked up, and headed for home. But he had not gone a block before the alley boys jumped him, knocking him down, beating him, kicking him with their pointed shoes, taking his wallet, and leaving him unconscious on the sidewalk. Guardsmen arrived too late to catch any of his attackers.

After Burdick had been carried away in an ambulance, rain began to fall, dissolving the crowd. Scarcely two thousand remained where earlier there had been five times as many, but those remaining were recalcitrant ones. When Superintendent Crowley drove up Broadway at about half past ten, he found the Tenth Regiment in well-organized control. A few revolver shots rang out in the darkness as his car neared F Street, and several sergeants with him gave chase without finding any trace of whoever had fired them.

There were no more shots. Most of the disturbances were now taking place in the streets and alleys off Broadway, small forays that the police and guardsmen easily broke up. Several false alarms were turned in. Small boys seized the opportunity to break a few windows in the Lawrence, Bigelow, and Hart schools. A convivial crew managed to filch two barrels of whiskey from a D Street saloon which they trundled to a vacant playground, broke open, and served out in pitchers stolen from the five-and-ten, an occupation that kept them from further mischief.

More serious trouble was obviously brewing in the section of West Broadway near E Street, where the gangs had consolidated. It boiled over at about eleven o'clock with the bellicose appearance of a band of toughs, some with pistols, who proceeded to rampage down Broadway away from the patrols. An isolated guard squad in front of adjoining O'Keefe's, the A & P, and Shea the Hatter proved a tempting target, and the toughs showered stones on the guardsmen, incidentally smashing the as-yet-undamaged windows. Hostile faces pressed in from all sides, and the amateur soldiers faced the throng with bayonets. The crowd yielded briefly to the leveled rifles, then pushed forward again, taunting, pelting the guardsmen with mud and stones, and daring them to "make something of it." One of the guardsmen by pointing his bayonet finally managed to work his way to Station 6 and call for help. Captain Thomas Hadley at once led out the Tenth Regiment's Company G in riot formation. At the sight of a company advancing in line, bayonets fixed, reinforced by riot guns, those threatening the isolated guardsmen temporarily retreated, but their blood lust was up and they soon returned more challenging than ever. As Captain Hadley placed his men in skirmish line across the wide street, there were more jeers. Hoarse voices dared him to fire. Even when the guardsmen raised their rifles for a volley in the air, the mob refused to take the gesture seriously. Several pistol shots echoed back in mocking reply, and stones continued to course through the air. Hadley then ordered those confronting him to disperse. As if in answer a stone struck him on the forehead and sent him spinning, even as the throng thrust forward. Staggering to his feet, he gave the command "Make ready!" There was the sharp click of bolts drawn back and cartridges thrust home. "Aim!" Then followed a staccato succession of shots as the guardsmen with rifles and riot guns fired directly into the encroaching mob. A wail went up, a long drawn-out echoing "Oh" of disbelief that ended in women's screams and was followed by a stampede to get away. Men and women were trampled down in the mad dash for cover. Five figures sprawled like rag dolls on the rapidly emptying boulevard. Anthony Czar, twenty-four, who lived on Broadway and who had been passively looking on from a doorway, lay dying from a bullet through the stomach. Robert Sheehan, sixteen, of L Street, shot in the back as he turned to run, would die a few hours later in the Carney Hospital. Twenty-one-year-old Robert Lallie, mortally wounded, would live until Friday. Thomas Flaherty, shot in the leg, and sixteen-year-old Helen Keeley with buckshot wounds in the head, would recover. Eight more, including two girls, escaped with superficial—mostly buckshot—wounds. Sergeant Hermann, leading his Twelfth Regiment platoon in clearing lower Broadway, was close enough to see the shadowy figures drop as the guardsmen opened fire. He concluded then and there that we were not as civilized as we ought to be.

As in the Boston Massacre a century and a half earlier, when the British troops had been baited into firing into a menacing mob on State Street, no one could say later who gave the order to fire. Captain Hadley denied that he had given it. Possibly—even as in that earlier confrontation—someone in the mob had called out the command in derision. Possibly a green young guardsman, fearful of the onrushing mass, had opened fire on his own and his fellows had copied him. But however fatal the result, it ended all disturbances in South Boston. The guardsmen, continuing their advance with rifles at the shoulder, encountered only fleeing individuals, whose belligerency had collapsed like a pricked baloon. "The firing," Adjutant General Stevens wrote smugly in his report, "had a salutory effect; it cowed the mob."

Beyond Scollay Square and South Boston there were only sporadic incidents in the city. Volunteers coming to report at Brighton's Station 14 during the afternoon were pelted with rotten eggs, yet there was no further trouble when they went on duty. Here and there a random holdup took place. John Kennedy of Roxbury was relieved by a gunman of twenty dollars and his watch near his home. A determined gang, after threatening to shoot the janitor of Maurice Keezer's suit-rental store on Columbus Avenue, made off with several thousand dollars' worth of dress suits. Several other small Roxbury shops were looted in quick sorties. Nevertheless the locale of the revolutionary Letts remained relatively quiescent. In the afternoon some 125 Roxbury merchants and businessmen met at the People's National Bank to organize a vigilante committee. Sworn in by Captain Skillings, given revolvers and badges, they encountered little opposition or disorder as they set out to patrol the streets near the Dudley Street el terminal. At Fields Corner a drunk, being taken by two subs to Station 11, was followed by a threatening gang who then began to stone the station, scattering only after a guard detachment had fired over their heads. Patrolman Francis McNabb—the solitary member of the policemen's union who did not go out on strike—assigned to guard the Park Square Theatre, had to be sent away when the Actors' Equity cast of *Buddies* informed the management that he must leave or there would be no show. Over thirty fire alarms were rung up in Boston, twenty-one of which turned out to be false. In Jamaica Plain, Captain Harriman, inspecting the rifles of his recruits, was shot in the thigh by a guardsman awkwardly presenting his weapon for inspection. Crap games continued across the Common, and lurking hangers-on obstructed the subway entrances. Guardsmen of Company L, Gloucester, broke up half a dozen such games but arrested only a sailor from the Hingham Naval Base, Harris Raymond, who had defied their order to move on. On Washington Street, a trooper sabered Cornelius Lynch of Charlestown in the back after Lynch had failed to get out of the way fast enough.

Long after the rest of the city had quieted down, a striking policeman, Richard Reemts, was fatally shot at the corner of Columbus Avenue and Buckingham Street in the South End. Reemts, from the Roxbury Crossing station and nine years on the force, along with Arthur Shea, another striking policeman, had led a party in two cars that pulled up beside volunteers John Reid of Belmont and Thomas Gannock, a Harvard student. Shea stepped out of the first car and asked the volunteers the way to Auburndale. As they attempted to explain, Reemts—one of the biggest men on the force—and several unidentified companions pinned them against the wall, slugged them, and seized their revolvers and badges. Sergeant John McDonald of Station 5, who happened to be close by, rushed to the rescue. He jumped on the running board of the first car and arrested Shea at pistol point. Reemts bolted down Columbus Avenue on foot, ducking as he ran. Abraham Karp, standing in front of his auto supply store with a revolver in his pocket, saw the bulky form hurtling toward him and feared he was about to be attacked. Drawing his revolver, he fired one shot. Reemts crashed down on the sidewalk, a bullet in his chest. By afternoon he would be dead. Shea, less than a year on the force, was held on a charge of robbery. Ironically enough he had been wounded in the right hand during the May Day disturbances and had returned to duty only two weeks before the strike.

By Thursday morning the state guard was in unchallenged control of the city. Olive-drab and khaki figures in felt campaign hats, with loaded rifles, bayonets, machine and riot guns, patrolled the streets, reiterating their one order: "Keep moving!" Later in the day many of the guardsmen would exchange their wide-brimmed hats for steel helmets, on loan from the army. Though Superintendent Pierce was still accepting volunteers, Crowley ordered them not to wear their by now provocative badges or flaunt their night sticks and revolvers. Some of the sub casualties had already dropped out. H. M. Chamberlain of Beacon Hill, hit on the head with a stone, returned to his Mount Vernon Street town house "to sleep off the dazed effect caused by the blow." Bill Hoffman and his friends were back in Cambridge, bruised, aching, and shaken, he with a split lip and a swollen nose but with no bones broken. Tack Hardwick had by his own proud admission "the biggest, ugliest and blackest bruised eye of the lot during valiant action in Scollay Square." The City Hospital, the Haymarket Relief, and the Carney Hospital were occupied by rioters, looters, guardsmen, and police in adjoining beds, suffering from glass cuts, bayonet jabs, bullet wounds, and bruises.

Banks, offices, and stores opened with revived confidence, some of the stores turning their losses into wry jests. Posner's advertised that any looted hats, shirts, or underwear that didn't fit would be gladly exchanged for the right size. The adjoining Coes & Young shoe store posted a sign on its boarded-up entrance: "We Are Open

But Our Shoes Are Too Valuable To Put In The Window." Merchants used their losses for informal advertising. Other signs read: "Our Merchandise Is Very Taking"; "Robbed But Opened For Business"; "They Took About 100 of our Umbrellas—We Hope It Clears Up."

Scollay Square, almost empty in the bleak morning aftermath, was heavily patrolled by both troopers and guardsmen. Pedestrians could cross only at designated points. Any three or more congregating individuals were instantly dispersed at bayonet point. No one could loiter. Sailors, usually so obvious in the square, were absent, the navy having suspended all shore leaves as of the night before. Regular army soldiers protected government property. On the waterfront, watchmen behind barricades guarded the wharves. At the State House the guards were doubled and strangers barred. Now that authority had reasserted itself, the indignation of established Boston over the two riotous nights had become virulently vocal. Business leaders, members of the chamber of commerce, and peaceable commuters, their fears abating, referred to the striking policemen as "deserters," "Bolsheviks," and "agents of Leninism." The *Transcript* underlined its photographs of looted stores with the remark that the situation in Scollay Square and on Washington Street had been as bad as on the Nevski Prospect during the October Revolution. Other Boston papers in their varying degrees emphasized the "lawlessness, disorder, looting . . . such as we have never known in this city."

Only on the Common at Brimstone Corner near the Neptune fountain did the diehards persist in their dice-rolling. Some forty crapshooters had formed a circle there, goggled at by about a hundred spectators, a number of whom were street urchins. Bills and coins dotted the center of the circle. The term "diehard" would take on a more literal meaning before the morning was over, for the order had come down from General Parker to clear the Common. Peripherally, the crapshooters had again started up on Avery Street, and the marathon game near the Dover el station was going into its third day, but the Common remained the center of defiance. Just before eleven o'clock Guard Lieutenant James Dooley of Cambridge marched his platoon of the Twelfth Regiment's Company F up the Long Walk from Boylston Street across the Common.

Halting his men briefly behind the Park Street subway entrance, he stepped out to reconnoiter. The ardent crapshooters by the fountain paid no attention either to him or his uniform. Quietly he advanced his men in extended order and surrounded the gamblers, then ordered them peremptorily to hold up their hands. When they hesitated, the guardsmen fired a volley over their heads, and the hands went up in a flash. One man, still hesitant, was struck down by a guardsman's rifle butt. Another, as he raised his hands, surreptitiously tossed away a revolver that skittered under a park bench and was retrieved by a small boy who scampered off with it. Dooley's men marched their prisoners away at brisk bayonet point, hands still in the air, toward Boylston Street en route to the LaGrange Street station. Urchins scrambled and scuffled for the coins and bills—the stakes of the game—abandoned on the pavement. A surly crowd followed the prisoners, growing so hostile that Dooley ordered another warning round fired. At the sound the crowd scattered, only to regroup again, hooting and jeering. Foremost in the crowd, Raymond Barnes, an eighteen-year-old merchant seaman in uniform, urged the others to spring the prisoners. The rear-rank guardsmen turned to face the oncoming threat, pulling back their rifle bolts and snapping them with ominous precision. "They're only shooting in the air!" Barnes shouted, making a dash at the line of guardsmen and waving his arms as if he were prepared to brush the rifle barrels aside. The nearest guardsman dropped to his knee, his rifle pointed upward, and as the sailor rushed at him, pulled the trigger. Barnes was only a few feet from the rifle barrel when the bullet went through him. The shot tore most of his throat away, and he sank to the ground. Appalled at what he had done, the young guardsman reached out to take the sailor's arm and steady him in his fall. Barnes collapsed and was carried into a Liggett's drug store across the street. He was dead by the time the ambulance took him to the relief hospital.

The killing marked an end of crowds and crapshooting on the Common. Other players in smaller circles quickly pocketed their dice and hurried away. Morbidly curious spectators gathered round the blood spot on the concrete, muttering to each other but no longer forming a crowd. Early in the afternoon the marathon crap game at Dover and Washington Streets was broken up by a naval provost guard, bringing Boston's open-air dice-rolling to an end. In the course of the day the provost guard also picked up several dozen AWOL sailors. Meanwhile Captain Thomas Goode of the Back Bay station had received a tip that New York gunmen were on their way to hold up the Fenway Park box office where, despite the strike, the till was bulging with receipts from the double-header baseball game scheduled that afternoon between the Red Sox and the St. Louis Browns. Captain Goode marched two state guard companies, a hundred volunteers, and a detail of loyal policemen to the park. No gunmen showed up, but the guardsmen and volunteers at least were able to see the home team beat the Browns 4–0, 6–0.

All day guardsmen lined Scollay Square at four-foot intervals, while a full company stood drawn up in riot formation in the square's center beside patrol wagons and military police vans. Pedestrians were hustled along the street with scarcely time to turn their heads, though if they did they were likely to see a bayonet pointed at them. There was no sign of resistance. In South Boston some twelve hundred guardsmen, a detachment of cavalry, three machine guns, and sixty riot guns made that turbulent area as tranquil as on Easter Sunday. Those on the sidewalks were kept on the move, householders not even being allowed to stand in their own doorways. The only incident to break the calm occurred when someone on a rooftop dropped a brick on the head of guardsman Lee Emery as he was patrolling his Broadway beat near D Street. Emery was taken to the hospital with a fractured skull.

Arrests in Boston, a mere dozen or so, were mostly for drunkenness. There was a slight flurry on the Common at midafternoon, when four Harvard volunteers, taunted by spectators, brandished their revolvers. Almost at once a state guard sergeant with his platoon surrounded them. The sergeant, after warning off the spectators, told the four to put away their guns, or he would haul them in for inciting to riot. Meekly they obeyed him. Nothing else happened except for a few small thefts in Roxbury—and a brief fracas involving a guardsman. The occupation and pacification of Boston seemed complete. Meeting in the city, the Grand Lodge of Masons in a unanimous rising vote pledged the support of Massachusetts's eighty thousand Masons to the governor and the mayor "in their efforts to maintain law and order."

Yet there was to be one final act of violence, one more death, before the day's end, this time in the well-to-do Jamaica Plain. Except for the wounding of Captain Harriman, the only other Jamaica Plain incident had occurred on Wednesday night when a Chinese laundryman on Green Street had been beaten and robbed. Tuesday's demonstration in front of Station 13 had been trivial, and on Wednesday the sedate residential district had kept its usual quiet. But on Thursday evening two guardsmen on patrol came across a handful of young men and boys hunched in the middle of Water Street around a manhole cover that they were attempting to pry open. As the men in uniform approached, the others scattered. The guardsmen shouted several times for them to halt, but they kept on running. Then, instead of letting them go, the guardsmen fired. The two shots brought down four men. Henry Grote, twenty, was killed outright. Carton McWilliams, eighteen, lay in the gutter dying. Two others, one of them only sixteen, were slightly wounded.

As spread across the press of the land, Boston's riot and disorder were magnified to insurrection, the realization of Fraina's reddest hopes. Headlines rang out like tocsins: *"TROOPS TURN MACHINE GUNS ON BOSTON MOBS"; "TERROR REIGNS IN CITY."* The San Francisco *Examiner* shuddered at the *"RIOTS IN BOSTON,"* where "Gangs Range Streets, Women Are Attacked, Stores Are Robbed, Shots Are Fired." For the Los Angeles *Times*, "no man's house, no man's wife, no man's children, will be safe if the police force is unionized and made subject to the orders of Red Unionite bosses." "Civic treason!" was the New York *World*'s opinion. The *Wall Street Journal* saw "Lenin and Trotsky on their way." Other papers predicted "Sovietism" in Boston, while several United States senators felt that "the effort to Sovietize the Government has started." Senator Henry Myers of Montana declared on the floor of the Senate that if the Boston strike succeeded, other police strikes would follow until within sixty days every town of more than three thousand inhabitants would have unionized police. Then "unionization" of the army and navy would follow, and "a Soviet government will be established in the United States before the next presidential election." He called the strike "one of the most dastardly acts of infamy that has ever occurred in this country since the act of Benedict Arnold."

President Wilson, touring the country in a desperate attempt to defend the peace treaty and his League of Nations, interpolated a reference to the police strike in a prepared speech after his secretary, Joseph Tumulty, had called his attention to the Boston crisis.

> I want to say this [the president told a Helena, Montana, audience] that a strike of the policemen of a great city, leaving that city at the mercy of an army of thugs, is a crime against civilization.
>
> In my judgment the obligation of a policeman is as sacred and direct as the obligation of a soldier. He is a public servant, not a private employee, and the whole honor of the community is in his hands. He has no right to prefer any private advantage to the public safety.
>
> I hope that that lesson will be burned in so that it will never again be forgotten, because the pride of America is that it can exercise self-control.

Eight persons died in the strike, twenty-one were wounded, and at least fifty injured. An estimated third of a million dollars' worth of property was stolen or destroyed, most of which, according to some obscure statute, had to be paid for by the city. So the riots came to an end in beleaguered Boston, the town that in its provincial pride had once called itself the Athens of North America and that now in the eyes of nervous Americans had come to seem its Petrograd.

LAW AND ORDER

Regrettable as the destruction and deaths of the last two nights had been—and no one regretted them more than the mayor of Boston—Peters could not conceal his self-satisfaction on Thursday morning. With corporation counsel Whiteside at his right hand and General Cole at his left, his city with its police was firmly under his control. Blame for the disorder he placed on Curtis. But order had been restored, and he could say he had been chiefly responsible for restoring it. Unless there was a declaration of martial law, the state guard under General Parker remained an auxiliary force subject to the mayor's command. Peters had been worried that the governor might indeed declare martial law, but Whiteside informed him, to his relief, that only the legislature was legally empowered to do this. Restoration of order came first, he told reporters authoritatively. Adjustment of the strike issues would have to come later. His most pervading fear was that the Boston Central Labor Union might stage a general strike before he could reach a settlement with the police. But with the obstructive Curtis out of the way, he felt that such a settlement, along the lines of the last Storrow Committee

171

proposals, was still feasible. However, as a precaution against any general strike, with its renewal and perhaps intensification of disorders, he appealed to the governor to request that federal troops be placed on the alert. Masking his impatience with the mayor, Coolidge telegraphed both the secretary of war and the secretary of the navy:

> The entire State Guard of Massachusetts has been called out. At the present time the city of Boston is orderly. There are rumors of a very general strike. I wish that you would hold yourself in readiness to render assistance from forces under your command immediately upon application, which I may be compelled to make to the President.

At noon, Peters busied himself with another press release, this time praising the nonstriking policemen, who "remained true to their oath of office." "They have faced not only physical danger," the mayor went on, "but, what is harder to a red-blooded man, the reproach of their lifetime associates that they have not stood by them, and they have done this without any hope or prospect of reward, except what comes from consciousness that they have done their duty and from the respect and gratitude which they will be accorded by their fellow-citizens." Following a lunch, brought in to his desk, the mayor held a conference with the four labor leaders —the AFL's Frank McCarthy, Boston Central Labor Union President Michael O'Donnell, CLU business agent Harry Jennings, and Councilor James Moriarty—who came to his office directly from the closing session of the Greenfield convention. Much chastened by the state guard's takeover, they now proposed a strike compromise: all the striking policemen would return to their posts at once; the mayor would dismiss the guard; a final settlement would be left to a board of arbitration. Jennings added that the policemen's union, even when affiliated with the American Federation of Labor, would agree never to take part in any sympathy strike. Peters, all affability, said he could not agree because he would then be exceeding the authority invested in him by the law under which he took over the police department. If, however, they would drop their demand for AFL affiliation, he thought a settlement might still be worked out. He agreed to speak to the delegates of the BCLU that evening at the Wells Memorial Building, where the entire body would vote on the edgy question of a sympathy strike. After his conference with the labor leaders Peters told reporters that "everyone present" expressed a desire "to avert such a strike."

Even as the mayor fumbled for ways to conciliate his labor constituents, Coolidge at the State House was preparing to cut the ground from under Peters's unsuspecting feet. The governor's sallow face flushed with rage as he thought of Peters now claiming credit for the state guard's restoration of order, his supplanting of Curtis by his own lightweight authority, and his subordinating General Parker to City Hall. Telephoning the suspended commissioner, Coolidge asked him rhetorically if he did not think the time had come "to take this thing over?" Curtis did indeed think so, as did even more emphatically the shadow at his elbow, Herbert Parker.

Far away in western Massachusetts, Murray Crane had followed the Boston disorders with dismay. Fearful of the effect they might have not only on Coolidge but on the fortunes of the state Republican party, he dispatched his iron-jawed envoy extraordinary, ex-Senator Butler, posthaste to Boston. Butler, Coolidge, and Herbert Parker mulled over the problem at lunch at the Union Club, Butler and Parker doing most of the talking. Finally Coolidge asked the others what they thought he should do. "I said that the governor should take over the situation," Butler recalled, ". . . and also take charge of the police affairs of Boston." Parker enthusiastically agreed. Later, after the three had returned to the executive suite, they were joined by pudgy-faced Attorney General Wyman and former Attorney General Pillsbury. Coolidge at his desk fingered a copy of the *Herald* with Peters's remark about receiving no help or practical suggestions from the governor. "I see," he remarked in his dry waspish voice, "that the mayor has taken a hand in this!"

What Coolidge and his advisers feared was that Peters would give in to the union, that the striking policemen would soon be back on their jobs, cocky and assured, ready to strike again whenever their demands were not met. Then, whatever the terms of agreement, the irresolute mayor might well emerge triumphant as the leader who settled the strike, a possible dangerous rival in the November annual gubernatorial election. The year before, Coolidge had just managed to squeak through with a 16,945 majority out of a total of 412,701 votes cast. This had never been far from his mind all during the strike, had made him at first so reluctant to have any part of it. Now, however, the moment of decision had indeed forced itself on him. He was ready, he told the expectant four, as commander in chief of the state's armed forces, to take over the state guard. They all but applauded in their agreement. His ensuing proclamation read:

> The entire State Guard of Massachusetts has been called out. Under the constitution the Governor is the commander-in-chief thereof by an authority of which he could not, if he chose, divest himself. That command I must and will exercise. Under law I hereby call upon all the police of Boston who have loyally and in never-to-be-forgotten ways remained on duty to aid me in the performance of my duty in the restoration of order in the city of Boston and each of such officers is required to act in obedience to such orders as I may hereafter issue or cause to be issued.
>
> I call on every citizen to aid me in the maintaining of law and order.

Without pause of pen he wrote out Executive Order Number One, through which he assumed control of the Boston Police Department, and he directed Curtis to return to his duties as commissioner, obeying only such orders as the governor might "issue or transmit." After he had finished preparing the two documents he turned to Butler, the thinnest of smiles breaking through his wintry features. "What further damage can I do?" he asked mockingly. Parker's legalistic mind was troubled, and he suggested that it might be tactful to inform the mayor what had been done. "Let him find it out in the papers!" the governor snapped.

Some time elapsed before the executive order arrived at City Hall, but rumors of it seeped through the corridors and offices and finally got to the mayor himself. Peters called the State House at once to ask whether it was true, and was shocked to learn that it was. Not long afterward a special messenger arrived at the mayor's office with the document itself. Peters, Whiteside, and General Cole spread it on the desk and examined it with increasing chagrin. At one pen stroke, the mayor found himself a supernumerary thrust aside by the rush of events, a commander without a command. Just as Curtis had done only two days before, Peters now wrote with ironically formal politeness to the man who had supplanted him, pledging his full support and cooperation. Privately and plaintively he continued to maintain that the governor had disrupted all his plans for the full restoration of law and order.

Law and order seemed only temporarily restored under the lengthening shadow of a general strike. The key firemen's union was still breathing fire. On Wednesday afternoon the union's president, Daniel Looney, after a long conference with Fire Commissioner John R. Murphy, told the reporters: "We are in the hands of the American Federation of Labor. It is for the Central Labor Union to take some action, and *what labor demands of us we will deliver!*" Commissioner Murphy thought that whatever labor demanded, there would still be enough loyal firemen to provide skeleton crews for any emergency. But Commissioner Curtis had thought the same thing about the police on Tuesday. As the Boston Central Labor Union met on Thursday evening, Bostonians, their nerves on edge, anticipated a sympathy strike that would shut down the city. For if there were no fire fighters, if the telephone service failed, if the electrical workers kept their promise to go along with the rest of labor, no one could guess what might happen in the darkened streets. At eight o'clock more than four hundred delegates representing 125 affiliated unions crowded into Wells Memorial Hall. The mood was militant. Among the most militant were the members of the newer unions; the carmen, the firemen, the "hello" girls, and the electrical linemen. Restlessly they waited the signal from the BCLU's committee of seventeen.

The somewhat unwieldy committee had been streamlined into a five-member executive committee consisting of President O'Donnell, business agent Harry Jennings, Councilor James Moriarty, AFL organizer Frank McCarthy, and former BCLU President Edward McGrady. Wise in the ways of the strikes, these elders were aware that whatever the inflammatory sentiments of the delegates, the police strike was faltering. What could be salvaged, should be, but it would have to be done discreetly. Cutting through the incandescent oratory, President O'Donnell ordered a secret ballot taken in which the delegates from each local would write down whether or not their union had voted for a sympathy strike. Eighty per cent of the delegates recorded themselves in favor of striking at once. O'Donnell and the executive committee decided to keep the results secret. Falling back on the ingenious excuse that some of the unions—actually fewer than fifty—had not yet committed themselves on the strike issue, the committee recommended soothingly that the BCLU continue "to work in conjunction with the Police Union, to the end that justice be given the members of the Police Union." To this was tacked the timeserving request that all locals not yet having done so would "have a vote ready for the next meeting of the Central Labor Union," the following week.

While the Boston Central Labor Union's committee of seventeen remained resolutely dilatory, Secretary of War Newton Baker reacted promptly to the Massachusetts governor's request. Major General Clarence Edwards, having emerged from his wartime eclipse to command the Northeast Department, placed the recently returned First Division on alert and ordered his scattered forces to hold themselves in readiness for riot and guard duty in Boston. He also ordered a large wire "Boche" cage to be built at Fort Devens, thirty miles northwest of the city, to take care of "radicals." The eight hundred men of the Thirty-sixth Infantry, already at Devens, readied themselves to arrive in Boston with Browning automatic rifles on three hours' notice. Rear Admiral Herbert Dunne, commanding the First Naval District, conferred with Edwards about sending naval detachments to the city. Between them, they assured the governor, they could muster ten thousand soldiers and sailors within twelve hours.

The Boston streets on Friday resumed the calm that was now beginning to appear customary. Most of the debris had been removed; the boards were being taken from the broken windows and new glass installed. State guard detachments continued to arrive, and armories were besieged by would-be volunteers, who to their disappointment had to be turned away. By the day's end there were six times as many guardsmen on the streets as there had been policemen the week before. Governor Coolidge, preparing for the ultimate emergency, ordered the demobilized Fourteenth State Guard Regiment of Fall River and Cape Cod back into service. He then instructed Brigadier General LeRoy Sweetser to reorganize the fourteen thousand troops of the old Massachusetts Volunteer Militia that had been absorbed by the National Guard in 1917. A number of volunteers, white handkerchiefs round their arms and wearing white hat bands, were still directing traffic, but this task was being turned over to the secretary of the Boston Automobile Association, Chester Campbell, who had organized a squad of fifty car dealers to take charge of traffic generally. Superintendent Pierce was continuing to enroll volunteers at the Chamber of Commerce Building, even though they were now destined mostly to sit round in station houses acting as reserves.

Friday morning also brought Curtis back to his desk at Pemberton Square, his jaw set in bulldog determination, his jowls wedged sternly into his wing collar. First he consulted with Attorney General Wyman, not with the intention of asking advice but for the legal backing to do what he had already determined to do. He then telephoned all his station captains, warning them that none of the policemen who had failed to report on Tuesday or since that time might return to duty under any circumstances nor were they to loiter on station premises. He personally would decide about those reporting back from vacation or from sick leave. The new minimum salary for policemen he now set at $1400 a year. As for the nineteen suspended patrolmen, he issued General Order Number 125, dismissing them from the force.

Coolidge, even though he was organizing some forty thousand reserves to fall back on—guardsmen, militia, and soldiers—nevertheless felt comfortably reassured that a general strike was only the remotest of possibilities. His friend Diamond Jim Timilty, the Roxbury Democratic ward boss, had tipped him off on Monday night, and where labor was concerned Diamond Jim knew what he was talking about. When Coolidge had been elected president of the Massachusetts senate, Diamond Jim—his nickname derived from the large diamond cuff links, stickpins, and rings he always wore—was senior senator. Cal and Jim had had their outward political differences, but privately the senate president granted his

Democratic colleague whatever favors he felt he could. Part of Coolidge's political success lay in his readiness to do favors, while almost never asking anything in return. Among the knife-wielding Democratic smilers on Beacon Hill he grew to be trusted. With the Timiltys of this world he had always felt more at home than he had with the Back Bay Brahmins. When Coolidge was president he placed three of Timilty's six children on the federal payroll. "I just went in to see my little pal," Timilty recalled to a *Post* reporter, "to tell him not to worry about a general strike. You know, I'm president of the largest labor organization in the state, the City and Town Laborers' organization, with the largest membership of any union in Massachusetts. I just told Cal that 'We won't go out,' and we have more votes in the Central Labor Organization than any of those others. You see, Cal's my kind of guy, and he's right about those damned cops!"

In spite of such reassurance, Coolidge with customary canniness ordered a survey of the Boston area public utilities by the engineering firm of Stone & Webster as a guide for action in the event of a general strike. In the late afternoon he held a press conference. By now and almost in spite of himself he had become the key figure in Boston's time of trouble. Peters was so thoroughly in eclipse that he had not even gone to the BCLU meeting, where he was scheduled to speak. The governor, all hesitancies at last thrust aside, faced the reporters with flinty aplomb, rasping out his laconic answers while at the same time adroitly shifting the responsibility for decisions onto the police commissioner and the law. His wish, he emphasized, was to support the commissioner "in any action he may take." Would he negotiate with the strikers? No. This was not a strike but—he hammered out the words—a "desertion of duty." If the police yielded, would they be taken back? "My personal opinion," said Coolidge, "is that they should not be taken back. You should keep in mind, however, that I have no authority over the matter. My only authority is over the police commissioner and when I have appointed him, it is his duty to administer the department." The governor said he could not think of any condition under which the police should be reinstated, but that it was a matter wholly beyond his control. As for affiliation with the AFL, he continued, "a rule of the police department, which is the law of the Commonwealth, provides that they shall not join any outside organization. That being the law, there can be but one reply to any such demand." Then, in a formal statement, he explained that in taking command he had acted to eliminate public confusion as to where the responsibility for community protection and the maintenance of law and order lay during the crisis. With stony malice he concluded by telling the grinning reporters that he and the mayor had been working together in "perfect harmony."

Long before the striking policemen had come to realize their waning fortunes, when talk of a general strike still boiled and bubbled, senior labor leaders elsewhere were developing second thoughts. Most prominent among the dubious was the diminutive sixty-nine-year-old Gompers, the frog-eyed, stubborn-jawed president of the American Federation of Labor for the past third of a century. A practical-minded craft unionist, distrustful of intellectuals and social theorists, he had prudently kept police unions at arm's length for decades. The present situation could not have arisen, he felt, if he had not been abroad in August at a meeting of the International Federation of Trade Unions in Amsterdam. On the very Tuesday that the Boston patrolmen had walked out, his father had died in the semi-suburb of Dorchester, and he had come to Boston in strictest secrecy to make the funeral arrangements and at the same time to size up the police situation. What he saw from behind his rimless spectacles more than dismayed him. Privately he admitted that the AFL had blundered in giving the police a charter. On Thursday, before his return to New York, his AFL vice-president, Matthew Woll, speaking before the National Civic Federation, sounded the first note of a tactical retreat. Woll blamed the "difficulty in Boston" on those in authority who refused to grant the police their right as Americans to organize and affiliate with the union of their choice, but he added significantly that the federation "discourages all government employees from striking."

On Friday, Gompers, faced with the added bleak prospect of backing a national steel strike that he considered doomed before it started, followed up Woll's ambivalence by urging the Boston policemen to go back to their posts. Unaware of how completely Peters had been shunted aside, he telegraphed the mayor:

> No man or group of men more genuinely regrets the present Boston situation than do the American Federation of Labor and I.

You have undoubtedly been apprised of President Wilson's suggestion to the commissioners of the District of Columbia, who
adopted a similar regulation to that adopted by the Boston authorities ordering policemen not to become members or to retain membership in a union affiliated with the American Federation of Labor.
The President requested that such order be held in abeyance and the
entire matter remain in *statu quo* until after the conference which he
has called for October 6 for the consideration of all matters affecting
the relations between workers and employers. The commissioner of
the District of Columbia complied with the president's request.

I therefore appeal to you and to the authorities who issued the
order that its enforcement be deferred until after the presidential
conference.

I am telegraphing the representative of the American Federation
of Labor in Boston, Mr. Frank McCarthy, 30 Wheatland Avenue, to
appeal to the Policemen's Union to cooperate and return to their
posts just as if the order had not been issued at all, upon information
that the enforcement of the order has been postponed to await the
outcome of the presidential conference.

Then he sent a copy of the telegram to McCarthy, at the same time
urging him to see that the policemen cooperated in carrying out
"the spirit and purpose" of his message.

Peters replied with petulant irrelevance that "the situation in
Boston differed from that of the District of Columbia as the policemen here left their posts and gave the city over to forces of disorder." "The governor as commander-in-chief of the state's forces,"
he concluded, "has now charge of the Police Department. Your
communications should be directed to him." Without bothering to
reply, Gompers sent off an identical telegram to Governor
Coolidge, who answered immediately:

Under the law the suggestions contained in your telegram are not
within the authority of the Governor of Massachusetts, but only of
the Commissioner of Police of the City of Boston.

With the maintenance of discipline in his department, I have no
authority to interfere.

He has decided that the men have abandoned their sworn duty
and has accordingly declared their places vacant.

I shall support the commissioner in the execution of law and
maintenance of order.

Meanwhile the members of the policemen's union met again in Fay Hall, where McCarthy read them Gompers's telegram. However equivocal it was, they sensed uneasily a bugle call for retreat. After listening grim-faced to half a dozen speakers, including the almost hysterical Mae Matthew, who promised the telephone operators' union's unconditional support, the patrolmen voted unanimously to go back to duty if the governor would cancel the commissioner's suspension order of September 8 and reinstate the nineteen union officers, "pending the adjustment of grievances at issue." There was still no apparent break in the strikers' ranks. But as their doubts expanded, they fell back on the consoling thoughts of labor rallying to their cause. Eighty-five per cent of the firemen were reported to be in favor of a strike. The percentage reached a hundred among the thirty thousand members of the United Hebrew Trade Unions. Boston bartenders through their local 77 declared that whenever the BCLU issued the call, their reply would be, "Ready, Sir." If the carmen and the electrical workers and the other Boston unions backed the police as the firemen and the telephone girls had so fervently promised, there was still hope.

Even among the most fervent, doubts were seeping in. Without explanation the Russell Club, the firemen's AFL-affiliated union, called off a meeting scheduled for Friday to vote on the question of a general strike. Union leaders, announcing that the meeting would be held on Tuesday instead, refused to say why it had been postponed and whether Gompers's telegram had had anything to do with it. At about the same time some two thirds of the Metropolitan Park policemen who had refused to go on duty in Boston on Tuesday night reported back to Metropolitan Police Superintendent Herbert West, expressing their regret at their earlier action and offering, if they were reinstated, to serve in any place they might be sent. West told them to put on their uniforms and report for duty at the Pemberton Square headquarters, and by evening the Metropolitan greycoats were patrolling the city streets. Those Boston policemen who had been on vacation or on sick leave and had been waiting to see which way the wind blew began to have second thoughts. Sometimes those thoughts proved of little avail. They were of small help to Patrolman Walter Crocket of the Field's Corner station. With almost twenty-five years of service, and with eight children plus his mother and mother-in-law at home to look after, he had refused to consider going on strike. But as his vacation was coming up anyway, he had left Tuesday morning for a three-day fishing trip down Boston Harbor. When he returned, he cut short his vacation, got into his uniform, and went down to the station house. Captain Reardon, with whom he had never hit it off, ordered him off the premises as a striker. Dejectedly Crocket handed over his badge and went home.

On Saturday morning Curtis received an official ruling from the attorney general:

> Confirming the oral opinion expressed to you yesterday upon the statement of facts as presented, I beg to advise you that the situation amply warrants a finding by you that the policemen in question have abandoned their offices. In the event of your decision that such abandonment has taken place, the offices abandoned are to be treated as vacant, to be filled by you as provided by law.

Armed with this, Curtis announced that

> the places in the police force of Boston formerly held by the men who deserted their posts of duty have by this action been rendered vacant. I am advised by the Attorney General that upon the existing facts the offices formerly held by the members of the police force to whom I have referred are in fact and in law, vacant. I shall accordingly proceed in accordance with law and in strict compliance with the requirements of the civil service laws to fill these vacancies with new men....
>
> I have further requested the Civil Service Commission to grant to me authority to appoint to the police force any veterans as defined by Chap. 150 of the General Acts of 1919. The Attorney General has ruled that such veterans must be a resident of the Commonwealth and need not be a resident of the City of Boston.

With the issuance of this statement, Curtis prepared to advertise for a new police force. In the postwar cycle of unemployment he expected a rush of ex-servicemen for the vacancies. He specified that recruits must have served honorably in the army, navy, or Marine Corps during the war, must not be under twenty-five or over thirty years, under one hundred forty pounds or shorter than five feet eight inches. In addition to the new starting wage of $1400 a year, he added that uniforms would now be furnished free. Those who could pass a noncompetitive civil service examination would be appointed at once.

While Curtis was laying out plans for recruiting his new police force, the leaders of the old striking force and the BCLU executive committee arrived at the governor's chambers to confront him with the resolution adopted by the police union the night before. From ten to eleven-fifty-five they sat before the unresponsive Coolidge, going over the same ground, asking for reinstatement of the policemen on the terms of the resolution, and getting the new threadbare reply that this was in the hands of the commissioner. McInnes was so wrought up on leaving that he could scarcely control his voice. "The situation is now in the hands of the governor," he told reporters. "You can make it plain that John F. McInnes, president of the Policemen's Union, will never go back on the police force of Boston except as a union policeman. The American Federation of Labor charter will never leave my hands!" From Coolidge came merely the brief statement that the committee of the policemen's union and the accompanying labor leaders had asked for another conference with him and Curtis and that he had undertaken "to transmit that request." Curtis on being notified replied that though he was willing at any time to confer with the governor, he did not "deem it advisable under the existing circumstances to join in the suggested conference." Later, at Coolidge's prompting, he unbent sufficiently to agree to meet with the group on Monday but *only* as private individuals, not as members or representatives of any labor organization.

Saturday afternoon the striking policemen held a desultory meeting at Fay Hall, then broke off for a long recess. The ensuing evening meeting had a sinister aspect to it. As the strikers filed in they found Captain John King and Sergeant George Augusta of police headquarters standing at the doors handing out discharge notices to the nineteen suspended union officers. Ranged on the street behind them, a crew of guardsmen had set up a machine gun to command the doorway. The delegates appeared agitated, but there was no sign of trouble as they took their places. Farther down the street several Roxbury Letts were distributing copies of *The*

New England Worker with articles denouncing the Boston press and calling for an immediate general strike.

The policemen did their best to keep up their spirits, but it was an increasingly forced effort. First, by a unanimous rising vote they pledged themselves to retain membership in the AFL and to do everything in their power to bring about their reinstatement. Then McInnes informed them that since he was no longer a member of the force, he could no longer preside over the meeting. He and his eighteen fellow officers offered their resignations. At once they were re-elected, again by a unanimous rising vote. Arrangements were then made to send a guard of honor to the funeral of Patrolman Reemts, the charges against him having been labeled fabrications. Delegates subscribed almost a thousand dollars for his family. For the rest of the evening speaker after speaker denounced Curtis and his order of that morning. At the end of the meeting the men filed out of the hall into the range of the machine gun, laughing and singing the wartime favorite, "Pack Up Your Troubles in Your Old Kit Bag."

McInnes himself was neither laughing nor singing as he left the hall. Stern-faced, more radical than he had ever been before, he told reporters that "the policemen are not wavering as in the false reports from the monied interests now so forcibly trying to deprive us of our American freedom. In the home and hearth of the policemen we remain undaunted in our struggle for the recognition of our union and our right to affiliate with the A.F. of L." But by the very tone of his voice the reporters sensed that he had come to doubt his cause.

By Saturday the pied khaki and olive drab of the state guard, the rifle and fixed bayonet had become taken for granted as part of the Boston scene. For the city, obviously and firmly under control, it was like awakening after a nightmare to the reassurance of daylight. Strollers again walked casually across the Common. Saturday morning shoppers took the el in from the suburbs. The stores, for all their shattered windows, did a rushing business. Under the shadow of Faneuil Hall the pushcart vendors held their weekly open-air market. Traffic under the direction of guardsmen and converted auto salesmen seemed to move more smoothly than it had before the riots. The danger points of Tuesday and Wednesday remained passive, inert. In South Boston a furtive figure threw a brick through the Waldorf Lunch window, one of the few intact windows on West Broadway. Nothing more. There was even less to report on Scollay Square, still occupied by a guard company with stacked arms. Loiterers, few in number, were urged on at bayonet point. Clusters of curious bystanders waited in front of the downtown police stations to see the soldier reliefs fall in, as if they were watching a ceremonial changing of the guard, but there was no hostility. Spectators lustily applauded as two battalions of the Twentieth Regiment went through close-order drill on the Common. Superintendent Crowley had forbidden open-air rallies "or anything calculated to draw a crowd." He now closed the all-night restaurants to disperse the "floating night population."

Trucks, blankets, uniforms, and additional equipment, even riot guns on loan by the state of Vermont, kept arriving in the city. The adjutant general was buying up boots at nine dollars a pair, the highest ever paid for army boots in the history of the state. Obviously the guard was preparing for a long stay. Understrength units filled up quickly. So eager were many recruits for this novel adventure that former officers even joined up as privates. The First Troop of Cavalry had two of its former captains serving in the ranks. In their summer encampments the guardsmen were allowed $.45 a day ration allowance. This was now raised to $1. Their daily base pay was $1.55. The Employers' Association of Eastern Massachusetts, comprising several thousand firms, announced that all members of the association would pay full wages to their employees on duty as guardsmen. A Fund for the Defenders of Public Safety was started to help the loyal police and their dependents and/or the families of less-favored guardsmen who might suffer through the absence of the breadwinner. Boston matrons who during the war had run Victory Court, the soldiers' and sailors' canteen on the Common, now reopened it for the members of the state guard.

Quickly, with makeshift ease, the guardsmen settled in for what seemed initially a lark, a novel exercise in authority before it became routine and finally a bore. Some eight hundred of the Twentieth Regiment, barracked in Faneuil Hall, were forced to make do with the decrepit single-gas-stove kitchen of the Ancient

and Honorable Artillery Company, while those who could not fit in
there found themselves in the easier quarters of the City Club. The
cooks at the huge East Armory kitchen began to prepare hot meals
for distribution at the various police stations. Nevertheless, in the
first day or two of mobilization, many guardsmen had to subsist on
coffee and doughnuts or sandwiches that they could snatch up
quickly at one-arm lunch rooms. The managers of the Waldorf cafeteria chain advertised that all guardsmen would be served at half
price. Company A's Flying Twenty at the Roxbury Crossing station
had to make shift with a secondhand gas stove to cook their meals.
The rest of the company, at Dudley Street, fared better after Captain Crowell commandeered the Waldorf Lunch across the street.
About a thousand men of the Eleventh Regiment were billeted in
the South Armory, where they slept on the ground on sacks they
themselves stuffed with straw. Not for another month would they
get cots. From the armories patrols were sent out for street duty
wherever needed. At first there were the inevitable confusions.
Chilled and hungry guardsmen found themselves patrolling without relief. Harry Cross went on duty at the corner of Summer and
Winter Streets at four in the afternoon and was not relieved until
eight the next morning. Company I of Lawrence was kept on con-
tinuous duty around City Hall for twenty-one hours. Such lapses
were soon corrected. By Saturday routine schedules had been
established by the guardsmen—eight hours of walking beats, sixteen hours in reserve, with three hot meals a day and sandwiches
and coffee brought to each man on street duty.

   In South Boston guardsmen of the Tenth Regiment were quartered in the two police stations and in the Municipal Building.
Colonel Sullivan set up portable messes on a vacant lot near the D
Street gymnasium and on Emerson Street to feed his five hundred
men. Within the nineteen police districts units were moved about
like pawns. Sergeant Hermann's Newton squad, after two days in
South Boston, found itself quartered in the Roxbury Boys' Club
and assigned to patrol the area of Roxbury's Station 9 along with
Captain Crowell's earlier arrivals. Sergeant John Underhill of
Newton's belatedly mustered Company B was quartered in
Mechanics Building and attached to Station 16 on Boylston Street.
His routine became as typical and uneventful as that of most of the

guardsmen called to duty. From four in the afternoon until midnight he and his men patrolled the Back Bay, from the Public Gardens to Huntington Avenue and beyond. The following day they covered the same route from midnight to eight in the morning. This alternation they would continue for the next six weeks.

Once bedded down and secure in rations, the guardsmen began to give some thought to recreation. Captain J. Randolph Coolidge, Jr., back from a year and a half abroad with the army engineers, started an entertainment program. Each armory soon had its evening moving-picture show. To those off duty the Shubert Theatre trust offered several hundred free tickets for the Wilbur and Plymouth theaters. On Saturday afternoon the men at the First Corp Cadet Armory organized an indoor baseball game. The various regimental and unit chaplains arranged services for Sunday.

Saturday, for all its apparent calm and orderliness, was still to take its toll of casualties. The fledgling soldiers showed themselves not only awkward in handling their weapons but occasionally—as in Jamaica Plain on Thursday night—trigger-happy. Sometimes the incidents were merely comic, as when a guardsmen at the corner of Milk and Federal Streets, on giving his officer a rifle salute, accidentally fired off the rifle. No one was injured. In South Boston a sergeant of the Tenth Regiment shot himself in the hand as he was demonstrating the stripping of a revolver, and a private in the Fifteenth Regiment wounded himself in the leg in cleaning his rifle. Such occurrences might be considered inevitable when large numbers of semitrained men are given weapons, but others could not be dismissed so casually, for one man was to die on the streets of Boston before the placid-seeming day was over, four other persons would be shot, and one would receive a bayonet slash in the cheek when he tried to snatch a rifle from a guardsman in front of Keith's Theatre on Tremont Street. The dead man was twenty-one-year-old Gustave Geist, who had served overseas with the Thirtieth Engineers. Geist, for no apparent reason, got into a violent argument with a guardsman at Brimstone Corner just before noon. As he raised his hands to grab the guardsman's rifle, another guardsman on the opposite corner dashed across the street and fired several shots at him. Geist fell dead near the subway entrance. A passerby, forty-two-year-old Mary Jacques, was hit in the knee and taken to the Haymarket Relief Station. Later in the day James McCourt of the South End was shot in the ankle by a guardsman he had challenged. In the North End, a small boy, Michael Russo, was hit in the left forearm by a stray bullet when overapprehensive guardsmen broke up an adolescent crap game. Saturday's final shooting took place in the evening as James Donnelly, twenty-two, was caught attempting to steal a car near the corner of Beach and Washington Streets. After he refused to obey the order to get out of the driver's seat, a guardsman shot him through the chest, the bullet piercing his right lung.

Sunday there were no more casualties. Crowds of sightseers came into the city to look over the damage and gape at the citizen-soldiers who had replaced the police. Throngs of friends and relatives crowded into the armories and stations to talk with the guardsmen not on duty. The strike was the principal topic of Boston sermons, and in almost every pulpit the police were condemned either directly or by implication. South Boston's St. Augustine's, St. Vincent's, and Gate of Heaven churches echoed with their priests' denunciation of the rioters, and though the police were not specifically mentioned, the congregations—with many a striking policeman squirming in his pew—understood that they were included in the denunciation. Cardinal O'Connell refused even to listen to any strikers' appeal. Episcopal Bishop William Lawrence, representing Brahmin Boston ex officio, condemned the erring police out of hand. The Reverend Dr. Edward Cummings of the Arlington Street Church, speaking for the Unitarians, accused them of betraying both organized labor and the public they had taken an oath to protect. At Episcopal Trinity Church on Copley Square the rector, the Reverend Dr. Arthur Mann, deplored the "muddy thinking" that led the police to believe they could serve two masters. Dismissing the matter of working conditions and the question of the union as irrelevant, he held that the strike posed the question of whether Americans would be governed by laws controlled by "constituted authority" or "controlled by some irresponsible organization." From Boston to the suburbs and beyond, the pulpit messages—backed by appropriate texts—were condemnatory. One had to go as far as St. Patrick's Church in Fall

River, forty-eight miles to the south, to hear Bishop James Cassidy speak the single clerical good word for the striking policemen.

Beyond Massachusetts, across the United States, luridly exaggerated reports of mob rule in Boston, of machine guns turned on crowds, of insurrection verging on civil war made the strike seem the climax of a perilous year, more ominous even than the Seattle strike because in Boston the law itself had abdicated. Haunting fears of Bolshevism, of revolution spreading from the streets to the seat of government, gripped the hearts and minds of ordinary Americans, who only ten months before had been hailing the war's end with such joyful optimism. "The situation in Boston is of the gravest kind," Senator Lodge wrote on Friday to his daughter, Mrs. Augustus Gardner. "It is a tremendous issue, and if the American Federation of Labor succeeds in getting hold of the police in Boston it will go all over the country, and we shall be in measurable distance of Soviet government by labor unions. I have faith to believe that the American people will not stand for it. It is hard to tell much at this distance but I think public opinion seems right and will win." Lodge's premonitions were echoed by editors and business and political leaders from coast to coast. Wilson in Spokane, Washington, continued to denounce the strike, calling it evidence of the "poison of unrest that is spreading to America from Europe."

Yet, whatever the extent of the violence, the rioting in Boston appeared chaotic, without a focal point, a blur of names and figures. Only after three days did an identifiable presence emerge in the resolute figure of the governor of Massachusetts. So it seemed from a distance. That was the way the press played it up. No one bothered to ask what the governor had been doing for the last month, what indeed he was still doing. When the ship of state had begun to founder, a leader appeared. That was enough. Hundreds of telegrams arrived at the State House congratulating Coolidge— from governors and United States senators, from the American Legion, the Masons, Granges, the Massachusetts Insurance Exchange, the Massachusetts Real Estate Exchange, chambers of commerce, business organizations, and the solid, articulate middleclass groups of middle America. Novelists Margaret Deland and Booth Tarkington added their approbation. A week before, scarcely anyone beyond Massachusetts had heard of Calvin Coolidge. Now he appeared full blown as a legend, his sharp-eyed Yankee features staring from front pages, a laconic presence, folksy, appealing, the minuteman from Vermont translated to Massachusetts. Round him sentiment rallied, coalesced. Who is this man Coolidge, they asked, the granite-faced Yankee with the quaintly nasal voice out of the New England past, the governor who still lived in a two-family house—as if the question answered itself. Across Washington they asked it, throughout the government departments, in clubs and hotels. Senators and congressmen buttonholed their Massachusetts colleagues to learn more about this governor. On Capitol Hill the talk was all of Coolidge, Democrats showing themselves as enthusiastic as Republicans. With little or no concern for facts, he was hailed as "the man who defied Bolshevism and more." The Coolidge myth sprang up almost overnight, rapidly eclipsing the man.

When Gompers on Saturday afternoon was told that Curtis had declared the posts of the striking policemen vacant, he muttered ominously, "I suppose he is willing to assume the responsibility for the consequences of his action." Then he gave out a prolix apologia, claiming that the unionization of the Boston police was not the AFL's doing but the "'natural reflex' of futile attempts by the policemen to improve their working conditions." Curtis, he reiterated, was the real culprit, since he "at any time might have honorably settled the dispute.... Even now vested with individual autocratic authority with which even the governor states he has no power to interfere, he declared the places of approximately 1400 policemen vacant. Surely there is some weight of justice in Boston that will prevent this individual whose vision and interests do not extend beyond the scope of the Boston Police area from openly antagonizing the great American labor movement." Gompers ended with the implied threat that "if the authorities give no consideration to the human side of the question or to the advice and suggestion which I had the honor to make, then whatever betide is upon the head of the authorities responsible therefore."

Before going on to his father's funeral, he drafted an answer to Coolidge's telegram, declaring that "the question at issue is not one of law and order, but the assumption of an autocratic and unwarranted position by the Commissioner of Police who is not responsible to the people of Boston, but who is appointed by you. Whatever disorder has occurred is due to his order in which the right of the policemen has been denied, a right which has heretofore never been questioned." He then appealed to the governor "to honorably adjust a mutually unsatisfactory situation in accordance with the suggestions by the President of the United States in a similar case.... May I not further appeal to you," he concluded, "to take a broad view of the entire situation and give the opportunity for cool deliberate consideration when the passions aroused shall have subsided."

Reading this over, Coolidge with his innate political awareness realized that Gompers had blundered into a web of his own spinning. Sunday, with Secretary Long at his side, he sat in his office in the empty State House drafting his answer with methodical slowness on heavy block paper, phrase by phrase, sentence by sentence. After he had finished, he showed it to Attorney General Wyman, who read it through but made no suggestions. Long then telephoned in the text to the telegraph office, taking care to send copies to the newspapers in time for the early Monday morning editions. In words as spare as the hill country of his native Vermont, in sentences devoid of the McKinley-baroque oratory of his contemporaries, Coolidge in unforgettable phrases justified his police strike actions.

> Replying to your telegram [he told Gompers], I have already refused to remove the Police Commissioner of Boston. I did not appoint him. He can assume no position which the Courts would uphold except what the people have by the authority of their law vested in him. He speaks only with their voice. The right of the police of Boston to affiliate has always been questioned, never granted, is now prohibited. The suggestion of President Wilson to Washington does not apply to Boston. There the police remained on duty. Here the Policemen's Union left their duty, an action which President Wilson described as a crime against civilization. Your assertion that the Commissioner was wrong cannot justify the wrong of leaving the city unguarded. That furnished the opportunity; the criminal element furnished the action. There is no right to strike against the public safety by anybody, anywhere, any time. You ask

that the public safety again be placed in the hands of these same policemen while they continue in disobedience to the laws of Massachusetts and in their refusal to obey the orders of the Police Department. Nineteen men have been tried and removed. Others having abandoned their duty, their places have, under the law, been declared vacant in the opinion of the Attorney General. I can suggest no authority outside the Courts to take further action. I wish to join and assist in taking a broad view of every situation. A grave responsibility rests upon all of us. You can depend upon me to support you in every legal action and sound policy. I am equally determined to defend the sovereignty of Massachusetts and to maintain the authority and jurisdiction over her public officers where it has been placed by the Constitution and laws of her people.

Featured on Monday's front pages from coast to coast, the telegram confirmed Coolidge as a national figure, a sudden folk hero. One sentence burned itself into the popular awareness: "There is no right to strike against the public safety by anybody, anywhere, any time." Those blunt one- and two-syllable words leaped out of the page.* Repeated, reiterated, they became part of the public vocabulary, a slogan that would head its maker toward a destiny far beyond Massachusetts. The response was like a whirlwind. All over the land men and women, from the famous to the unknown, dashed off letters and telegrams to express their admiration for the champion of law and order. Sixteen deliveries a day were not enough to bring the laudatory mail to the State House. The governor's staff was swamped in trying to get out replies. Telegrams arrived by the thousands; telephone lines were jammed by eager well-wishers.

The strikers were now looked on as their country's enemies, as base and evil as the wartime Germans. Their grievances were not considered worth discussing. No issue remained but the challenge to authority and Coolidge's response. "The nation has chosen," the Philadelphia *Evening Public Ledger* editorialized. "If it was ever vague in its conception of the Bolshevik horror, the vision is clear-cut now." The *Ohio State Journal* felt that the striking policemen "should consider themselves lucky if they are permitted

---

* They would eventually find their way into most dictionaries of quotations.

to escape with only the loss of their positions. When a policeman strikes, he should be debarred not only from resuming his office, but from citizenship as well. He has committed the unpardonable sin; he has forfeited all his rights." Democratic Senator Charles Thomas of Colorado, eulogizing Coolidge on the floor of the United States Senate, told his fellow senators, "It is to such men that we must look for the preservation of American institutions," and he asked that Coolidge's telegram to Gompers be inserted in the *Congressional Record*.

While Gompers prepared to leave on Sunday evening for Washington, his secretary, the oddly named Guy Oyster, was making ready to take the midnight express for Boston with Frank McCarthy, who had come to New York the day before, ostensibly to attend the elder Gompers's funeral. The AFL head had taken him aside and told him flatly that there was not going to be a general strike in Boston and that he had better get back in a hurry and explain this fact of life to the BCLU and the Russell Club. Oyster, a head taller than Gompers, was a dapper, not to say sportive presence, from the cut of his sleek double-breasted suit to the moiré bow tie that set off his high collar. Square-jawed, his wavy hair parted in the middle, his fingernails ostentatiously manicured, he looked less like a labor official than a reincarnation of Richard Harding Davis's Van Bibber. Meeting him, one had the uneasy feeling of having seen him somewhere before, until one suddenly remembered—the Arrow-Collar Man! Deftly, urbanely, he stood beside the stubborn Gompers, guiding him as one might guide an irascible uncle. To the reporters who flocked to AFL headquarters after word of Coolidge's Sunday message, Gompers said that he had sent a telegram in reply. Oyster interrupted emphatically to say that the telegram had been rescinded. "Yes," said Gompers lamely, "it has been rescinded." Then Oyster, as he left for Boston, glanced down at his manicured nails and murmured, "There will be no general strike."

When Oyster and McCarthy arrived at the South Station early Monday morning, they were met by O'Donnell and Jennings. On seeing Oyster, the other two could scarcely trust their eyes—his pearl-grey hat, his double-breasted suit with the jacked-up shoulders, his yellow gloves, and—to top it off—spats and a malacca cane. A dude no less! In the obsolescent term of their younger days, a lounge lizard! The four walked to AFL headquarters in the Kimball Building. Oyster, swinging his cane jauntily, did not fail to notice the red-and-black IWW stickers pasted on many of the poles. At the mention of a general strike, his all-American face turned hard. "That would be," he told the others, "most unfortunate."

Vahey and Feeney were waiting for them at headquarters. For the inner circle of labor leaders the question of union affiliation and the redress of grievances had already become subordinate to the cold practical problem of how to help the striking policemen retain their jobs. An AFL official in New York had already let reporters know that Gompers "does not want a general strike and the Federation does not want a general strike." One of the purposes of Oyster's visit was to relay this message even more bluntly to the firemen. After a by-now ritual denunciation of Curtis, the lawyers discussed the possibility of getting the police reinstated through court action, but it seemed a forlorn hope, scarcely worth pursuing. While the leaders and their lawyers conferred, Richard Reemts's funeral was being held at St. Joseph's Church in Roxbury. The pallbearers were officers of the policemen's union. A hundred striking patrolmen formed a guard of honor. After the service the men, all in civilian clothes, stood in line at either side of the church entrance as the coffin passed.

At midday McCarthy, O'Donnell, Jennings, and the dapper Oyster were joined by McInnes in Pemberton Square for their conference with Curtis. Briefly they reproposed Gompers's terms: the police to return at once to duty, and no further action to be taken until after the October 6 Washington conference. The commissioner listened to them, aloof and silent. "I have heard whatever you may have wished to say to me," he wrote immediately afterward to O'Donnell in a letter that he at the same time made public. "The action which I have taken is the only one I could take under the law and the obligations of my office. I shall be guided in further official action by the same requirements of the law in every particular. It is to be always remembered that I exercise only those authorities which the law of the Commonwealth have imposed upon me. I could not even if I would permit any other considerations to control or direct my action."

Curtis felt much encouraged by the mail he was receiving praising his stand. Heads of firms wrote him to say they were gladly paying the differences in salary for their employees in the state guard. Others were organizing a committee for various kinds of assistance. An optician offered free eye examinations to prospective policemen. Again and again writers expressed their fears of a total breakdown in the government if the strike succeeded. Through the letters ran a streak of nativism. "Would it not be a fine thing," E. L. Thompson of Baldwinville, Massachusetts, wrote, "when appointing new police officers to select a few old-fashioned Yankees—full blooded Americans on the force to instil a little Americanism into the situation? There seems [sic] to be altogether too many Irishmen in these positions to impart the true Americanism which we so much need in these trying times." James Grimes of Boston urged the commissioner to "discharge every one of the strikers and go back in the country towns and get some husky Yankee boys to put in their places. Good Americans and Yankees do not strike. The Public is with you." A. H. D., who preferred to shelter behind his initials, admired Curtis's courage "to stand out with that bunch of Irishmen." A scattering of union members wrote in their congratulations, but there were few Irish names among them. What Curtis most prized was a telegram from the faculty of Bowdoin College praising his handling of the strike as "in accordance with the best traditions of your college, the kind of courageous citizenship which Bowdoin has endeavored to teach her sons."

Later in the afternoon, Oyster and his reluctant labor associates conferred with Peters at City Hall. But the mayor told them no more than that he could do nothing for them, since the governor's action had placed matters beyond his control. McInnes and his union officers still pinned their final hope on union solidarity. Mae Matthews had come running to him as he left the commissioner's office to assure him that the telephone girls were massively behind the police. The firemen's vote on Tuesday would be crucial, but had not Looney, their president, promised that what the police demanded of them they would deliver?

On Tuesday morning, Oyster talked on the telephone for a long time with Gompers, still in Washington. What they said remained a secret, but following consultation of Oyster with union officials the scheduled meeting of the firemen's union was canceled. The counsel for the union, former Assistant District Attorney Thomas Lavelle, then stated that "the firemen have not voted on the question of a general strike. They will not vote. There is no need. They have decided not to strike and they have decided not to participate in any way in a general strike." Suddenly the fire-breathing firemen, who the week before had been raging like lions, turned meek as lambs. Their formal statement declared that

> There is a provision in the constitution of this association which provides as follows:
> "It shall be deemed inadvisable to strike, or take active part in strikes, as our position is peculiar to most organized workers, as we are formed to protect the lives and property of the communities in case of fire or other serious hazards."
> This position we shall keep. Organized labor and its representatives have not sought to change that position and we make this statement so that the public may know just where the firemen stand. If it tends in any way to allay fears of a firemen's strike, we want to emphasize it in large letters.

The statement concluded with expressions of sympathy for the police and the hope that "a calm and careful survey of present events when it is made, as undoubtedly it will be made, will take the human element into consideration with reference to the Boston police and their strike."

Firemen were swayed as well by certain practical considerations, not the least of which was the volunteer fire-fighting force formed from the state guard, First Motor Corps, and instructors from the Massachusetts Institute of Technology. Then, too, many firemen had been so harassed by false alarms and hostile crowds during the two nights of disorder that their sympathy for the striking police had soured. In addition, there were minor but telling incidents such as the wrecking of a newsstand run by a fireman's widow across the street from a fire station.

Taking their cue from the firemen, the other unions of the BCLU proceeded to backtrack vigorously. The telephone operators, who had been balloting all that day, now decided to withhold the results of their balloting and to strike only in case of "a general strike ... not confined to any particular group of unions." Other unions followed suit. The bartenders, the Hebrew traders' union, the electrical workers, and the rest were willing to take action, but only if the others did. No one union expressed any wish to start a sympathy strike on its own. The Boston typographical union referred the strike question to its various chapels. Members of the municipal sewer workers' union declared themselves unalterably opposed to a general strike. Earlier in the week the carmen, in a mass meeting at Fay Hall, self-righteously announced that they owed their first duty to the public and hence could not strike.

McCarthy still insisted that the policemen's struggles for "right and justice" would continue "until victory perches on their banner." At the same time Oyster, Vahey, and Feeney renewed talk with police union officers about petitioning for a writ of mandamus to demand reinstatement for the discharged men. In a Wednesday afternoon press release, Oyster described the policemen as the "finest body of men as ever I saw. Three hundred of them ex-doughboys in Uncle Sam's army, and their president, John F. McInnes, the proud possessor of four honorable discharges from the U.S. army, and four wounds received while fighting under the Stars and Stripes, now being called 'deserters' because they had the manhood and the courage to strike, after two weeks' notice, for their human rights and constitutional guarantees, after being assured by the statements of the police commissioner that any situation caused by the form of protest then adopted, could and would be taken care of."

He did admit, however, the impossibility of a general strike of Boston's organized labor. His chief would not come to Boston, Oyster explained loftily, because "the situation is sufficiently delicate without implicating matters." On leaving that evening on the *Federal Express* for Washington to report to Gompers, he called out to waiting newspapermen, "You can say that we [the AFL] are a hundred per cent behind these policemen in their fight to maintain their rights as American citizens and that we will be with them to the finish." What he meant by this enigmatic pledge no one really understood, least of all the striking policemen.

Oyster's weasel words, the firemen's broken pledge, and the backtracking by other unions meant that any real chance of a successful outcome to the police strike was gone. Talk of court action, the only alternate recourse left, was a mere whistling in the dark. Public opinion had congealed in anger against the police, and that anger—fanned by the press—was something the other unions had no wish to court. Coolidge underlined this on Wednesday in a letter to Fire Commissioner Murphy thanking the firemen for their "loyalty to the city in its time of need." At a press conference in the afternoon an out-of-town reporter asked him if he had not "always been a friend to the working man since becoming governor." Coolidge replied wryly that he had signed every bill that had come before him for the benefit of the working people, "except to raise the pay of the members of the legislature."

While the unions were disengaging themselves from the police imbroglio, Curtis continued his preparation for enlisting a new force. Replacements for those passing their summer examinations had been negligible, and the commissioner needed a thousand additional recruits. On Friday he placed advertisements in all the Boston papers asking prospective volunteers to report Monday morning to former Superintendent Pierce at Kingsley Hall in the Ford Building on Beacon Hill. Determined to tighten discipline, he amended Rule 40, which had allowed him to punish members of the force only by discharge, a reprimand in general orders, reduction in rank, or punishment duty. He now restored fines or suspension up to thirty days in his list of punishments—something that O'Meara had eliminated because of the hardship to the men's families. He also announced that the new force would have a new uniform of a more modern cut, with a short tunic and a military-type visor cap to replace the high-domed helmet. Then he sent loyal policemen to the homes of the strikers to collect their brass uniform buttons, the property of the department.

Even as the commissioner's advertisement appeared in the papers, forty-six Metropolitan Park patrolmen were appearing on trial before the Metropolitan Commission, charged with refusing to go on street duty in Boston on September 9. The next day, nineteen of them were dismissed from the service; the other twenty-seven, being found guilty of insubordination, were merely reprimanded and fined thirty days' pay. There was no further talk among the park police of solidarity with their striking brothers.

That afternoon McInnes, in an effort to persuade ex-servicemen not to join the new police force, spoke to the All-Dorchester Post of the American Legion at the Strand Theatre, Uphams Corner. He charged that the attempt to recruit a new force from servicemen was meant to split the ranks of labor. "Are you going to keep a Kaiser licked," he asked the legionnaires, his voice hoarse from days of speaking, "or are you going to keep a Kaiser in existence? Are you going to take the bread and butter out of the mouths of the men who fought with you?"

On that very afternoon, President Wilson sent a telegram from California to the commissioners of Washington, D.C., saying that the organizing of the police forces of the country to bring pressure against the public "should not be countenanced or permitted." Harvard's President Lowell at about the same time made public the "pride of the university in the men who did duty during the police strike." Vahey and Feeney, announcing that they had given up any attempt at legal action, made public an indignant letter they had written to Peters, Curtis, Herbert Parker, and Storrow demanding that they tell the truth about how and why the compromise plan was turned down. The letter had little effect. The striking police were scapegoats.

This was unhappily clear to the members of the BCLU gathering at Wells Memorial Hall on Sunday. Their meeting was the largest in the central union's history. Every seat was taken, and delegates wedged themselves onto windowsills and in odd niches, even on the fire escapes. President O'Donnell, after calling the meeting to order for some brief routine business, turned it over to his vice-president and retired to the BCLU's general offices on the floor above with the committee of seventeen and representatives of the police union. There they remained in seclusion for an hour and a half while various delegates reported on the actions taken by their unions. Six young women delegates then took up a collection for the police, and $220.30 was donated. As the speakers droned on unheeded, all eyes kept fixed on the closed door at the end of the hall. There was a sign of anticipatory relief when the door finally opened and the committee, led by O'Donnell, filed in. Congratulating the delegates, the president admitted that the member locals—he did not name them—had almost all declared their willingness to respond to a general strike if the BCLU demanded it. Nevertheless, he and the committee had decided that "the time is not opportune for ordering a general strike." O'Donnell tried to palliate the reversal by telling the delegates that they must realize that "the eyes of the nation are upon this meeting today—for this and other reasons we are to act in a manner that will not give the prejudiced press or the autocratic employers a chance to criticize us.... We don't intend to give anybody a chance to say we have not used good judgment, as has been said of the police." Resignedly the delegates voted to accept the committee's recommendations. From now on they were willing to continue to give the police "their moral and financial support"—but nothing more.

Doubt and dismay were spreading among the strikers in spite of McInnes's bold words. Edward Kelleher, a striking policeman who had been three times wounded as a soldier overseas, told reporters:

> I want to say that I joined the union because we could not get our grievances redressed, or even listened to, any other way.
>
> I didn't want to strike, and I don't know any other man who did want to. I went out because 19 men were discharged by the commissioner because I and the others had elected them officers of the union. They were no more guilty than I was and I wouldn't be yellow enough to leave them to be the goats for all of us. I'm proud of it.
>
> I wouldn't have gone on a strike if I thought the city was undefended and there was going to be a riot, and neither would the rest of the fellows.
>
> I want to go back to my work. I think it is honorable work. But I don't want to go back unless the whole crowd goes back.

Recruiting for the new force began on Monday morning. By eight-forty-five when the doors opened at Kingsley Hall, candidates had formed a long line in front of the Ford Building. A number of them still wore their army uniforms, and one man even appeared in the dress blues of a Marine Corps sergeant. They were first given a physical examination and then screened by an examining committee whose key question was, "Have you ever stated that in the event of a so-called strike of the Boston Police you would not accept a position?" Those who passed were sent to the State House to apply for noncompetitive civil service examinations scheduled for Friday.

By five o'clock, 180 aspirants had passed their preliminary tests. Guardsmen patrolled the Ford Building and the route to the State House all day, but there was no trouble either from the police or from organized labor.

Contributions for the striking police were niggardly, yet a quarter of a million dollars had already been raised for the guardsmen through the Fund for the Defenders of Public Safety. In the cold aftermath of the second week, destruction in the city appeared far less than the original heated estimates. Claims filed by merchants with the city clerk for damages amounted to only thirty-five thousand dollars. Monday also marked the beginning of the great steel strike, a labor struggle that overshadowed the dwindling news from Boston, even though there were rumors that Gompers might try to tie it in with the Boston strike.

Tuesday, September 23, was primary day in Massachusetts. Although the weather was seasonably mild, the voting was the lightest in years, the only extraordinary feature being the presence of guardsmen with bayonets at the polling places. Coolidge remained unopposed for the Republican nomination, as he had been the year before, but he received almost thirty-five thousand more votes than he had in 1918. His Democratic opponent was again Richard Henry Long, who had overwhelmingly defeated the elderly and discredited Old Boy Foss for the nomination with the tacit support of the Democratic leaders. They particularly favored Long, since he was ready to finance his own election campaign.

Coolidge, fortified by the primary results, was irritably aware of rumors, promoted by police-union officers, that there would still be a general strike, that Gompers would act after all, that the climax of the struggle was still in the offing. Blown about in gusts, the rumors were mostly the wishful thinking of defeated men, yet they created an uneasy mood in a city that would not readily forget those two nights of violence. Grasping at any straw now, the striking policemen saw Curtis's amendment to Rule 40 as a back-door way to their reinstatement; however, the commissioner scotched this the next day by announcing that his new rule did not apply to the strikers, who would never be reinstated. There was talk among the politicians at the State House and in City Hall of a belated compromise, hints that state and city officials would soon meet with union heads and that most of the policemen would be taken back, gossip that the canny Coolidge would not want to alienate the labor vote just before an election. McInnes predicted knowingly that his men would be back at work on Saturday. Coolidge himself feared that sentiment in the state might be turning against his stand, and he felt the need to justify himself against charges that he had been a tyrant.

The evening of the primaries he listened to the returns with Frank Stearns and William Butler in Stearns's library. The fussy Lord Lingerie had grown to be the governor's most intimate associate, his closest friend—if he could be said to have a friend—while Butler was a confidential adviser second only to Murray Crane. Yet never could Coolidge bring himself to call them by their first names, never break that formal barrier. They would remain "Mister" to him, while for them he was "Governor." As they sat tabulating the results that evening, Coolidge mentioned the movement to reinstate at least the more innocent strikers. Then he said with sudden vehemence: "This propaganda is still going on. I think I must say something publicly."

Neither Stearns nor Butler made any comment at the time, but Stearns mulled the matter over all night and at breakfast time he telephoned Butler. "I have thought the matter over and I believe the governor should say something," he told the other breathlessly. "I agree," Butler replied, "only tell him to make it strong!"

Fretful as ever, Stearns was waiting in the anteroom when Coolidge arrived at his office at nine o'clock. He told of what had been bothering him all night, of how he feared the strike might damage Coolidge's re-election chances and added, "If you do decide to speak, make it strong and, if proper, put it in the form of a proclamation by the governor, and then you will get the front page of the newspapers for it."

Cautiously Coolidge asked, "What does Mr. Butler think of it?"

Sterns, fiddling nervously with his expensive watch chain, answered, "Why not call him on the telephone and find out?"

After talking briefly to Butler, Coolidge turned to Stearns and said, "If possible, Mr. Butler is even stronger than you about it."

A glowingly relieved Stearns then trotted off to his Tremont Street department store. Within an hour Coolidge sent for him, gave him several typewritten pages, and remarked dryly, "That has gone to the newspapers. You can show it to Mr. Butler if you want to."

Stearns hustled down to Butler's State Street office and handed him the proclamation. Butler read it aloud, then, as he finished, remarked dubiously, "I wanted it strong, but he can't say that!"

"There's no help now," Stearns told him; "the newspapers have it."

Coolidge's statement was indeed front page news to vie with the national accounts of violence and death as two hundred seventy-nine thousand steelworkers left their jobs. The governor had proclaimed:

There appears to be a misapprehension as to the position of the police of Boston. In the deliberate intention to intimidate and coerce the government of this Commonwealth a large body of policemen, urging all others to join them, deserted their posts of duty, letting in the enemy. This act of theirs was voluntary, against the advice of their well wishers, long discussed and premeditated, and with the purpose of obstructing the power of the government to protect its citizens or even to maintain its own existence. Its success meant anarchy. By this act through the operation of the law they dispossessed themselves. They went out of office. They stand as though they had never been appointed.

Other police remained on duty. They are the real heroes of this crisis. The State Guard responded most efficiently. Thousands have volunteered for the Guard and the Militia. Money has been contributed from every walk of life by the hundreds of thousands for the encouragement and relief of these loyal men. These acts have been spontaneous, significant and decisive. I propose to support all those who are supporting their own government with every power which the people have entrusted to me.

There is an obligation, inescapable, no less solemn, to resist all those who do not support the government. The authority of the Commonwealth cannot be intimidated or coerced. It cannot be compromised. To place the maintenance of the public security in the hands of a body of men who have attempted to destroy it would be to flout the sovereignty of the laws the people have made. It is my duty to resist any such proposal. Those who would counsel it join hands with those whose acts have threatened to destroy the government. There is no middle ground. Every attempt to prevent the formation of a new police force is a blow at the government. That way treason lies. No man has a right to place his own ease or convenience or the opportunity of making money above his duty to the State.

This is the cause of all the people. I call on every citizen to stand by me in executing the oath of my office by supporting the authority of the government and resisting all assaults upon it.

Once more the press of the nation poured out its praise for the strong man from Massachusetts—as he seemed from afar. Coolidge's words had a tocsin ring: "There is no middle ground"; "That way treason lies"; "No man has the right ..."; "The cause of all the people ..."; brief, resounding phrases, blunt, direct. Such a man, many were soon saying, ought to be the next President of the United States. Without fully realizing the effect of his words, Coolidge had dramatized the issue, simplified it, turned it to a legend. After his proclamation the striking policemen, although they were slow to face the fact, had lost their last shred of hope.

AFTER
THE STRIKE

As if Coolidge's proclamation had not been sufficiently mortal, Gompers in Washington that same day gave the strikers what seemed to them the ultimate stab in the back. Speaking to the Senate Committee of the District of Columbia against a bill to withhold the salaries of policemen who affiliated with any labor organization, he defended the Boston police as sacrificial victims. Their strike had benefited the police all over the country, he told the senators, by calling attention to such matters as pay and working conditions, but he ended lamely by saying that he did not recognize the right of a police force anywhere to strike.

The governor's proclamation had stunned the Boston labor leaders. O'Donnell replied tentatively that the labor movement would answer it after the Storrow committee had made its report to the public. Feeney said he could not reply until he had read it more carefully. Vahey and McInnis were not accessible. McCarthy refused to discuss it. Finally Vahey and Feeney sent an open letter to Peters, Storrow, Curtis, and Parker calling for the truth about the strike and denying the still-current story that the union had been hostile to the compromise plan. Since their letter remained unanswered, they followed it up with a second letter to Peters and Storrow asking why they had not responded to the request for "a truth-telling party," complaining that the "police officers of Boston ... have been assailed with a ferocity, injustice and lack of Christianity unparalleled in our life time" and asserting that the governor's "slandering and villifying [sic]" of them as "traitors and deserters" was "as false as hell." The police were being made "the football of political greed and ambition." The letters and a long covering statement published at length in all the Boston papers drew only a feeble response within the city and scarcely any at all outside. Except for the police themselves the strike was over, done with, settled. Other things engrossed the public. President Wilson's collapse in the West took over the headlines. The steel strike with its growing violence commandeered the labor news.

After the first rush of candidates for the new police force there was a certain falling off in recruits at Kingsley Hall. Some held back out of fear that the old police might, as was rumored, soon get their jobs back. Strikers did their best to discourage and intimidate prospective patrolmen, threatening them as they stood in line before the Ford Building or harassing them at their homes. The governor's proclamation reassured the candidates and swelled their ranks. To increase the total still further Curtis requested the Civil Service Commission to expand the age limits from twenty-two to thirty-five years, lower the height minimum to five feet seven inches, and the weight to one hundred thirty-five pounds. Any such change required the approval of the governor's council and the governor, and usually took several bureaucratic months. But since the state guard was costing the Commonwealth twenty thousand dollars a day, everyone from the governor to the commissioner was anxious to set up a new police force as quickly as possible, and approval for Curtis's proposed modification came within a week. On September 24 the commissioner released the last of his civilian volunteers. Although his search for applicants outside of Boston was not very successful, by November he had in all five hundred recruits enrolled. Ten days later he discontinued his newspaper advertising. By the month's end his new force was almost complete, and by December 13 the last group of men sworn in brought the

total patrolman strength to 1574—more than had been on the force
when the strike began. Since the United Garment Workers in their
solidarity with the old police refused to make uniforms for the new,
many recruits had to go on duty in civilian clothes. Curtis shipped
three thousand yards of blue cloth from headquarters to an
unknown destination outside the state where, it was hinted, new
uniforms would be made by convict labor. Wherever they might be
made, Curtis expected to have all his men properly outfitted by
New Year's.

As the police in impotent anger watched their cause collapse,
they came to feel increasingly, beyond any question of grievances
or union affiliation, that what they wanted most was once again to
wear a policeman's uniform. Labor they now accused of betraying
them. Two weeks after the BCLU vote against a general strike, the
delegates met again at Wells Memorial Hall to discuss the police
situation. Three striking patrolmen who were not delegates—
Boston Social Club President Michael Lynch, Charles McGowan,
and John Mahoney—made their way into the hall and, after listening impatiently to a timeserving report by the committee of seventeen, stood up and furiously attacked the central union for its
failure to make good on its promise. Lynch shouted from the floor
that he wanted to know "where the organized labor movement
stood in relation to its pledge of full moral and financial support."
Mahoney asked what the BCLU had done to stop the opponents of
the policemen's union from poisoning the public mind. McGowan
reminded them that on the second day of the strike McCarthy had
told the police that "we would have to extend our lines and further
extend those lines if necessary to win the fight." Bitterly he concluded, "I am now satisfied that someone failed him."

The three impassioned patrolmen so stirred the delegates that
even on that belated date they were ready to vote a general strike.
President O'Donnell did his best to calm them down, assuring
his dubious audience that friends in high places were still working
hard for the police and were making real progress. McCarthy told
them that the situation was "unusually bright for the policemen"
and hinted that "something is about to drop that may result in
somebody, now seemingly all powerful, walking the plank."
Jennings explained soothingly that "the question now is one of

adjustment. The people who talk general strike are in my opinion not safe, sound or sure." O'Donnell kept the matter from coming to a vote, but he could not keep the rank-and-file resentment from spreading. The next day the police union members meeting in Fay Hall voted their confidence in the BCLU, but it was confidence in the Pickwickian sense.

After Coolidge's proclamation few expected the Storrow committee to issue any further statement, and in fact the committee, meeting a day later, voted not to make a public report. However, at Peters's request, on October 4 the committee members finally did issue their report, explaining that it would have been inopportune to release one earlier, "while the state was still engaged with the immediate tasks of asserting its sovereignty, defeating the strike and re-establishing law and order." The committee resolved "that the policemen of Boston were unjustified in leaving their post," and that they should not have been permitted to join an outside organization whose interests might interfere with their duty. Furthermore the committee "fully support the acts of the authorities in preserving law and order and toward defeating finally and conclusively the efforts to enforce by strike the right of the policemen to join the A. F. of L." Nevertheless the committee did admit that Curtis, and not the police union, had rejected the compromise and that Coolidge had stepped in only after order "had been generally restored." Placatingly if not wholly accurately the report concluded that

in justice to the commissioner it should be stated that at no time during the progress of the affair did counsel for the union or officers of the union or men upon trial take any position with the commissioner other than to insist upon continuing and retaining their membership in the union.

And in further justice to all parties it should be stated that the Governor, the Mayor, and the Commissioner, in the opinion of the committee, acted at all times from the highest motives and with but a single thought, namely the welfare of the Commonwealth and its people.

Vahey and Feeney were enraged by the report. Not only did they question the "highest motives" of the commissioner and the governor, but they denied that the union had insisted on retaining membership in the AFL. Several weeks later they challenged Coolidge, Curtis, Parker, and former United States Senator John W. Weeks—who publicly asserted that the police department had done much for the benefit of the patrolmen—to debate the following six topics with anybody the others might select before a bipartisan group of citizens interested in getting at the facts:

1. Who is responsible for the strike of the Boston policemen?
2. What was done to prevent it?
3. What was done to protect the lives and property of Boston citizens?
4. Did Commissioner Curtis grant relief to the policemen of Boston as stated by the Hon. John W. Weeks and if so what did that relief really amount to?
5. Should the striking policemen be restored to their jobs?
6. Are the striking Boston policemen deserters or traitors?

To this challenge there was no reply either from Pemberton Square or the State House.

Interest in the police strike would have subsided much sooner if it had not been for the November election, but with Coolidge inevitably cast as the law-and-order candidate, the strike became the central, in fact the sole, issue of the campaign. By pre-empting the conservatives and the moderates, the governor forced his opponent into an increasingly radical position. That acute Democratic journalist Michael Hennessy considered Coolidge "easily the most popular public figure in the State," whereas Long "was quite generally supported by the leaders of the police strike and their friends." The *New York Times* correspondent went even further, holding that among Long's adherents were "all the Bolsheviki, the Soviets, the I.W.W. . . . the striking policemen and all their disorderly followers." Charles Baxter of the Republican State Committee predicted that Coolidge would win by as much as fifty thousand votes.

Suffering from the after-effects of influenza, Coolidge made only a few speeches during the campaign. In the clipped generalities that came so readily to him, he defended his strike stand as if he were more concerned with the principles of free government than with party politics. "The forces of law and order may be dissipated," he told an applauding Republican State Convention; "they may be defeated; but as long as I am their commander-in-chief, they will not be surrendered." To an audience gathered to honor Theodore Roosevelt's sixty-first birthday, he grew even more emphatic. "We are facing an issue which knows no party," he said. "It is not new. That issue is the supremacy of the law. On this issue America has never made but one decision." He did not attack Long. He did not so much as mention his name. Only at the end of the campaign did he refer to "a rash man ... seeking to gain the honor of office by trafficking in disorder." To his fellow Republicans he explained that "the issue is perfectly plain. The government is seeking to prevent a condition which would at once destroy all labor unions and all else that is the foundation of civilization, by maintaining the authority and sanctity of the law. When that goes, all goes. It costs something, but it is the cheapest thing that can be bought." His earlier hesitancies forgotten, he insisted that once the policemen had struck he could give no "aid and comfort ... to support their evil doing." Yet, he continued, he was no foe of labor; in fact his administration had more than any other in the state's history "passed laws for the protection and encouragement of trade unions."

The rare speeches that Coolidge did make were received with tremendous enthusiasm. A decade later he wrote in his *Autobiography*: "Though I was hampered by an attack of influenza and spoke but three or four times, I was able to make the issue plain even beyond the confines of Massachusetts.... I felt at the time the speeches I made and the statements I issued had a clearness of thought and revealed a power I had not been able to express, which confirmed my belief that when duty comes to us, with it a power comes to enable us to perform it."

The Democratic platform had neither condemned nor condoned the strike, but the Democrats found it a touchy issue, one they preferred to keep at arm's length. They went so far as to admit that the police were wrong in leaving their post but balanced that by condemning Coolidge for his failure to protect the lives and property of the city of Boston. Long himself was more intemperate, stumping the state, and in increasingly violent language accusing

Coolidge and Curtis of deliberately goading the police into striking. "Governor Coolidge," he told one audience, "has shown himself to be the most helpless and incompetent governor that our
state has ever had." Nearly a hundred members of the policemen's
union campaigned for Long with desperate fervor, traveling about
the state to interrupt Coolidge rallies and heckle the speakers and
visiting factories to urge the workers to "get Coolidge" on election
day. Their wives and relatives formed a Women's Committee for
Public Safety to stir public opinion in favor of the discharged men
and to drum up votes for Long. Nevertheless, Long for some time
avoided saying whether or not he favored reinstating the police.
Finally Chairman Herman Hormel of Boston's Republican City
Committee pinned him down. Hormel demanded flatly to know
whether he as governor would restore the policemen to their old
posts. Long at last came out and said that he would.

In the last weeks of the campaign Long, stung by Coolidge's
steady disregard of his challenges, played the rabble-rouser. He
promised if elected to reinstate the struck policemen and remove
Curtis, to give all veterans of the World War a year's pay, and to
abolish the poll tax and force the rich to make up the difference in
revenue. Coolidge, he charged, was the governor for Standard
Oil and the beef trust, a coward who had hidden away during the
crucial stages of the strike, then afterward used "Prussian methods" to deal with it. As Long ranted, many of the Democrats who
heard him deserted their party. The supporters of Colonel Gaston
had in any case never forgiven Long for usurping the nomination
in 1918 and were only waiting for a chance to even the score.
Democratic papers such as the *New York Times*, the New York *World*,
the Boston *Post*, and the Springfield *Republican* crossed party lines
to endorse Coolidge. From all over the country attention again
focused on Massachusetts, where, it seemed, the final act of Law
versus Anarchy was about to be played out. Even the *New Republic*—besides the *Nation* the only journal that had any use for the
striking police or doubts about Coolidge—felt that Massachusetts
held the chief interest of the nation on election day. In the last
hours of the campaign ex-President Taft came on to speak for
Coolidge as did Governor Bartlett of New Hampshire and Allen of
Kansas and Senator Poindexter of Washington. Republican elders

Elihu Root and Nicholas Murray Butler telegraphed their support. Mayor Ole Hanson called from Seattle to tell the Republican State Committee that "the people of Massachusetts must stand by Coolidge." Senator Lodge, masking his personal distaste for Coolidge, struck a Verdun stance at the election eve rally in Tremont Temple, declaring dramatically that "they shall not pass!" Republican leaders were now predicting that Coolidge would carry the state by a hundred thousand votes.

On Sunday, November 2, two days before the election, sermons on the virtues of Coolidge resounded from Boston pulpits. The local papers each carried a full-page admonition that "*THE NATION WATCHES*," under which were printed the names of a dozen governors from Maine to California who were endorsing the Massachusetts governor. Next day an advertisement appeared in the form of a collage of the headlines of the *Herald*, *Post*, *Globe* and *American*, as they appeared during the strike. Above it windswept letters proclaimed, "*REMEMBER SEPTEMBER THE 9TH*," while at the bottom there loomed the warning, "*DON'T LET IT HAPPEN AGAIN! FOR LAW AND ORDER VOTE FOR CALVIN COOLIDGE.*"

On election day itself the *Herald* ran a cartoon of a steamer, "The Pilot Who Weathered the Storm" in which the frail slack-muscled governor was transformed into a sturdy figure in oilskins standing rather oddly in the bow rather than on the bridge of the steamer *Law and Order*. Not to be outdone, the Los Angeles *Times* ran an eight-column headline, "*REDS RUN ELECTION ISSUES —BATTLE IN BAY STATE*," and asked "Shall the state of Massachusetts be governed by law or mob rule?"

From the earliest returns on election night, it was clear that Coolidge was winning, but even the Republican optimists were astonished at the size of his victory. Carrying the entire Republican ticket with him, he defeated Long with 317,774 votes to the latter's 192,673, a majority of 125,101 and one of the most sweeping electoral triumphs in the history of the Commonwealth. That evening, when sufficient returns had come in to make his victory certain, he looked up for a moment at his associates with the thinnest of smiles. "Three words tell the result," he said in his most aphoristic manner. "Massachusetts is American!"

With the result finally tabulated, congratulations again poured in from all over the country. "A shining triumph for straight Americanism," the *Transcript* called the election. On the other side of the United States, the Los Angeles *Times* hailed it as "a defeat of the Soviets." Charles Evans Hughes, ex-President Taft, Will Hays, and other Republican luminaries added their good wishes. The *Herald* quoted from fifteen leading newspapers, all of them hailing Coolidge's victory as the triumph of law and order and the vindication of conservative principles against "violence and wild innovations." Republicans and Democrats in both houses of Congress applauded the Massachusetts outcome. Theodore Roosevelt, Jr., wired that "the American people have vindicated themselves by their support of you." Governor William Sproul of Pennsylvania found the result "a body blow to radicalism and irresponsible democracy." Nicholas Murray Butler thought it "a truly impressive victory of American principles." From his sick bed in the White House the stricken Wilson telegraphed: "I congratulate you upon your election as a victory for law and order. When that is the issue, all Americans stand together."

On election day the state guard was still on duty at the polling

"The Pilot Who Weathered the Storm"

places, motor corps guardsmen with white hat bands still directed traffic, but elsewhere in the city the brown uniforms were thinning out. From the original 4768 guardsmen called into service the total had increased in two weeks to 7567 officers and men. But by the end of September, as the threat of a general strike passed, the adjutant general had curtailed the enlistment drive.

With its uniformed presence the state guard had brought a brief renewal of wartime fervor and excitement, as if the guardsmen were the soldier boys of 1917–1918 all over again. Hospitality huts reopened on the Common. The YMCA, Salvation Army, and other social organizations distributed coffee, doughnuts, candy, gum, cigarettes, magazines, and newspapers, just as they had done during the war. There were state guard entertainments several times a week, as well as passes to the Shubert, Colonial, Boston, and Plymouth theaters. On September 21 a three-hour benefit performance was held at the Colonial Theatre with vaudeville turns, variety acts, and community singing. General Parker and his staff attended. Anything the guardsmen did was newsworthy. For weeks the daily papers were full of the casual details of what it was like to eat and live in an armory, what the men did for recreation, their various Sunday religious services, the small accidents and incidents of barrack life. Minor disturbances were blown up into major human-interest stories. There were special articles on the men's backgrounds, their families, and the personal hardships brought on by their enlistments.

Among the men themselves something of the holiday atmosphere of a summer encampment persisted. In their spare time those with a knack for such things wrote jingles and ditties or made up songs. There was usually one versifier to each company. After the messing problems were straightened out, guard life became freer as it became more routine. Many of the older men and those with families grew restive as the weeks passed, but most of the younger unmarried ones, in spite of the confinement and the incidence of "armory bronchitis," enjoyed their temporary authority. Harry Cross, now quartered at the Naval Service Club at the foot of Beacon Street, was one of them. He had been shifted to traffic duty just outside the South Station, conveniently near the Wentworth Lunch. Whenever four or five men came out of the lunchroom together, he would bring his rifle to the port and order them to "break it up!" He also kept people from loitering in doorways. At first he was on a daily eight-hour shift, but this was changed to four hours on and eight hours off. Every other week he had a forty-eight-hour pass. Sometimes a striking policeman would come up to him and in a quite friendly way give him a few tips on the district. There was no trouble at all.

The usual mishaps continued. A guardsman at Scollay Square accidentally fired off his rifle through a Painless Dentist sign, an incident his comrades labeled the Battle of the Signs. Ever since autos had first appeared in any number, Boston acquired a well-deserved reputation as the home city of the anarchic pedestrian. This, General Parker now decided to alter. One morning just after midnight the First Motor Corps spent four hours painting white lines at street corners from curb to curb—"Dead Lines" they were called, where motor vehicles must stop to let pedestrians cross. Crossing at any other point, Parker announced at guard headquarters next day, was forbidden. Jaywalking would cease!

The guardsmen's most pervasive complaint was that their families were suffering. Then, too, some employers were hinting they might have to discharge their absent guardsmen unless they returned to work. The adjutant general threatened legal action against such unpatriotic taskmasters. As for the families, the Fund for the Defenders of Public Safety had reached $500,514.22 by October 24.* Over a hundred thousand dollars were dispersed to the families of 516 guardsmen. At the same time, the trustees announced that they would give a $200 bonus to each nonstriking policeman. All the guardsmen had a flattering sense of having done their duty. They agreed fully with Governor Coolidge when he addressed a group of them at Faneuil Hall, conveying the people's gratitude for their service, which "spoke more eloquently than

* By 1959 the trustees had dispersed about $400,000 and they petitioned the state Supreme Court to terminate the trust by giving $75,000 to a police-administered athletic program for Boston's teen-agers, $90,000 to five hospitals for medical care of police officers and their dependents, and $10,000 to the Boston Police Relief Association. Surviving guardsmen and widows objecting, the court refused to grant the petition. In 1963 the fund still amounted to $191,900 in spite of annual disbursements of over $12,000. Grants continued to loyal policemen and their widows and to the guardsmen who "performed police functions during the crisis." By 1973 the fund had diminished to $90,150. Grants that year were $13,301.

words of the dignity and strength of the Commonwealth of Massachusetts." The mayor and other speakers said the same thing in more ornate language. In a more tangible expression of gratitude, the governor called a special session of the legislature, to raise the pay of the state guard from $1.55 to $4. a day and to make this retroactive from the day the guardsmen reported for duty.

On October 24 the guard received its first reduction in strength. Almost half the men were released. At Newton's Company A the men drew lots, those left behind calling themselves the Army of Occupation. Thirty-eight men remained in the South Armory of Company A's original seventy-one. On November 16 came a second cut and this time twenty-seven men marched away, leaving eleven of Company A in the Second Army of Occupation. On November 23 after a third cut, only three men remained, and in a few days they were ordered to their home station and placed in reserve. Finally on December 21, following a mustering-out parade of the First Motor Corps on Boston Common, the last units of the state guard were demobilized after 102 days of consecutive duty.

The day after his re-election, Coolidge wrote that he was willing to help the unemployed police to jobs "where they can bring forth works meet for repentance." He and Curtis encouraged the chamber of commerce to find places for the financially pressed patrolmen, few of whom had had any outside skills and many of whom now found themselves unable to support their often large families or keep up their rent or mortgage payments. The chamber set up a special committee to assist them. However, the men in their pride and anger wanted no "charity" from an organization they had found so hostile, and by a unanimous vote their union rejected the chamber's aid, making this statement: "Now you offer to get us jobs while at the same time you condemn us. If we are not fit for our jobs as policemen, we are not fit for any job and if you think you can put us in the position of accepting charity from you after the hypocrisy and double-crossing you have indulged in with us, all we can say is that you don't yet know the kind of men we are."

Nevertheless, Coolidge continued surreptitiously to do what he could for the stranded policemen, and they with quiet reluctance accepted his assistance. They had not many places to turn.

Employers generally were reluctant to hire them. Some of the men even conceived the notion of taking examinations for the new police force, but this notion was at once vetoed by the Civil Service Commission. Except for the six patrolmen who did not join the union and go on strike until after the initial walkout and who managed to retain their jobs on a technicality, none of the strikers were ever taken back. On October 15 at Fay Hall, the Women's Committee for Public Safety heard the English expatriate, Harvard professor Harold Laski, defend the striking police and denounce Curtis as the real deserter. But Laski's was a solitary voice. Labor support remained tepid. Not long after Coolidge's re-election the Boston firemen returned their union charter to the AFL's International Association of Firefighters. In a desperate reversal Vahey filed a petition with the Massachusetts Supreme Court for a writ of mandamus to compel Curtis to restore the nineteen discharged officers to the force, claiming that the commissioner's Rule 35 was "invalid and unreasonable, and contrary to the Constitution of the United States." On November 7 the court denied the petition. There were occasional briefer flurries. The day of Governor Coolidge's second inauguration, Samuel Gompers spoke at a luncheon of the Boston Chamber of Commerce and caused a sedate uproar when he accused Curtis of being responsible for the strike. A month later, on February 18, 1920, Feeney, testifying before the Legislative Committee on Metropolitan Affairs, gave Peters the credit for quelling the strike troubles and told the legislators that the policemen's union would have accepted the Storrow compromise plan.

The police union lingered on in a state of dormancy. At a meeting on February 22, McInnes resigned as president, saying that he was returning to his trade of bricklayer. In December the union became the Association of the Former Police of the City of Boston. Later it was absorbed into the Boston Social Club. Long before this, a majority of the discharged policemen had found other jobs for better or worse, though in the beginning generally for worse. Some became bank guards in the city, the State Street Trust Company alone refusing to employ them. Others joined the police forces in other parts of the state or even outside Massachusetts. For most of them the need of a job was so pressing that they took anything that came to hand. Thanks to another discharged colleague at Station 15 who had been a steam fitter, Frederick Claus became a steam fitter's assistant at Wellesley College, then a few months later a milkman for the Whiting Dairy Company. James Long, with two children at home, went round knocking on doors asking for work only to be turned down as a "striking cop" until finally he was taken on as a driver for the Bond Bread Bakery. Two children would have been only a prelude for Iron Mike Fitzgibbon's large brood in Mattapan. To provide for them he managed to get a job as a meatcutter on Blue Hill Avenue while all the time looking for another police post. Many were not even as lucky as Iron Mike. Walter Crocket was broken by his discharge. "He was never the same man again," his fifteen-year-old daughter Mildred wrote years later. "He was so proud of that uniform." For months he could find nothing to do, and to keep the family going his oldest daughter, Alice, had to leave high school to work as a messenger girl in a hospital at $7.50 a week. All he could get in the end was a job as an attendant at a Jenney filling station. Hundreds of the discharged men had similar fates. Yet though they had cast off the union, they still kept their cause alive in the Boston Social Club, and they refused to give up the hope of one day being vindicated.

Of the three principals in the police strike, Commissioner Curtis had the briefest further history, for he died on March 28, 1922. After the strike, in spite of his increasingly grave heart condition, he continued at his Pemberton Square office, seldom missing a day. With the zeal of a younger and healthier man, he reformed and reorganized his department. Every applicant had to be interviewed by him personally, every discharge had to be initiated by him. After his death the *Transcript* printed under his sternly Roman features: "No soldier in battle ever made a more gallant sacrifice than the head of the Boston Police Department, whose long career in public service was one of splendid achievement."

On a chill and glowering March afternoon, Curtis, in his office, had a sudden heart seizure that he must have sensed was fatal. Stoically saying nothing to anyone, he summoned his car and had himself driven home. On their reaching the house the chauffeur tried to help him out, but Curtis brushed him aside. "Don't take my arm until we get inside!" he ordered. Somehow he managed to walk up the steps unaided. Once the door closed behind him he collapsed, and died a few minutes later.

In the aftermath of the strike, while the state guard still patrolled the streets of Boston, the Union Club became an unofficial mess for its higher-ranking officers. General Parker and his staff dined there. At mealtimes the coat hooks in the dressing room were weighed down with Sam Browne belts and pistol holsters. Governor Coolidge arrived almost daily for lunch, accompanied by an extra bodyguard for the emergency. While he ate, his two guards would wait in the reception room with their revolvers on the table. A new attendant, George Simpson, one day gave the thin-lipped governor the customary brass check for his overcoat, which he indignantly refused to take. A governor was a governor! Coolidge's outside popularity did not penetrate within the club walls. Never did he speak to the waiters or any of the other help except to give an order. "Lemon-puss," they used to call him behind his back.

The police strike and Coolidge's stunning election victory left him a figure of national interest and national goodwill. More than once during the winter he was mentioned as a possible presidential candidate. Charles S. Baxter wrote in the November 5 edition of the *Transcript* that "Governor Coolidge now looms so large before the nation with his wonderful triumph and so impressive a verdict by the Massachusetts electorate behind him that he must be given serious consideration by the Republican Party in the selection of its national leaders for the presidential campaign of next year."

Frank Stearns opened his heart and his pocketbook at the prospect. Even before the election he had arranged with Houghton Mifflin to publish a selection of Coolidge's speeches under the title *Have Faith in Massachusetts*, and he himself bought over sixty-five thousand copies to distribute to libraries, schools, newspaper editors, and above all politicians. After the election he opened a Coolidge-for-President headquarters in Washington and was preparing to open one in Chicago when Coolidge issued a flat statement that he refused to enter any contest for delegates. He did not, he said, wish the governor's office to be used "for manipulative purposes." "I have not been and am not a candidate for president," he announced, to Stearn's chagrin. Yet the Massachusetts governor remained an enigma. Did he, after all, have secret presidential ambitions? Did he think by remaining an enigma he might be drafted? In his *Autobiography* he wrote, "I did not wish to use the office of Governor to prosecute a campaign for nomination to some other office." The *Herald* observed shrewdly: "Although Governor Coolidge has withdrawn as a presidential candidate, he remains available for dark horse purposes.... You can never tell what will happen at a convention. The Governor is among the possibilities."

As the months of 1920 moved on toward the Republican National Convention, General Leonard Wood was unquestionably the leading Republican candidate. A widely popular independent-conservative, scornful of politicians, the friend of the late Theodore Roosevelt, and the choice of the Roosevelt family, his nomination seemed inevitable. Branches of the Leonard Wood League were springing up all over the country. William Allen White saw him as "the political man of the hour." The pols, the party wheelhorses, and the old guard of the McKinley era did not. Wood might collect more delegates than any other candidate, but the politicians would do their best to see that he lacked a majority. The general's closest rival was the reform governor of Illinois, Frank Lowden, who was hampered not only by his independence of the party bosses but by his wealth and his marriage to the daughter of that notably unpopular capitalist George M. Pullman. Astute political observers saw the Wood and Lowden forces fighting each other to a standstill at the convention, and the weary delegates turning to a dark-horse candidate in the ensuing stalemate. Harry Daugherty, that wily Ohio political confidence man, was the first to sense this possibility. Long before the convention Daugherty had traveled round the country buttonholing Republican state leaders and city and county bosses, praising Wood and Lowden and local favorite sons to the skies while at the same time collecting second and third and fourth choices among prospective delegates for his own favored candidate, the amiably insignificant Senator Warren G. Harding of Ohio.

A few days before the convention's opening the *Literary Digest* poll placed Wood unassailably at the head of the list of possible nominees. Harding rated sixth, Coolidge seventh. But once the convention met, Daugherty's long-odds hunch proved uncannily accurate. The delegates, during four days in the smoke-heavy flatulent air of Chicago's barn-like Coliseum, with the temperature often above a hundred, sweated in frustration as Wood and Lowden canceled each other out in ballot after ballot. Sour and disgusted, short of funds and short of patience, the men on the floor had come to feel it might as well be the innocuous Harding, the second-third-fourth choice, as anyone. It was a feeling shared by a group of senate elders whose inconsequent discussion that night at the Blackstone Hotel would give rise to the "smoke-filled room" myth. But as George Harvey, in whose room the discussions were held, explained afterward, "Harding was nominated because there was nothing against him and because the delegates wanted to go home."

The demonstration following Harding's nomination the next day was more of relief than enthusiasm. Most of the delegates nursed the frustrated image of their own rejected candidate. There was still the minor matter of the vice-presidential candidate to consider. During the roll call on the final ballot, the senate hierarchs had huddled in a small alcove concealed under the speakers' stand and decided on the old Bull Mooser Senator Irvine Lenroot of Wisconsin. Besides being a trusted senator, Lenroot would add a progressive balance to Harding's machine conservatism. It was arranged that Senator Medill McCormick of Illinois would make the nominating speech, to be seconded by H. L. Remmel, an old-line politician from Arkansas. The word was passed along to the delegates, some of whom were already drifting out of the darkening hall.

Senator McCormick duly mounted the platform and in a perfunctory two-minute speech nominated Lenroot. The florid old-pro Remmel seconded the nomination. With contemptuous indifference the permanent chairman, Senator Henry Cabot Lodge, turned over the gavel to Ohio's hog-calling ex-governor Frank Willis; then he and McCormick left the platform. The vast Coliseum echoed to the tramp and shuffle of feet and the clatter of chairs as more and more of the delegates and onlookers in the galleries made their way toward the exits.

Scarcely anyone could catch what the speakers were saying, nor did it seem to matter. Suddenly on the far side of the hall a stocky, red-faced man bellowed for recognition. Affably, the substitute chairman recognized Wallace McCamant of Oregon, assuming that his was merely one more seconding voice for Lenroot.

There is a moment when the whip cracks and the animal, instead of jumping, turns on the ringmaster. Chairman Willis did not recognize that moment until it was too late. The voice from the floor was no casual approval of an accomplished fact. McCamant had angrily talked the matter over with his delegation and decided to have none of Lenroot. In the last year he had been sent three complimentary copies of *Have Faith in Massachusetts*. Coolidge was the man he thought of now—"Law and Order" Coolidge.

McCamant's voice rumbled on in indistinguishable phrases, then broke clear with, "I nominate for the exalted office of Vice President, Governor Calvin Coolidge of Massachusetts." The murmuring hall suddenly resounded with a thunder of applause followed by shouts of "Coolidge, Coolidge." For the first and last time in his life Calvin Coolidge had become a symbol of revolt in the most spontaneous convention action since the nomination of James Garfield in 1880. The week-long frustration of the delegates, their sense of impotence as the whip cracked, their rage at being forced through the hoops, suddenly spilled over at the mention of Coolidge's name. Quickly the nomination was seconded by the delegations of Michigan, Maryland, North Dakota, Arkansas, and Connecticut—all supposedly under senatorial control. Remmel, the old professional, knew a bandwagon when he saw one. As soon as he could get the attention of the chair, he announced that he was withdrawing his seconding of Lenroot in order to second the nomination of Coolidge.

Only the day before, a friend of Coolidge's had remarked to the *Outlook* editor, Frederick Davenport: "If Calvin Coolidge were nominated for the vice presidency, I wouldn't take the presidency for a million dollars. Because I would die in a little while. Coolidge has been lucky politically. Everything comes to him in a most uncanny and mysterious way. Excuse me from the presidency with him in the vice-regal chair!" It was a hauntingly flip prophecy, for on August 2, 1923, the flaccid Harding died suddenly and Coolidge became President. Luck was with him even in the timing, for he had fifteen months to replace the tarnished Harding administration with his own prim Yankee image. Burgeoning prosperity made him invincible. Nominated in 1924 without opposition, in the election he carried thirty-five states, defeating his Democratic opponent, the conservative New York lawyer John W. Davis, by 7,339,417 votes, a triumph marred only by the personal tragedy of the death of his younger son during the summer.

Late in the campaign the Democratic National Committee attempted to make an issue of the police strike, charging that Mayor Peters alone by his "courageous, drastic action" was the hero of that event in contrast to the dilatory and inactive Coolidge. Former attorney general Wyman denied this on behalf of the Republican National Committee and blamed the violence on Peters. In reply the Democrats offered a thousand dollars to any-one who could prove its version untrue, an offer at once taken up by the Boston *Post*. In a lengthy editorial the *Post* claimed that Coolidge had been willing to assume authority at the beginning of the strike but that "Peters was not willing to let it pass from him." Peters, now out of office, wrote a letter challenging the *Post*'s state-ment. Wyman then challenged Peters. The month passed with Wyman and Peters writing indignant letters and the *Post* printing new editorials defending Coolidge and castigating the ex-mayor. Even within the state this word battle echoed hollowly, for Massa-chusetts gave Coolidge 63 per cent of its vote.

"No doubt it was the police strike of Boston that brought me into national prominence," Coolidge wrote later. "That furnished the occasion and I took advantage of the opportunity." His opinion was shared, if mordantly, by a number of strike participants such as James Vahey, who shortly after Harding's death ran into Herbert Parker at the Parker House. "Oh, Mr. Parker," he called to him, "see who we made president!"

The parsimonious Yankee in the White House, presiding over a period of unexampled affluence, soon came to be regarded with affection as a cracker-barrel sage. His laconic remarks were widely quoted and later even collected in a short volume, *Coolidge Wit and Wisdom*. To the Jazz Age he seemed an amusing anachronism. What was later seen as a fleeting Indian summer then appeared the bright midseason of permanent prosperity, with Coolidge as the pilot who weathered the calm. In 1928 President Coolidge could have had the nomination and the election at the nod of his head. But while spending the summer of 1927 in the Black Hills of South Dakota, he one day handed the reporters at his daily press conference slips of paper with the twelve-word sentence: "I do not choose to run for President in nineteen twenty eight." He refused to explain his enigmatic statement further, perhaps out of Yankee puckishness, despite all the debate it caused. Some thought he did not mean it, that he was waiting to be drafted. In any case he was not a candidate the following year, whether from weariness of office, considerations of health, or grief for his dead son, of whom he wrote in his autobiography, "When he went, the power and the glory of the Presidency went with him." But beyond his more personal feelings, Coolidge was no doubt impelled by his singular political instinct that so often translated itself into the Coolidge luck. Before he left the White House his wife remarked to a friend, "Poppa says there's a depression coming."

In March 1929 Coolidge turned over the presidency to his unfortunate successor, Herbert Hoover. He lived out most of the Hoover administration in retirement in Northampton, dying suddenly of a coronary thrombosis on January 4, 1933. He was buried in the Vermont hills that he had never really left.

By a special act of the Massachusetts legislature in 1918, the mayor of Boston was made ineligible for immediate re-election. This was not aimed at Peters, for there was never any possibility of his being re-elected, but at the feared political buccaneer James Michael Curley. No act of the legislature could prevent Curley from running again in 1921, after a four-year lapse, against John R. Murphy, Peters's fire commissioner. Murphy, a man of intelligence and integrity, the highly respected son-in-law of John Boyle O'Reilly, was narrowly defeated in a contest called "the most vicious and vituperative in Boston's history."

Peters left office discredited in almost all eyes but his own. As the Boston newspaper man Joseph Dinneen wrote of him, he was, as mayor, "one of the most trusting souls ever placed in a job that required the quick eyes, ears and instincts of an honest poker player among cardsharps. He believed implicitly everything he was told. He signed his name to documents without reading them, and even repeated into a telephone acknowledgments and commitments which his secretariat called to him, an innocent dupe for a conscienceless corps of bandits. . . . He never took a wrong nickel while in office and a time came when he looked around blinking, bewildered and uncomprehending, not knowing what had happened. He never did figure it out."

After quitting City Hall, Peters went back to his Federal Street office and the practice of law, devoting most of his time to estate management. For a time he was president of the Boston Chamber of Commerce. He also became a director of the First National Bank. Yet visions of political sugar plums still occasionally danced in his head, as he admitted in a little poem, "Reflections Upon Running for Office," that he dashed off several months after retiring from public life:

> I've done my job as Mayor
> And they say I've done it well,
> So I'll give up public life
> And rest and play a spell.
>
> I'll return to private practice,
> The practice of the law,
> And with my little graflex
> I'll literally wage war.
>
> I may become the president
> Of a small but growing Trust—
> Or I may pull together
> One which recently went bust.
>
> I may take a fling upon the Street
> With partners all well-known,
> Or maybe run a banking shop
> That's really quite my own.
>
> I've chances quite a few
> To go out and try my luck
> With just enough of gamble in them
> To let me test my pluck.
>
> And of course I've done my bit
> To keep the Nation going—
> So I've no interest at all
> In political winds a-blowing—
>
> No none at all—and yet—
> There's the Gold Dome on the hill,
> Perhaps a couple years up there
> Would really fill the bill?

Not too arduously occupied at the office, he continued his pleasant routine of sailing and yachting, spending long summers in Maine, and enjoying the social life of his various clubs. He also continued his relations with Starr Wyman, who had taken the name of Starr Faithfull after her divorced mother had married Stanley E. Faithfull, a crank inventor, and moved to New York. During her teens Starr had periods of queerness which her family could not understand. Sometimes she would slip away to see Peters, whom she continued to regard with fear and affection. Once, after spending two nights with him in a New York hotel, she broke down and told her mother about their affair. Either Faithfull or his wife then confronted Peters. The result was that, after signing a formal release of all liabilities for damage done to Starr, the Faithfulls received a large sum of money. Faithfull—who always referred to Peters as Mr. X—said it was twenty thousand dollars. Other sources indicated that it was closer to eighty. In any case it was for years the Faithfull family's sole apparent source of income. The sedate Boston law firm that negotiated the payment and release merely observed that "if Faithfull wants to say it was only twenty thousand dollars, then we're satisfied to let it rest at that."* When Starr was nineteen she spent nine days in a Boston mental hospital. Later she was under the care of various psychiatrists. Once after being found drunk, naked, and apparently beaten-up in a New York hotel room, she was taken to Bellevue. At other times and places she appeared outwardly normal, handsome, well dressed, even vivacious. She had periods of extended gaiety, particularly in London, a city she visited twice. But on her second trip she swallowed twenty-four grains of allonal and was barely revived.

In the spring of 1931, when she was twenty-five, she fell heedlessly in love with the ship's surgeon of the Cunard liner *Franconia*. He neither reciprocated her feelings nor appreciated her all-too-voluble attentions. At the end of May, noticeably tipsy, she boarded the *Franconia* in New York a few hours before sailing time and made her way to the reluctant surgeon's sitting room. He tried to send her away just before the ship sailed, but instead she mingled

---

* A full account of Starr Faithfull is given by Morris Markey in his chapter in *The Aspirin Age*.

with the passengers, and after an embarrassing scene with the doctor, had to be put ashore by tugboat when the *Franconia* was down the harbor. The next day, she wrote him a letter, two days later a second, two days after that, on June 4, a third. In her last letter she wrote that she was giving herself twenty-four hours and that she would never see him again. Four days later her body, in a silk dress and nothing else, was washed up on the sands of Long Beach twenty miles from New York.

Her death was a three-day tabloid sensation, with headlines of rape, murder, and other unfounded suppositions. Somehow she had drowned herself; just how or where would remain a mystery. A policeman going through her possessions in the Faithfull family's flat found her "Mem Book," containing scattered sexual passages and references that even the tabloids would not venture to print. In these fragments from a bitter and broken life, one set of initials kept cropping up: AJP. "Spent night AJP Providence. Oh, Horror, Horror, Horror!!!"

Reporters were not long in associating the letters AJP with that distant relative Andrew J. Peters. No one was ever brash enough to question Peters to his face about the connection, but so widespread were the scandalous innuendoes that he felt compelled to make a formal denial to the press that he had ever had improper relations with Starr Faithfull.

His personal reputation blackened, he could sense the whispers behind him now when he entered any of his clubs. Yet a certain residual political aura managed to surround him. In 1928 he had been picked to second the nomination of Al Smith for President at the Houston Democratic National Convention. In 1933 he was appointed to the Massachusetts Advisory Committee of the Home Owners' Loan Corporation. His last years were sad. In the summer of 1932 his two boys John and Alanson died of polio. Then his son Bradford was killed in a car crash. He himself died of pneumonia on June 26, 1938.

Under their mild-mannered president, Michael Lynch, the members of the Boston Social Club continued to hold monthly meetings in Hibernian Hall, Roxbury. Each year they commemorated the strike by holding a memorial mass at St. James Church on Harrison Avenue for their comrades who had died in the preceding twelve months. They remained closely knit, fiercely loyal, and stubbornly determined to vindicate themselves by getting their old jobs back or at least the recognition that they could have them back. Their wives formed a ladies' auxiliary. At its annual June convention, held in 1920 in Montreal, the AFL had pledged the discharged policemen its "moral support," but this buttered no bread. Over four hundred of them were then still out of work. In 1921 Lynch appealed to Coolidge's successor, Governor Channing Cox, to give the strikers a second chance, saying that they were now truly repentant. Cox would not even discuss the matter. At last, in the winter of 1923, the policemen appealed directly to the legislature. The Republican majority in the House of Representatives refused to consider a bill to reinstate them. Even those strikers settled down in other careers still felt the sting of the labels "traitor" and "deserter," still agitated for the vindication that never came. Although barred from the Metropolitan District Police and the newly formed state constabulary, a number of them did find police work in other towns and cities of the state.

Iron Mike Fitzgibbons and two other Mattapan patrolmen, James Hogan and Daniel Rowley, ended up on the police force of Walpole, a small milltown eighteen miles south of Boston. There on the outskirts Iron Mike bought a run-down farm which he proceeded to restore while raising still more children. In the thirties he became a sergeant and was even offered the job of chief of police but turned it down because there were no civil-service benefits. When he died in the late forties he was a much respected and honored man in that small community, and his funeral was one of the largest that the town had ever seen. Dan Rowley did become Walpole's chief, while Jim Hogan became police chief of neighboring Medfield. Others were chiefs in Cambridge, Medford, Millis, Sharon, Provincetown, Vineyard Haven, and across the country in California, where Thomas Noone was appointed chief of police of Los Angeles. Several former patrolmen later rose to the rank of captain in the Boston Fire Department. James Long left his bakery route for the New England Telephone Company, where he would stay until he was pensioned thirty years later. Mayor Curley, reelected mayor in 1921, made jobs for a number at City Hall. Still others became court-house attendants, postal workers, clerks in the

Internal Revenue Service. Several built up trucking firms. A few grew rich.

Among the more unusual transformations was that of rookie Patrolman Frank Lynch, once of Station 7, East Boston, who ended as Brother Timothy of the Redemptorist Order in Asunción, Paraguay. Another rookie, John Rooney, went to medical school and became a well-known Dorchester general practitioner. Patrolman Edward J. Carroll turned to undertaking and later was elected to the state senate. His striking brother Daniel made a fortune as a prize-fight promoter. Frederick Claus was not so fortunate. He left his milk route for a job as carpenter, traveling all over the country in the slacker seasons. After he had located a nearby job, his brother found him night work with the United Fruit Company unloading fruit boats on the East Boston docks, and with this extra money he was finally able to pay off the mortgage on his house. During World War II he made templates at the Boston Navy Yard until, following an operation for a strangulated hernia, he developed cancer, living another tortured two years. In his later years he became president of the Social Club. When he first struck he had thought he would be back in uniform in a few days. Always in after years, whenever he saw a policeman, he would count the service stripes on his sleeve, and if the man had enough to indicate he had been serving at the time of the strike, he would cross to the other side of the street to avoid him.

In 1931 a legislative committee held another hearing to determine whether the 1919 strikers should be given the right to be restored to the force. Former patrolman Thomas Dowling testified that the "old time policemen would clean up things" if they were given the chance that two hundred fifty to three hundred of them were still waiting for. Though it was opposed by the Civil Service Reform Association, the legislature, on the committee's recommendations, authorized the police commissioner to reinstate the strikers at his discretion. However, the police commissioner then in office, Eugene Hultman, turned down all 147 applications that he received. In November 1934, after finishing a third flamboyant term as mayor, James Michael Curley was elected governor. In his campaign he had promised—among a multitude of other promises

—to reinstate the ex-policemen. Once in the governor's chair he sacked the Yankee police commissioner James Leonard,* replacing him by the more amenable Boston politician Eugene McSweeney. Some months afterward he notified his new commissioner that he expected at least twenty-five of the old police to be restored to duty, that it was a matter of honor—or so he told a delegation of former policemen headed by Senator Edward Carroll. Yet somehow McSweeney did not get the message. Curley complained that his commissioner had snubbed him and broken his word. McSweeney denied that he had agreed to take any of the 1919 strikers back. He had never yet said what he would or would not do, and he was not going to be "stampeded or hurried" in making his decision. He declared he would conduct his department in his own way "even if it costs me my job." That is just what it did cost him, for Curley finally forced the disappointingly unamenable commissioner out of office, replacing him with his military aide, Diamond Jim's son Joseph Timilty.

With Timilty's arrival in Pemberton Square, the policemen of 1919 thought their long-postponed hour had at last struck, particularly since Mayor Frederick Mansfield had assured the new commissioner that he would be allowed a budget increase sufficient to add one hundred fifty new patrolmen to the force. But instead of action there was hesitancy. All Timilty would say was that he was not ready to make known whether he intended to reinstate any of the former police. In the end he would prove as disappointing as Hultman and McSweeney to the now middle-aged men, almost eight hundred of whom had filed application for reinstatement.† For his belated decision was to take none of them back. As he explained to the president of the Boston Social Club, John Counihan, the average age of his force was already forty-four, whereas the ideal age was thirty. To take on a group of older men would raise his average to fifty. "If this decision were dictated by

---

* Curley's predecessor, Joseph Ely, though a Democrat, detested and was detested by Curley. As Governor Ely left office, he and Curley exchanged blows within the State House. Knowing Curley's hatred of Hultman, Ely moved the commissioner to the chairmanship of the Metropolitan District Commission and replaced him with Leonard.

† A number of these of course merely wanted formal reinstatement but had no intention of going back into uniform.

my heart I would restore them," he told Counihan. But his policy called for the appointment of "young, vigorous, alert police officers who will be readily responsive to the training and discipline of modern police methods." The reinstatement of the strikers "would not be in accord with views I hold relating to the maintenance of an efficient police force."

This rebuff ended the striking policemen's last effort at vindication, although they continued to meet each month, invited political candidates to address them at election time, and endorsed their choices. During World War II the more active served as air-raid wardens and even as members of Boston's auxiliary police. Thirty years after the strike, half of those who had walked out in September 1919 were still alive. That year 375 members of the Boston Social Club held their annual reunion and banquet at Elks' Hall on Huntington Avenue. From then on their numbers dwindled with actuarial speed. Their monthly meetings were now more veterans' get-togethers than discussions of strike issues. Even vindication was no longer a vital concern. Many were growing too old to attend the meetings, and in 1963 the Social Club ceased, although the survivors continued to send each other Christmas cards and sometimes a few of them managed to meet informally. They still continued their memorial mass, holding it now on September 9, the anniversary of the strike.

By the beginning of the seventies the Social Club, the memorial mass, and the strike as an event had faded away. Every few years a feature writer would resurrect the police strike for an article in the *Globe* or the *Herald*. For a time it became almost a fad for college term papers and master's-degree theses. Nothing more, except a few old men—living in the more anonymous suburbs with their children or grandchildren if they were lucky, or in a Medicaid-financed nursing home if they were not—thinking back through a haze of years to the time when they were young and patrolled the streets of Boston.

From being one of the most respected police forces in the country, the Boston Police Department after 1919 became one of the least, often accused—according to the candid admission of its own commissioner—of "corruption, dishonesty and inefficiency." Lacking the morale of the old, the new force bent to the temptations of the lax Prohibition era, something that even O'Meara's men might not have been wholly able to resist. It took the department a decade to recover from the effects of the strike. The hasty recruiting brought in numbers of unsuitable men. In the year following the strike 238 patrolmen resigned, many with only a few days' or a few months' service, and 73 were discharged. The commissioner's report for 1921 concluded: "The period following the strike was one which tried the mettle of overburdened officers and loyal men. Many of the new men were unequal to their tasks and had to be watched with special care. The police officials felt that they were doing well if they kept the system from breaking down completely."

In 1920 the department numbered 1846 men of all ranks. Fifty years later it had increased by only about four hundred, and the foot patrolmen and even the traffic officer had all but disappeared. In 1962 the power of appointing the police commissioner was restored to the mayor of Boston. Once a means by which the Republican state administration kept a leading string on City Hall, such control had no meaning in a solidly Democratic state, even though the electorate out of whimsy or pique occasionally elected Republican governors. This same year President Kennedy's executive order allowing federal workers to organize was followed by the collective-bargaining law giving these rights to state and municipal employees as well. For a long time after the 1919 strike Boston policemen had shown little inclination to form any kind of internal organization, but under the spur of this new law they founded their own union in 1965, the Boston Police Patrolmen's Association. The BPPA immediately began to demonstrate that it was no company creature but as militant as any union with outside affiliations in standing up for what it considered the rights of its members.

In 1968 the patrolmen's association secured a labor contract with the city. Later in the year the 1919 statute forbidding the police of Massachusetts to affiliate with an outside labor organization was repealed, except for the state police (the former state constabulary).* After half a century the state's policemen were free to affiliate with the AFL. They showed no great eagerness to do so.

* In 1972 the law was amended to include the state police.

The six hundred members of the Metropolitan District police—the old Metropolitan Park police—did join the American Federation of State, County and Municipal Employees, as did the hundred or so patrolmen of the State House's Capitol police. But the chief recruits were the minuscule forces of the small towns of southeast Massachusetts: Swansea, Rehoboth, Dighton, Westport, and several others. The police of the larger cities such as Fall River, Worcester, and the mill cities of the north remained aloof. That the Boston police declined to affiliate with the State, County and Municipal Employees was explained by one of the officers of the patrolmen's association, who said that they felt that no outside union could do so much for them as an inside one knowing all the intricacies of the department. Since the police were in any case barred from striking, an outside union had nothing much to offer them.

In 1973 the patrolmen's association turned its official newsletter into a tabloid newspaper, *Pax Centurion*. Since its first issue the paper has been savaging Mayor Kevin White for his forced economics in the police department which it claims are endangering the safety of the city. But *Pax Centurion* reserves its particular venom for the new police commissioner, Robert di Grazia, a "small-time sheriff faced with problems he can't handle." Di Grazia, a man of pleasant personality but limited police experience, who sees his present post as a stepping stone to things higher, has been in controversies with his department ever since Mayor White imported him two years ago from the West. He is probably as disliked as was Curtis at the beginning of the 1919 strike, and less respected. *Pax Centurion* does not spare him.

Statistically speaking there have been four police strikes in the country's history. Actually there have been only two, for the first and the last were merely small-town comic interludes. The first police strike took place in Ithaca, New York, in 1889, when the city council voted to lower the men's pay. The police thereupon resigned in a body, the pay cut was hastily rescinded, and the men returned to work.

The second strike, the first police strike to cause any national interest or concern, broke out in Cincinnati, Ohio, on September 14, 1918, after four patrolmen who had conferred with an AFL organizer about forming a union and obtaining pay increases were suspended for "conduct unbecoming an officer." Eight hundred policemen walked out in protest on the day set for a parade of fifty thousand draft registrants, the largest parade in the city's history. Their places were at once taken by three thousand members of the home guard who had been armed and drilled for just such an emergency. Though the streets were thronged, there was not even a semblance of disorder, much less any rioting or looting. The patrolmen claimed they had a right as American citizens to form a union, but they found public opinion against them and when they learned that plans were being made for a new police force, with preference being given to returned soldiers, they went back to their jobs before they could be replaced. All were allowed back except for the four who had been suspended. The Cincinnati police were then required to take new oaths that they would not affiliate with any outside labor organization, though even as they did so an American Federation of Labor charter was on its way to them.

The last strike, in the little town of Rockville Centre, Long Island, in January 1920, was farcical. Six of the nine members of the police department walked out demanding fifteen dollars a month pay increase. Chief Joseph Russ planned to raise a volunteer force, but the men returned to duty next day before anyone realized there was a strike on.

Following the Boston Police Strike, laws were passed in a number of states forbidding the police to join unions. Even when those laws were relaxed or repealed, the policemen showed none of the compulsive union enthusiasm of 1919. As a publication of the International Association of Police Chiefs observed in 1949, "Through the years it [the Boston strike] has served as a public reminder to police employees of the nation that divided allegiance can bring nothing but sweeping public resentment against, and destructive criticism of, the police profession as a whole." Twenty-five years after the police of Boston struck, at a time when organized labor claimed some fifteen million members, there were a mere fifteen police unions chartered by the AFL in the 168 American cities with a population of over fifty thousand, and of these only three—Augusta, Georgia; Flint, Michigan; and Portsmouth, Virginia—had been recognized by city officials. After

World War II, leaders of the AFL-CIO toyed for a time with the idea of a national police union but gave it up for lack of response. The Service Employees International Union does have a branch, the National Union of Police Officers, that has granted charters to a negligible number of police departments, but most of the police prefer to remain independent. And whatever their attitudes today toward union affiliation, they do not conceive of any circumstances that would justify a strike. Those few departments with AFL-CIO affiliations are barred by their charters from striking. No American city in over half a century has again been threatened by a walkout of its police. This, at least, is the legacy of the Boston Police Strike.

THE
GHOST OF
SCOLLAY SQUARE

For a generation after the police strike (granted a generation is about thirty years), downtown Boston remained unchanged except that each year it grew a little shabbier, a little dirtier. The flaking grey paint on the State House dome—the gilt having been camouflaged over in World War II—seemed in its morose way a symbol of the fading seaport. As if to sum it all up that aged blusterer James Michael Curley was rounding out his fourth term as mayor amidst the encrusted grime of City Hall, broadcasting that he was going to stay there until he was 125 to bury all his enemies. Boston was too poor for a new City Hall, too poor to refurbish the old, too poor to do anything but to elect Curley and decay.

Suddenly, like a pantomime transformation scene, everything changed. Curley, five months of his four-year fourth term having been spent in the Federal Correctional Institute at Danbury, was out of office, defeated in 1949 by his own city clerk. Then Edward Logue arrived fresh from demolishing and more or less rebuilding New Haven to take charge of the Boston Redevelopment Authority. Deft manipulator of the federal money spigot with its gold pipeline running to Washington, Logue turned that spigot on in Boston full force. A Danaän shower! Suddenly, a municipal government that could not keep up its moldering City Hall found itself presented with a streamlined modern one; a city that could not afford the old was demolished by the new. For several Logue years much of inner Boston resembled sections of London hit by the Blitz: gutted houses, bare walls traced with the outlines of vanished rooms and stairs, piles of brick and rubble, gaping holes where streets had been. Scollay Square, that hazard point of revel and riot—its name derived from a sedate eighteenth- century merchant—magnet for men in uniform and for the seamen of the world, was high on the demolition list of those with the gleam of alabaster cities in their eye. When James Michael gave his last hurrah in 1958, forty-two years before he had promised to, a whimsical suggestion was made to change the ill-reputed name to Curley Square. To the urban renewers the remedy seemed worse than the disease. They were resolved to obliterate both the name and the place. So effectively did they carry this through that today it requires an old map and a compass to trace where Scollay Square really was.

As I walk up Tremont Street on this February midmorning, a northeast wind cuts against my face from across the brick acres of the Government Center plaza that has absorbed the lower end of what was once Scollay Square. T. S. Eliot must have known the square as a Harvard undergraduate, recalling in his exile the

> ... faint stale smell of beer
> from the sawdust-trampled streets.

Even those streets have been bulldozed away, along with the gaudy landmarks. They are all gone—if not into the world of light, at least gone—the Crawford House, vibrating to the raucous intimacy of its floor show; the musties* slopped on the counter of the Hotel Imperial across the street with its fly-specked crayon sketches of Generals Patton and Ike in the twin windows; the flaring lights and

---

* "Mustie" was the indigenous name for a glass of half-ale, half-beer. When James Michael Curley went to Washington as a congressman and first dined at the Willard, he is said to have asked the wine steward for a mustie.

brassy countermen of Joe & Nemo's all-nite hotdog stand; the Star
Theatre, admission a dime, its interior a blended odor of the
Franklin Park elephant house and the gents room at the South Station, showing old films twenty-four hours a day, seven days a week,
but shutting down for twenty minutes at 1:00 a.m. to see if anyone
had died there the previous day; the huge steaming kettle hanging
over the entrance to the Oriental Tea Company, its claimed capacity 227 gallons, 2 quarts, 1 pint, 3 gills, or 8 men; the musky—
or perhaps "mustie"—dungeon that was the New Ritz Café; the
tattoo parlors, passport photographers, shooting galleries, penny
arcades, painless dentists, instant oculists, poolrooms, bars, cafés,
flophouses, and the unforgettably named St. Marx and St. Leon
hotels. And above and through it all a kind of gusto. Scollay Square
was brash and bawdy, like the Old Howard round the corner, the
former Millerite Tabernacle that, after the Second Coming proved
a dud in 1844, became the staid Howard Athenaeum and then in a
more raffish day, the Old Howard—home of burlesque, where the
striptease originated, where something was always doing "from 9 to
11."

There are congealed patches of dirty snow in the gutter as I
cross through the stalled traffic. The yellow light flashes DON'T
WALK. No one in Boston bothers with that. In 1919 the state guard
was going to put down jaywalking once and for all, but over half a
century later it is still an ingrained Boston habit. Picking my way
among the cars I find myself walking over the very ground where
the First Troop of Cavalry charged so gallantly across the cobble-
stones on that September night to set the rabble flying. Not a
marker to remember that charge! The wind picks up, curling across
the brick expanse between the new City Hall and the John F.
Kennedy Federal Building. The sunken fountain is still snowbound.
A splay-rumped girl in a miniskirt shivers as she dashes for the shelter of the Kennedy Building past the bronze lump of abstract sculpture in front of it. How many tons of metal went into that lump, and
what was it Bishop Berkeley said about abstractions? More than
anything else the sculpture looks like a foundering three-legged
horse with an erection. The girl has reached the entrance—neither
the rear end nor the weather for that kind of costume! Floor after
floor the stone-and-glass Kennedy cube rises to some sort of metal

grill at the top, white, austere, functional, like an up-ended air conditioner. Not quite opposite is the state's similarly white, similarly angular Leverett Saltonstall Building, named after the retired senator. A fair enough pre-humous memorial. For in the second evacuation of Boston some of the retreating Yankees showed a belated talent for taking advantage of Democratic intratribal conflict and conning the Irish into voting for them. Senator Saltonstall was among the earliest and the deftest.*

The Kennedy and Saltonstall buildings are one thing. The new City Hall is something else again. Those sandwich slabs of concrete on stilts, those brick wedges, that disornamentation. It must easily be the ugliest building in Boston, perhaps in New England. As I look at it in the morning cold, my mind stirs, a layered memory slowly emerges. Something like it I have seen before. Then all at once I know. The new City Hall is a cubistic version of East Prussia's Tannenberg Memorial!

What then endures from the great strike? A vague if haunting memory, yet something more substantial as well. Because of it a conservative Yankee became President instead of the Western progressive Irvine Lenroot. Under President Lenroot the country might have been different, though in the end the false summer of prosperity would probably have been too much for him. If the strike had not occurred in Boston, it would have occurred in some other city, though possibly with less violence. That the police should insist on affiliation with the AFL was part of the labor mood of 1919. That they were slated to fail was part of the larger public mood. After the Boston disorders and the ensuing outcry, other police unions turned in their AFL charters.

Curtis's disciplinary stand, for which he felt ready to die, in which he felt he had triumphed, did not endure. The principle for which the defiant patrolmen lost their jobs did them no good even though in the end it prevailed. Ironically, Boston policemen who may now, if they choose, affiliate their patrolmen's association with the AFL-CIO, do not so choose. Though they vilify Commissioner

---

* Oddly enough, in the first evacuation of Boston in 1776, among the loyalists who sailed away into exile rather than renounce their allegiance to King George was one Leverett Saltonstall.

di Grazia in each issue of *Pax Centurion*—the November issue had
a fold-out cartoon of a naked di Grazia as Playmate of the Month—
they recoil at the word "strike."

How it dates one actually to remember the police strike! I think
of that as I walk from the Kennedy Building toward the subway
entrance. The old tea-kettle of the Oriental Tea Company, regilded
and with the dents removed, again gives out steam above the
entrance to a coffee bar. It is probably the only Scollay Square
object left from the riots. The subway entrance is new, massively
brick, cubistic, like an air raid shelter for an atom-bomb attack.
The old one with its gothic turrets and finials could have served as
a chapel for the bones of St. Botolph. Or for the five anonymous
bodies found during the leveling of the square.

Though Scollay Square is only a ghost, I cannot pass this way,
walk across the Government Center plaza or past the Pemberton
Square Courthouse and down School Street to the old City Hall
without thinking of the strike, without remembering the amateur
soldiers in their misfit uniforms who loomed so heroic to my child's
eye. The principals have lost any currency. Curtis is forgotten;
Peters is forgotten; Coolidge is vaguely recalled in the presidential
sequence as the predecessor of the unlucky Hoover, a wooden-
Indian profile on a postage stamp. Yet that strike, overlaid now by a
half century of more massive world disorders, did settle something,
did make its axiomatic point in history.

It was a point not so well understood north of the Canadian
border. For the Montreal police, who had struck in 1918, struck
again in 1946. Then on October 6, 1969—Montreal's Black Tuesday—the city's Policemen's Brotherhood Union, in a sudden gesture of impatience following a wage dispute, called a third strike.
Early in the morning the men quit their posts, returning to work at
midnight only after the Quebec legislature ordered them back
under penalty of heavy fines and prison terms. During that long day
and evening a mob formed, turning quickly violent. Two miles of
shops were looted along St. Catherine Street, the pavement strewn
with glass fragments and discarded merchandise, a large garage
burned to the ground, and over a million dollars' worth of damage
done. Two men died, forty-nine persons were injured. The police
themselves were dismayed at the sudden consequences, the chas-

tened head of the brotherhood union remarking on the "thin blue line" that separates civilization from chaos and anarchy. Below the border one might tend to forget how thin that blue line is—until one remembers Boston.

POSTSCRIPT
IN BALTIMORE

On Thursday evening, July 11, 1974, and after I had finished writing my last chapter, a police strike occurred in Baltimore, the first such in a major American city in fifty-five years. According to officials of the American Federation of State, County and Municipal Employees—of which a slight majority of the Baltimore police were members—1300 to 1500 of the 2800-man force quit their jobs. Police Commissioner Donald Pomerleau, however, gave out the total as 457 strikers.

The municipal workers' strike began on July 1 with a walkout of garbagemen in protest against what they considered the inadequate offer by Mayor William Schaefer of a twenty-five cents an hour pay increase. The mayor explained that the city lacked the money for an additional increase and could not count on any supplementary state or federal funds. In spite of a Maryland law forbidding strikes of municipal employees the garbagemen were joined by the unionized jail guards, park and zoo keepers, and highway and sewer maintenance workers. Then, as garbage and refuse piled up in the streets, after several days of a police slowdown in which the mayor's official car was twice tagged, the more militant policemen made a delayed gesture of solidarity by walking out.

Their walkout was the signal for young blacks to take to the streets, smashing windows and looting, their target chiefly liquor and jewelry stores. Over two hundred stores were vandalized that night. Hundreds of trash fires were set in the streets. Two men died in the tumult, one a looter shot down by an on-duty policeman.

On Friday Governor Marvin Mandel ordered a hundred state troopers of the special tactical force to Baltimore along with an armored police car and a detachment of police dogs. He also alerted the National Guard. Mayor Schaefer, after recalling the Boston strike, accused the police of failing their obligations and betraying their oaths. During the morning he and the commissioner and the governor toured the city. "I have a great deal of emergency power in this situation," the governor warned union officials, "and I will have no hesitancy in using it." Commissioner Pomerleau said that the city was under control—as indeed it proved to be—and remarked that the police who stayed on the job were superior to those who struck. During the day many strikers returned to duty. Meanwhile City Circuit Court Judge James Murphy threatened to fine and jail the three top union leaders unless the men were back on their jobs by Monday.

The sweltering weekend passed calmly if odiferously, while mayor and commissioner negotiated with the union leaders. The mayor was willing to make some wage concessions, but the commissioner refused to consider a general amnesty for the strikers. Those, he said, who continued to stay out would be dismissed, including eighty-two probationary patrolmen who had joined the strike.

By Monday afternoon most of the municipal workers, as well as the police, were back on the job. On Tuesday the union leaders, to the indignation of the younger patrolmen, yielded to the commissioner on the amnesty issue as they signed a new contract that increased the pay of officers with five years' experience. Whatever their private feelings the union members ratified the agreement. At the time the vote was taken, only twenty-four policemen had failed to return to work. An hour later Judge Murphy fined the staff director of the union's Maryland Police Council $10,000 for one day's contempt of his back-to-work injunction and fined the police local $25,000.

The Baltimore strike lacked wider implications. Compared with the riots in Baltimore following the murder of Martin Luther King or the uprisings in Watts and Detroit and Harlem, it seemed a minor incident. In half a century the country had become acclimated to riots, mob violence, cities under siege. Most papers beyond the state did not consider the Baltimore strike newsworthy. Mayor Schaefer, Commissioner Pomerleau, and Governor Mandel made no names for themselves nationally. Nevertheless the shadow of that Boston strike, attenuated though it might be, impressed itself on Baltimore in those five days. The mayor and the governor and the commissioner sensed it as they drove through the streets on Friday morning. The officials of the union sensed it, as did Judge Murphy. It gave the striking policemen a feeling of uncertainty to the point that other striking municipal employees felt uncertain of them. "I feel terrible about this strike," one policeman told a reporter. "It's the most terrible thing I have ever done." But he added, unconvincingly, that he felt he was right. Police Commissioner Pomerleau announced that "there will be no general amnesty for those police officers who have failed their responsibility to the public," though there would be "degrees of consideration" to those who returned promptly. But for the memory of the Boston Police Strike it seems unlikely that the commissioner would have ventured on so fixed a course and even more unlikely that union officials would have acquiesced. Nor would there have been such quick cooperation between the mayor and the governor. Several lessons, at least, had endured, whatever the rights and wrongs.

ACKNOWLEDGMENTS

To the many who were kind enough to reply to my requests for information about the police strike I am most grateful, in particular to Helen C. Bailey, Mildred Beverly, Richard Courtenay, Harry Cross, Alan F. Flynn, A. H. Hermann, John Heskell, Catherine Knapp, James A. Long, John B. O'Neil, Richard M. Russell, Commander Joseph Siano of the Massachusetts State Guard Veterans, George Simpson, and John Underhill. I am also indebted to my uncle Charles Herbert Kent, to Anne Lydon, to Francis Moloney and the staff of the Boston Public Library, and to Bob McLean and David Farrell of the Boston *Globe*. The Boston Public Library with its microfilms of newspapers, the Massachusetts State House Library, and the Boston Athenaeum have been indispensable to me. But my most enduring gratitude is to those long dead, my grandfather, my father, my Aunt Amy, and others the memory of whom has sustained me in this work.

SELECTED
BIBLIOGRAPHY

Books

Ables, Jules. *In the Time of Silent Cal.* New York, 1969.

Allen, Frederick L. *Only Yesterday.* New York, 1931.

Boston Tercentenary Committee. *Fifty Years of Boston: A Memorial Volume Issued in Commemoration of the Tercentenary of 1930.* Boston, 1932.

Coolidge, Calvin. *The Autobiography of Calvin Coolidge.* Boston, 1929.

———. *Have Faith in Massachusetts: Addresses and Proclamations of the Governor.* Boston, 1919.

Curley, James Michael, with John Henry Cutler. *I'd Do It Again.* Englewood Cliffs, N.J., 1949.

Cutler, John Henry. *"Honey Fitz"—Three Steps to the White House.* Indianapolis, 1962.

Dates, Data and Ditties: Unofficial Record of the Tour of Duty of A Company, 11th Regiment Infantry, Massachusetts State Guard, During the Strike of the Boston Police. Boston, 1920.

Fosdick, Raymond B. *American Police Systems.* New York, 1921.

Friedheim, Robert. *The Seattle General Strike.* Seattle, 1964.

Fuess, Claude M. *Calvin Coolidge: The Man from Vermont.* Boston, 1940.

Gilfond, Duff. *The Rise of Saint Calvin: Merry Sidelights on the Career of Mr. Coolidge.* New York, 1932.

Gitlow, Benjamin. *I Confess*. New York, 1940.

———. *The Whole of Their Lives*. New York, 1948.

Harrison, Leonard V. *Police Administration in Boston*. Cambridge, Mass., 1934.

Harvey, R. H. *Samuel Gompers: Champion of the Toiling Masses*. Palo Alto, Calif., 1935.

Hennessy, Michael E. *Massachusetts Politics 1890–1935*. Norwood, Mass., 1935.

Hopkins, Ernest J. *Our Lawless Police: A Study of the Unlawful Enforcement of the Law*. New York, 1931.

Lane, Roger. *Policing the City: Boston, 1822–1885*. Cambridge, Mass., 1967.

McCoy, Donald R. *Calvin Coolidge: The Quiet President*. New York, 1967.

Malkin, Maurice. *Return to My Fathers*. New York, 1972.

Markey, Morris. "The Mysterious Death of Starr Faithfull" in *The Aspirin Age*. Edited by Isabel Leighton. New York, 1949.

Murray, Robert K. *Red Scare: A Study in National Hysteria, 1919–1920*. Minneapolis, 1955.

Russell, Francis. *The Great Interlude*. New York, 1964.

———. *The Shadow of Blooming Grove*. New York, 1968.

Savage, Edward H. *Police Recollections, or Boston by Daylight and Gaslight*. Boston, 1873.

Slosson, Preston W. *The Great Crusade and After*. New York, 1930.

Sullivan, Mark. *Our Times*, volume vi: *The Twenties*. New York, 1935.

White, William Allen. *A Puritan in Babylon: The Story of Calvin Coolidge*. New York, 1938.

Wood, Charles G. *Reds and Lost Wages*. New York, 1930.

Zizkind, David. *One Thousand Strikes of Government Employees*. New York, 1940.

Newspapers

Boston *American*. Boston *Evening Record*. Boston *Evening Transcript*. Boston *Globe*. Boston *Herald*. Boston *Post*. Boston *Traveler*. Los Angeles *Times*. New York *Herald Tribune*. *New York Times*.

Articles

Bartlett, Randolph. "Anarchy in Boston." *American Mercury*, XXVI (December 1935).

"Harvard Men in the Boston Police Strike." *School and Society*, X (October 11, 1919).

Lyons, Richard L. "The Boston Police Strike of 1919." *New England Quarterly*, XX (July 1947).

Mason, Gregory. "No Bolshevism for Boston." *Outlook*, CXXIII (September 24, 1919).

"Police Strike in Boston; and Other Labor Problems." *Current History*, XI (October 1919).

"Policemen's Right to Strike." *Literary Digest*, LXII (September 27, 1919).

Public Documents and Official Reports

Miscellaneous circulars, pamphlets, and journals in the State House Library, reports of the adjutant general of the Commonwealth of Massachusetts, annual reports of the police commissioner, Harvard class reports, and so forth.

Unpublished Material

Coolidge, Calvin. Collection of clippings and miscellaneous papers, vol. IV. State House Library.

Curtis, Edwin U. Four bound volumes of letters to Curtis on his handling of the strike. Boston Public Library.

Koss, Frederick Manuel. "The Boston Police Strike." Ph.D. dissertation, Boston University, 1960.

Littauer Public Administration Library, Harvard University. Collection of material on the strike.

Long, Henry F. "The Boston Police Strike." Mimeographed pamphlet. Boston, 1920.

O'Meara, Stephen. Papers. Boston Public Library.

Peters, Andrew J. Papers. Boston Public Library.

Peters, Robeson, "The Boston Police Strike of 1919." Master's thesis, Columbia University, 1947.

INDEX

Allen, Henry J., 211
Ambulance Corps, 156
American Defense Society, 10, 17
American Federation of Labor (AFL),
25, 54; Boston police vote to join,
73–74; Coolidge addresses, 115–16;
demands removal of Curtis, 119;
general strike and, 172, 175, 179–80,
197; membership in a hindrance to
police duties, 75, 79, 91–92; opposes
radicalism, 24; praised by Mayor
Peters, 93; rejects right of police to
strike, 205; reverses policy on police
unions, 58; Storrow committee and,
98, 100–102
American Legion, 17
Aspirin Age, The, 226n
Association of the Former Police of the
City of Boston, 217
Augusta, George, 183
Australian ballot, 45

Back Bay, 121, 127, 168, 187
Baker, Newton, 21, 176
Ballam, John J., 115, 157
Ballard, John, 28
Baltimore, Md., 242–44
Bancroft, Charles, 95, 103
Barnard, John, 27
Barnes, Raymond, 167
Barry, Edward, 151
Bartlett, John Henry, 211
Baxter, Charles, 209, 219
Beacon Hill, 125
Bigelow, John Prescott, 30

Billings, Warren, 23–24
Billings, William, 28
Bolshevism, 12, 17, 189–90, 192
Boston *American*, 110, 212
Boston Central Labor Union (BCLU),
79; condemns police commissioner,
82; general strike and, 110, 113, 127,
171–76, 193, 199–200, 207–208;
meets with Coolidge, 88; policemen
delegates to, 86; votes to support
police strike, 89–90
Boston Chamber of Commerce, 94, 217
Boston Common, 131, 166, 168,
184–85, 214
Boston *Daily Advertiser*, 45, 80
Boston Elevated Street Railway
Company, 13, 95
Boston *Evening Transcript*, 76, 111, 117,
166
Boston *Globe*, 11, 13, 37, 42, 65, 110,
143, 145, 212
Boston *Herald*, 25, 76, 80, 88, 110, 144,
212, 220
Boston *Journal*, 37, 40–41, 76
Boston Police Department, *passim*;
corruption in, 39, 70, 231–32;
grievance committee, 56–58; history
of, 26–46; integrity of, 39–41, 231–32;
Irish and, 34–38; joins AFL, 78;
recruiting for new force, 200–201,
206; salaries, 47–50, 54–56, 58;
station houses, 51–52; unions' support
for striking, 90–91,125, 147, 175,
177–79, 181, 195–98, 217; votes to
strike, 113

Boston Police Patrolmen's Association (BPPA), 232
Boston *Post*, 110, 211, 223
Boston Social Club, 25, 101; former policemen and, 217–18, 227, 231; formation of, 38; joins AFL, 78; rule against unions and, 73–74; salary dispute and, 48–49, 54–56, 58
Boston *Social Register*, 68
Boston Stock Exchange, 145
Boston Watch, 28–31
Bowdoin College, 44, 195
Bowles, Francis, 142, 144
Brahmins, 44, 114
Brighton, Mass., 125
Brock, George, 99
Brogna, Vincent, 95
Brown, William, 85
Bryan, William Jennings, 61, 146
Bryce Report, 8
Buffalo, N.Y., 102
Burdick, Stephen, 161
Burke, Billie, 146
Burleson, Albert S., 20
Burns, James, 134
Bussey Institute, 68
Butler, James L., 85
Butler, Nicholas Murray, 212–13
Butler, William M., 106, 173–74, 202
Byrne, Patrick, 123

Cabot, Godfrey Lowell, 142
Campbell, Chester, 177
Canada, 21, 240
Canney, James, 126
Carroll, Daniel, 229
Carroll, Edward J., 229, 230
Cassidy, James, 189
Catholicism, 110, 113–14
Chamberlain, H. M., 165
Chapin, Arthur, 118
Chaplin, Charlie, 8
Charlestown, Mass., 123, 159
Choate, Charles F., Jr., 95, 104, 106
Cincinnati, 233
City Club, 94, 98
City Hall police, 126
Civil War, 32–33

Clarke, Christopher, 28
Claus, Frederick, 122, 218, 229
Clemenceau, René, 18
Cleveland, Grover, 36
Coes & Young, 165–66
Cole, Charles, 95, 106, 139, 141, 149, 171, 175
Collins, Patrick, 36–37
Colonial Theatre, 214
Communist Labor party, 16
Communist party, 11, 16, 114–15
Coolidge, Calvin, 1, 13, 25, 55, 147, 198, 209; addresses AFL, 115–16; attacked by BCLU, 90; background, 58–67; Commissioner Curtis and, 80, 82, 84, 87, 103, 116–18, 128–29, 180; general strike and, 177–78; issues proclamation against strikers, 203–204; learns of police strike, 127; Mayor Peters and, 120, 129–30, 148–50, 172–74; meets with union leaders, 183; as national figure, 189–92, 219–21; offers help to policemen, 216–17; becomes President, 223–24; re-election campaign, 201–202, 209–13; Storrow committee and, 116, 118–20, 208; tours state, 108–109; vice-presidential nomination, 222
Coolidge, Grace Goodhue, 62
Coolidge, John, 148
Coolidge, J. Randolph, Jr., 187
Coolidge, Julian, 64
Coolidge, Mary, 148
Coolidge Wit and Wisdom, 223
Coran, Helen, 142
Counihan, John, 230
Cox, Channing, 228
Crane, Murray, 65, 106, 109, 117, 173, 202
Crap games, 131–32, 145, 164, 166–68
Crawford House, 158
Crocker, Alice, 218
Crocket, Mildred, 218
Crocket, Walter, 181–82, 218
Cross, Harry, 155, 186, 214
Crowell, Henry, 154, 186
Crowley, Michael H., 84, 89, 104;

background of, 81; interrogates union leaders, 86, 89; riot duties of, 135, 137–39, 145, 152, 161,185; signs suspension notice, 78
Cummings, Edward, 188
Curley, James Michael, 94, 114; corruption in City Hall under, 38; denounces Mayor Peters, 151–52; elected mayor, 224; elected governor, 229–30; opposes "Honey Fitz," 95; police salaries and, 51; re-elected mayor, 228, 236–37; runs against Peters and loses, 67, 69
Curran, George, 82
Curtis, Edwin Upton, 67, 100, 121,127, 205, 209, 217; advertises for new police force, 182–83, 198, 206–207; background, 43–46; Coolidge supports, 116–20, 128–29, 148, 150, 173–74; death, 218; as election issue, 211; general strike and, 175, 177, 183–84, 190; Mayor Peters and, 128–30, 171,173; meets with union leaders, 194–95; police salaries and, 49, 54–57, 73; police union and, 58–59, 70–72, 75–93, 101; Storrow committee and, 101–108, 110–11, 208; suspends policemen, 112–13
Curtis, George, 44
Curtis, John, 44
Curtis, Margaret Waterman, 43
Cutler, John, 37
Czar, Anthony, 163

Dailey, Matthew, 121
Dalton, R. O., 118, 121, 127, 129
Dana, Richard Henry, 40
Daugherty, Harry, 220
Davenport, Frederick, 222
Davis, John W., 223
Davis, Laurence, 142, 152
Debs, Eugene V., 10
Decrow, John, 156
Deland, Frank, 135
Deland, Margaret, 189
De Valera, Eamon, 146
Devens, Fort, 176

Devlin, James H., 91–92, 98, 104
di Grazia, Robert, 223, 240
Dinneen, Joseph, 224
Donnelly, James, 188
Dooley, James, 166–67
Dorchester, 34, 137
Dorr, Arthur E., 134
Dowling, Thomas, 229
Driscoll, Dennis, 77
Driscoll, Thomas J., 86
Dudley, Thomas, 26
Dunne, Herbert, 176

Edwards, Clarence, 13, 19, 176
Eisner, Kurt, 18
Eliot, Charles W., 67
Eliot, John, 44
Eliot, T. S., 237
Ely, Joseph, 230n
Emergency Fleet Corporation, 15
Emery, Lee, 168
Empey, Arthur Guy, 8
Employers' Association of Eastern Massachusetts, 185
Endicott, William, 67
Executive Order Number One, 174

Fairbanks, Douglas, 8
Faithfull, Stanley E., 226
Faithfull, Starr. See Wyman, Starr
Farrar, Geraldine, 8
Feeney, John P., 89, 91, 93, 194, 197, 199, 205, 208; Storrow committee and, 98–100, 102–106
Fenway Park, 168
Ferreira, George E., 86, 121–22
Field, Henry P., 60, 62
Filene, A. Lincoln, 95
Firemen, 80, 175, 181, 195–98
First Naval District, 176
Fisher, Bob, 143
Fitzgerald, John F. ("Honey Fitz"), 37–39, 51, 69–70, 94–95, 114
Fitzgibbon, Mike, 4–6, 218, 228
Fitzgibbon, Susy, 4
Flaherty, Thomas, 163
Flynn, Alan, 145, 152
Flynn, Elizabeth Gurley, 17

Ford, Francis, 76, 86
Fosdick, Raymond B., 39
Foss, Eugene, 40, 201
Fraina, Louis, 11, 21, 24, 114–15, 157
Franconia, 226
Frothingham, Louis, 142
Fuess, Claude, 104
Fund for the Defenders of Public Safety,
    185, 201, 215

Gallivan, James A., 69
Gallup, Dana, 130
Gannock, Thomas, 164
Gardner, Mrs. Augustus, 189
Garfield, James, 222
Garrison, William Lloyd, 29
Garrity, Hugh, 86
Gaston, William, 44, 67–68, 211
Geist, Gustave, 187
General Acts of Massachusetts, 128
General Order Number 119, 87
General Order Number 125, 177
General Order Number 129, 53–54
Giovannitti, Arturo, 17–18
Gitlow, Ben, 16, 24, 114
Goff, Michael, 123
Goldman, Emma, 16
Gompers, Samuel, 13, 24, 179–81,
    190–91, 201, 205, 217
Goode, Thomas, 168
Good Government Association, 41, 69
Goodwin, Robert, 107*n*
Great Boston Fire, 33–34
Greenhalge, Frederick, 43
Greenwood, Levi H., 65
Grimes, James, 195
Grote, Henry, 169
Groupa Pro Prensa, 18
Guild, Curtis, 36, 38
Gustin Gang, 124

Hadley, Thomas, 162–63
Hague, Frank, 74
Hale, Harry, 19
Hall, Edwin, 102–103
Hammond, John C., 60
Hampshire Gazette, 61
Hanson, Ole, 15–16, 17, 19

Harding, Warren G., 14, 220–23
Hardwick, Huntington ("Tack"), 141,
    152–53
Hardwick, Thomas, 19, 165
Harriman, Captain, 164
Harrison, Leonard, 42
Hart, Thomas N., 45
Harvard University, 142–43
Harvey, George, 221
Have Faith in Massachusetts, 219, 222
Hayden, A. F., 21, 22
Hayes, Bartlett, 141
Hayes, Charles, 147
Hays, Will, 213
Haywood, Bill, 10, 17, 20
Hearst, William Randolph, 146
Hennessy, Michael, 209
Hermann, Augustus, 155, 163, 186
Hesketh, Jack, 155
Higginson, Francis Lee, 144
Hitchcock, Raymond, 146
Hoffman, Bill, 143, 158, 165
Hogan, James, 228
Holmes, Oliver Wendell, 20, 44
Hoover, Herbert, 224
Hopkins, Ernest, 41
Hormel, Herman, 211
Horrigan, Edward, 148
Hospitality huts, 214
Howe, Frederick C., 20
Hughes, Charles Evans, 213
Hultman, Eugene, 229–30
Human Life, 42
Hunneman, Frederick, 152
Hyde Park, 126

Industrial Workers of the World (IWW),
    10–11, 15–16, 17
Irish, 34–38, 45
Ithaca, N.Y., 233

Jacques, Mary, 188
Jamaica Plain, 68, 126, 169
Jennings, Harry, 172, 175, 193–94,
    207
Jersey City, N.J., 74
Jewett, Henry, 146
Johnson, James Weldon, 22

Jordan Marsh, 119, 135
Joyce, Michael, 86

Kaplan, Ime, 18
Karp, Abraham, 165
Keeley, Helen, 163
Keezer, Maurice, 164
Keliher, Sheriff, 147
Kelleher, Edward, 200
Kennedy, John, 163–64
Kennedy, John F., 232
King, John, 183
King, Michael L., 85
King, Patrick, 103
Kuhlman, Patrolman, 157
Ku Klux Klan, 23
Kun, Béla, 18

Laffey, James, 147
La Follette, Robert, 10
Lallie, Robert, 163
Landis, Kenesaw Mountain, 20
Larkin, Jim, 16, 18
Laski, Harold, 217
Lavelle, Thomas, 196
Lavequist, Edwin, 125
Lawrence, William, 188
Lawrence, Mass., 17–18, 74
League of Nations, 57
Lee, Higginson & Company, 94
Lenroot, Irvine, 221, 239
Leonard, James, 230
Lettish Workmen's Association, 11, 21, 157, 183
Lewis, Gertrude, 158
Liberty Bonds, 8
Lincoln, Frederick W., 32
Literary Digest, 220
Liverpool, 74
Lodge, Henry Cabot, 37, 39, 57, 113, 189, 212, 221
Logan, Edward, 147
Logue, Edward, 236
Lomasney, Martin, 45, 94
London, 74
Long, Henry, 58, 108, 118, 129, 148, 191
Long, James, 50, 52, 126, 136, 218, 228

Long, Richard Henry, 66, 201, 209–12
Looney, Daniel, 175
Looting, 133–38, 159–62, 165–66
Los Angeles Times, 169, 212–13
Lowden, Frank, 220
Lowell, A. Lawrence, 142, 199
Lusitania, 8
Lynch, Cornelius, 164
Lynch, Frank, 229
Lynch, Michael, 49, 54, 73, 78, 207, 227–28

Mahoney, John, 207
Maloney, John, 85
Mandel, Marvin, 243–44
Mann, Arthur, 188
Mansfield, Frederick, 230
Markey, Morris, 226n
Martens, Ludwig C. A. K., 115
Massachusetts Police Association, 74
Massachusetts State Guard, 153–56, 159–64, 184–87, 214–16; demobilized, 216; Eleventh Regiment, 153–54, 186; Fifteenth Regiment, 155, 187; First Cavalry Troop, 129, 152, 157, 185; makeup of, 140–41; Tenth Regiment, 153–54, 160–62, 186–87; Twelfth Regiment, 155, 166; Twentieth Regiment, 155, 185
Massachusetts Volunteer Militia, 177
Matthew, Mae, 125, 181, 195
Matthews, Nathan, Jr., 45
"May Day" bombs, 20
McCall, Samuel, 13, 42, 46, 53–54
McCamant, Wallace, 221–22
McCarthy, Frank, 74, 113; announces police union, 87; asks for other unions' support, 127; denounces Rule 35, 75, 79; general strike and, 172, 175, 193–94, 197, 205, 207; objects to volunteer police, 90
McCormick, Medill, 221
McCourt, James, 188
McDonald, Francis, 39
McDonald, John, 165
McElwain Shoe Company, 150
McGill, Arthur, 158
McGinniskin, Barney, 35

McGowan, Charles, 207
McGrady, Edward, 175
McHugh, Peter, 127
McInnes, John F., 112; background, 85; elected union president, 85–87; general strike and, 183–84, 194, 197, 199–200, 205; meets with Commissioner Curtis, 92; postpones strike vote, 113; during riots, 125, 127, 147; Storrow committee and, 99–100
McKinley, William, 37
McLaughlin, John, Jr., 158
McNabb, Francis, 164
McSweeney, Eugene, 230
McTiernan, John, 157
McWilliams, Carton, 169
Mechanic's Building, 136, 186
Mercier, Cardinal, 146
Metropolitan Park Police, 74, 127, 135, 138, 181, 198, 233
Meyer, George von L., 144
Mob action, 122–26, 133–38, 150–52, 156–64, 167–68
Montreal, 240
Mooney, Tom, 20, 23
Morgan, J. P., 20
Moriarty, James, 76–80, 83, 90, 100, 110, 127, 172
Morse, Arthur, 151
Motor Transport Corps, 156
Muck, Karl, 9
Munsey, Frank A., 37
Murphy, Daniel, 151
Murphy, James, 243–44
Murphy, John R., 175, 198, 224
"Mustie," 237n.
Myers, Henry, 169

Nation, 211
National Civic Federation, 17
National Peace Jubilee, 33
National Police Magazine, 47
National Security League, 17
National Union of Police Officers, 235
Nawn, Harry, 95
New Bedford, Mass., 74
New England Worker, 184

New Republic, 211
New York City, 14, 20, 23, 102
New York Times, 211
New York World, 169, 211
Noone, Thomas, 228
Northampton, 60–62

O'Brien, Hugh, 34–35, 36, 45
O'Brien, Robert Lincoln, 109n
O'Connell, Cardinal, 46, 57, 188
O'Donnell, Michael, 110, 113, 127, 172, 175–76, 193–94, 199–200, 205, 207–208
Ohio State Journal, 192
Oliver, Andrew, 28
O'Meara, Stephen, 36–43, 48, 51–53, 84, 198
O'Reagan, Florence, 124
O'Reilly, John Boyle, 36
Our Lawless Police, 41
Oyster, Guy, 193–95, 197

Palmer, A. Mitchell, 20, 22, 24
Parker, Herbert, 209, 214, 223; appointed chief legal adviser to commissioner, 92; background, 83–84; establishes "Dead Lines," 215; general strike and, 173–74, 205; Storrow committee and, 103–106, 110–11
Parker, Samuel, 140, 149, 159, 166, 171, 173
Parkman, Henry, 45
Patterson, George, 161
Pax Centurion, 223, 240
Peabody, Francis, 9, 142, 144
Peabody, Francis, Jr., 45
Pelletier, Joseph, 21
Perry, John, 154
Pershing, John, 146
Peters, Alanson, 227
Peters, Andrew J., 13, 81, 86, 140, 152, 205; background, 67–70; blames Curtis for riots, 171; Coolidge and, 128–30, 141, 148–50, 173–75, 178–80, 223; leaves office, 224–25; meets with union leaders, 171–72, 195; mobilizes state guard, 149–50; police salaries and, 49, 54–55, 139;

police union and, 93; scandal involving, 70, 226–27; Storrow committee and, 95–96, 100, 103–104, 110, 116, 118–20, 208, 217
Peters, Bradford, 227
Peters, James G., 86
Peters, John, 227
Peters, Martha Phillips, 68
Phelan, James J., 95, 99
Philadelphia *Evening Public Ledger*, 192
Pierce, Henry L., 33, 34
Pierce, William H., 89, 106
Pillsbury, Albert, 76, 173
Plain Words, 22
Plumb Plan, 24
Poindexter, Governor, 211
Police Administration in Boston, 42
Pomerleau, Donald, 242–44
Posner's, 165
Powers, Leland, 22
Progressivism, 63, 66
Prohibition, 132*n*, 232
Pulitzer, Joseph, 37
Pullman, George M., 220
Puritan in Babylon, A, 43, 63

Quincy, Josiah, Jr., 30
Quincy, Josiah, III, 45
Quincy House, 79

Race riots, 23
Ratshesky, Abraham, 95, 109
Ray, Joseph, 126
Raymond, Harris, 164
Read, Charles, 146
Reardon, Charles, 122, 182
Reed, James, 146
Reed, John, 16, 24
Reed, William G., 44
Reemts, Richard, 164–65, 184, 194
Reid, John, 164
Remmel, H. L., 221
Revised Laws of Massachusetts, 128
Revolutionary Age, 11, 17
Richardson, John, Jr., 141
Rockefeller, John D., 20
Rockville Centre, N.Y., 234

Rooney, John, 229
Roosevelt, Franklin D., 22, 149
Roosevelt, Theodore, 37–38
Roosevelt, Theodore, Jr., 213
Root, Elihu, 212
Rowley, Clarence W., 55
Roxbury, 11–12, 34, 44, 123, 137, 168
Roxbury Historical Society, 146
Rowley, Dan, 228
Rule 35, 75, 79, 86, 88, 91, 117, 217
Russ, Joseph, 234
Russell, Richard, 160
Russell Club, 80, 181, 193
Russo, Michael, 188

Salvation Army, 214
Sandburg, Carl, 17
San Francisco *Examiner*, 169
Scalizy, John W., 136
Schaefer, William, 242–44
Scollay Square, 132–34, 145, 151–53, 157, 159, 166, 168, 185, 215, 237–40
Seattle, 15–16, 115
Seattle *Union Record*, 15
Seaver, Benjamin, 31, 35
Seemes, Captain, 28
Service Employees International Union, 235
Shea, Arthur, 21, 164–65
Sheehan, Robert, 163
Shephard's, 119
Shubert Theatre, 187
Sibley, Frank, 11
Sidis, Willy, 21
Simpson, George, 219
Skillings, Perley, 123, 155
Slattery, E. T., 119
Smith, Al, 227
Smith, Jerome Van Crowninshield, 35
Socialist party, 10–12, 16–17, 114
Soldier, Patsy, 142
Sousa, John Philip, 9
South Boston, 124, 137–39, 147, 150–51, 160–63, 168, 185, 186
Soviet Russia, 11, 16–17
Springfield, Mass., 74
Springfield *Republican*, 211
Sproul, William, 213

Stearns, Frank Waterman, 109, 127, 202, 219
Stevens, Jesse F., 118, 129, 149, 153, 163
Stone & Webster, 178
Stores, looting of, 133–38, 159–62, 165–66
Storrow, James Jackson, 93–110, 116, 118–20, 205
Storrow Committee, 95–110, 208; compromise plan, 106–108, 116, 171–72
Street and Electric Railway Employees of America, 75
Street Carmen's Union, 76, 78, 95, 147
Strike, general, 173, 175, 177–79, 181, 195–98
Sullivan, Jeremiah, 125
Sullivan, Thomas, 140, 144, 151–52, 158, 186
Sweetser, LeRoy, 177

Taft, William Howard, 211, 213
Tague, Peter, 69
Tarkington, Booth, 189
Telephone union, 125, 181, 195, 196
Theaters, 146, 164, 187, 214
Thomas, Charles, 193
Thompson, E. L., 195
Timilty, Jim, 177–78
Timilty, Joseph, 230
Treadway, Allen, 65
Tresca, Carlo, 17–18
Tukey, Francis, 30–31, 35
Tumulty, Joseph, 170

Unamuno, Miguel de, 114
Underhill, John, 186
Union Club, 66, 219
United Garment Workers, 207
United Hebrew Trade Unions, 181
United Shoe Machinery Company, 66
United Textile Workers of America, 18

Vahey, James, 75, 89, 91, 93, 125, 194, 197, 199, 205, 208, 217, 223; Storrow committee and, 97–100, 102–106
Valdinoce, Carlo, 22
Valdinoce, Susie, 22n

Van Dyke, Henry, 11
Victory Court, 185
Violence, acts of, 122–26, 133–38, 150–52, 156–64, 167–68
Volunteer police: advertisements for, 89; composition of, 102–103, 141–44; riot duties of, 118–19, 151–53, 158, 161, 164–65, 168, 177

Wall Street Journal, 169
Walsh, David Ignatius, 65
Warren, Fort, 33
Warren, Winslow, 67
Washington, D.C., 74, 102
Watkins, James, 126
Weeks, John W., 209
Wellesley, Mass., 74
Wendell, Barrett, 59
West, Herbert, 181
West Roxbury, Mass., 126
White, Edward Douglass, 9
White, Kevin, 233
White, William Allen, 43, 48, 63, 220
Whiteside, Alexander, 140–41, 171, 175
Whitten, John F., 85
Willis, Frank, 221–22
Willis, William P., 85
Wilson, William B., 18, 20, 24, 69
Wilson, Woodrow, 9, 14, 18, 57, 170, 199, 206, 213
Winnipeg Trades and Labour Council, 21
Winthrop, John, 26
Wobblies. See Industrial Workers of the World
Wogan, Lawrence, 130
Woll, Matthew, 179
Women's Committee for Public Safety, 211, 217
Wood, Leonard, 220
World War I, 7–13
Wyman, Henry, 127, 173, 177, 191, 223
Wyman, Starr, 70, 226–27

Yankee Division, 11, 19, 95
YMCA, 214
York, Alvin, 57
Young, Mathew, 27